Due Return	Due Return
Date Date	Date Date

citizen politics

second edition

citizen politics

politics

an introduction to political behavior

second edition

james david barber
yale university

MARKHAM PUBLISHING COMPANY / Chicago

MARKHAM POLITICAL SCIENCE SERIES
Aaron Wildavsky, Editor

For D. B. B.

acknowledgments

I am glad to thank John Applegath, Nathaniel Beck, Murray Edelman, William H. Flanigan, Fred I. Greenstein, Charles E. Lindblom, Kevin L. Mc-Keough, Aaron Wildavsky, Martha Bond, Pat Froelich, Tina Miller, Patricia Welter, and Ann Sale Barber for thoughtful comments, some of which have led me to change the original text.

For special help with the Second Edition, I thank Carl Akins, Susan Fergenson, Mark Levy, Harry G. Matthews, J. Sliwa, Bobbie Smetherman, John Sullivan, and Goetz Wolff, and particularly two loving critics, Jane Lewis Barber and Sara Naismith Barber.

preface to the second edition

Citizen Politics is not a book about current events, but there are two good reasons for the changes in this new edition. First, there are some striking new developments in politics that illustrate how theory, facts, and action fit together. The sudden expansion of the electorate to include millions of new voters, the role of youth in politics, the resurgence of interest in preparing for a future beyond the war, and other changes show the dynamism and interplay of politics. New cultural themes and institutional inventions have appeared and shaken the system. Millions of people are questioning the virtues of old-style politics-as-usual, the ceaseless round of bargaining for minor gains. Most of what I wrote a few years ago still holds (I have updated the evidence where possible), but these new themes need looking at.

Second, the book has been widely used and the publisher has energetically sought the criticism of its readers. These comments from students and faculty have been extraordinarily helpful to the revision. Although I have not always followed their suggestions, I have made numerous changes in content and language where others helped me see a better way. I still seek guidance from you readers who, in the end, give meaning to these labors.

J.D.B.

contents

introduction

Increasingly, citizens turn to the social sciences for answers to political problems. Too often, what they get back are statements, couched in fancy language, about how complex politics is. Or they are shown high theories or little experiments which seem only distantly relevant to the tough issues. Or they are given a list of basic concepts or methods to be memorized, or ancient history to be understood, in the faith that later the importance of these will become evident. Meanwhile, the gap between the citizen's interest in today's challenges and the scientist's passion for eternal truth widens.

This book takes a different tack. It is an attempt to close that gap by starting with questions many citizens are now concerned with and then moving directly into the most relevant discoveries and theories about political behavior. This is Plato's idea: education moves from opinion to knowledge, from the question of the day to the answer for tomorrow, from a concern with issues to a concern with the underlying forces that shape politics. For example:

From the late 1960's onward, hot issues about *who* should decide *what* in American politics have come to the fore. The idea of participatory democracy, that the people affected by a policy ought to have a hand in making that policy, has caught hold—and has been challenged as unrealistic. Who should be included in deciding when, where, and how a slum is to be rebuilt? The people who live there? The experts? The politicians? What is the citizen's role in such matters? In chapters i and ii, we move from this question into facts about the present patterns of actual citizen participation, including the ways motives, opportunities, and resources work together in special combinations.

"Old enough to fight, old enough to vote?" Should the draftable eighteen-year-old have a right to full participation in politics? What do votes for the eighteen to twenty year olds mean for American politics in 1970's? In particular, what intellectual qualities—knowledge, the ability to think systematically, and so on—are necessary for effective political thinking? In chapters iii and iv, we look first at individuals and then at collections of individuals to see how, in fact, the typical citizen thinks about politics. Chapter iv takes up a specific system for increasing the rationality of choice: the debate. How close do our political fights at campaign time come to an ideal model of informed controversy?

Under what conditions is it legitimate to resist the government? When one disagrees with a policy? When one judges the policy to be immoral? When one sees that a policy threatens his existence? These problems—brought forward in our time by resistance to war and domestic injustice—relate directly to the basis for government authority in the loyalties of citizens. Loyalty, in turn, is one of several related political feelings that bear on the stability and productiveness of democracy. These themes are developed in chapters v and vi. We see there how opinions help people—to make sense of politics, to get along with others (sometimes by fighting them), and to express emotion.

What is the effect of the clever propagandist, using all the means of persuasion at his control, on the democratic citizen? Is it now the case, or soon to become so, that the mass public is at the mercy of the "hidden persuaders," the public relations men and television image-makers? Chapter vii turns that question around to look at it from the viewpoint of the persuader. The problems he faces in gaining attention, in fitting his message into the citizen's set of wants and needs, and in defining a course of action he wants the citizen to take are analyzed. It soon becomes clear that political persuasion (and, more broadly, power in politics) is much affected by cultural setting; chapter viii explores connections between culture and power in four communities.

"Given all these forces for stability, how do we get any action out of politics?" is the question that begins chapter ix. Modern experience shows that governments which fail to adapt – quickly – to rapid, fundamental social changes are in danger of their lives. Contrary to the picture painted by much social science, change is always a feature of politics. But how does it happen? How do new power groups come into being? Why do they fade away? In particular, what do the massive changes taking place in American society portend for the future of a political system organized around a static factor: geography? These questions set the stage for chapter x, where the darker side of change – and the power of groups to resist unwanted change – is explored.

The overall framework of the book, then, should give you a strong start on five basic themes in the study of political behavior. You should see how comparisons among categories of citizens can bring forth the main outlines of *political participation* – of who takes part in what and why. Then, by means of a model or abstract picture of the process, you should get a grasp on the nature of *political thinking,* of how some measure of reason is possible amid widespread ignorance. The character of *political feelings,* especially the reasons why people hold and express their political sentiments, emerges from a tested approach: the search for the benefits people derive from their life experiences. Behind the analysis of *political persuasion* is the larger theme of power; this exploration should acquaint you with the main dimensions of this basic political factor and show you how the definition of power depends upon the questions you want to answer and upon the political system where the answers lie. Finally, in the discussion of *political change,* the time dimension comes in; the dynamic relationships among what just was, what is now, and what is just about to be highlight the developmental quality of change. Each of these larger themes has uses throughout the study of political behavior.

I hope that you will find these pages interesting and useful and that they will make you want to know more about political behavior. If you see ways to improve the book for the benefit of students in the future, I would appreciate learning of your ideas.

James David Barber

October, 1971

chapter i

Taking Part

Participatory democracy, like most new ideas in politics, is a battle cry with a wide variety of meanings. In the late 1960's, activists in the civil rights movement, the war on poverty, and student politics used it to express anger and frustration at officials in power who seemed to want to do things *for* the Negro, the poor, and the student, but not to let these disadvantaged groups really participate in making the key decisions. Free speech, they said, was not enough; nor was being listened to or kept informed or even taken into account. Real freedom seemed to imply, for champions of participatory democracy, power to make the decisions — real decisions — in the hands of the people the programs were supposed to help. In poverty programs, the poor them-

1

selves would organize their neighborhoods and direct activities to improve their lot. Negroes would run civil rights agencies, not through white liberal leaders, but by common action at the grass roots, and students would select which of their professors would be granted tenure. Fed up with being led by strangers, the people would lead themselves.

Is that what democracy means? There is a different democratic vision, one that might be called "potential democracy." The people themselves, this argument goes, lack the skills, the resources, or indeed the inclination to run the government—most of the time, in most of the complex decisions that need to be made. Government of, for, and by the people does not require continuous, sustained attention by the average citizen, nor does it require him to take responsibility for detailed planning and administration. Real democracy, according to this view, is a set of institutions, the most important being free elections, through which the people can choose their leaders—and throw them out if they fail to deliver satisfactory results. Most people, most of the time, won't care. When enough do, the machinery is there for them to work their will.

For a very long time, these controversies and others like them have been part of the political struggle. They are ideas with consequences. They grow directly out of practical contests for political power and practical demands that political power actually produce a better life for citizens now alive. In modern form, these ideas express an eternal concern of democrats with participation: in fact, from Plato (no democrat) on, no one has managed to think clearly about democracy without positing or assuming some position on how many should participate how much in what. The history of democracy is a history of progressive inclusion. The propertyless, the women, the Negroes, the illiterate gradually and with many a hard fight have been admitted to the game and have established their claims on the government. No debate on including a new group has gone by without predictions about their actual performance as participants in the democratic process.

All of these arguments contain at least two common components. One is the *value* component expressed in statements about what ought to be. For example, should every citizen vote? Should the major decisions in a democracy be made by the citizens themselves, by their representatives, or by others ruling in their interest? Should the commoner leave government to his betters, should the worker take over from the exploiters?

The other component is *factual,* expressed in statements about what is. How many citizens vote? Who are they? Why do some go beyond voting to other forms of participation?

These two components are intimately linked. Only a person out of touch with the facts discusses whether or not China *should* be the fifty-first of the United States. Assumptions about political reality are implicit in every responsible value statement; they shape and limit the agenda of moral debate. Similarly we do not (or should not) waste much time on questions of fact which have no relevance to our larger purposes. For political scientists, the percentage of citizens who are left-handed would appear to be a trivial matter of fact. But many other fact questions are of critical importance to value judgments on the goals and policies governments pursue, and in this book we shall focus on a good many of them.

To begin with, how much participation is there in the American democracy? Since the days of the Founding Fathers (and probably before), Americans have been deploring political apathy and exhorting one another to take an active part in government, in public service—even in "politics." How does our record today compare with that of the past and with participation in other democracies?

how much participation?

By far the easiest form of political participation to measure with some precision is voting, and this is no doubt one reason why so much research has been done on voting behavior. Another reason is that votes are decisive politically: they determine which people hold most of the key, authoritative offices. Rarely in political science do we find this happy combination of readily available, quantified data and obvious political significance. Votes are counted and votes count. Considered in the context of the citizen's total life activites, voting may seem trivial. It amounts to taking a few minutes every year or so to cast a ballot. Other forms of political participation in the broadest sense, such as reading newspapers and watching the news on television, take up much larger proportions of his time. But in the aggregate, the millions of individual voting decisions shape the course of government by suddenly dividing the ins from the outs.

In the United States, the active electorate is far larger today than it used to be; barring disaster or radical changes in population rates, this statement will be valid for all major elections to come. Table 1.1 shows the general magnitude of change in number of votes for President in the Lincoln-to-Kennedy century.

TABLE 1.1
Votes Cast for President, 1860–1960

1860	4,677,000
1880	9,208,000
1900	13,965,000
1920	26,705,000
1940	49,901,000
1960	68,833,000

Sources: For 1860–1940, Robert E. Lane, *Political Life: Why People Get Involved in Politics* (New York: Free Press, Macmillan, 1959), Table 2.2, p. 21; for 1960, Elmo Roper, "How to Lose Your Vote," *Saturday Review*, March 18, 1961.

In 1964, the Presidential vote broke 70 million (70,913,673, to be exact). The 1968 vote was 73,211,562 (Nixon won by approximately seven-tenths of one percent of the vote).

That rapidly increasing population means a rapidly expanding electorate is as obvious as it is important. For it impels the candidates of the two major parties to reach an immense number of people. In the century from 1860 to 1960 the number of votes for President increased nearly fifteenfold; the number of major candidates remained the same. This gross expansion has at least these large implications:

1. The growing importance of money in politics. The cost of reaching and stirring to vote 70 million people is of an order of magnitude far different from turning out 4 or 5 million. This is not to say that money *wins* elections—marginal differences between candidates in expenditures may mean little—but that a candidate for President or any other *national* office has to be able to attract a large amount of money.

2. The growing importance of the mass media in politics. Two men cannot shake 70 million hands. As we shall see, the effects of media messages on voting can easily be overestimated. But simply to get the attention of the electorate these days requires campaign methods undreamed of in Lincoln's day.[1]

3. The growing importance of organization in politics. Much that can be done informally on a small scale requires extensive organization in the large. As numbers increase — especially when they increase in such vast proportions — new organizations proliferate and old ones get more complicated. The array of committees, clubs, societies, chairmen, directors, assistant captains, and so forth that appears every election year is in part a response to the voter explosion. These practical implications (and there are many more) add up to a continuing revolution in politics.

rates of participation

For analytic purposes, we want to know not only how many people vote, but also what *proportion* of those eligible to vote actually do so, and how that has changed historically. In Table 1.2,

TABLE 1.2
Percentage of Adult Civilians Who Voted, 1944–68

1944	56.3%
1948	51.5
1952	62.0
1956	60.1
1960	63.8
1964	62.1
1968	61.8

Sources: For 1944–60, *Report of the President's Commission on Registration and Voting Participation,* November, 1963; for 1964, Theodore H. White, *The Making of the President 1964* (New York: Atheneum, 1965), p. 381; for 1968, U.S. Bureau of the Census, *Statistical Abstracts of the United States, 1969* (Washington, D.C.: U.S. Government Printing Office, 1969), p. 368. The 1964 election was the first in which citizens in the District of Columbia, 198,597 of them, voted for President.

[1] Alexander Heard, *The Costs of Democracy* (Chapel Hill: University of North Carolina Press, 1960).

the percentage of the voting-age population which actually voted is shown for the Presidential elections since World War II.

Since the low-turnout election in 1948, these percentages seem to have stabilized around the low 60's. Is that high or low? The answer, of course, depends on one's basis for comparison. Those who speak of "merely" or "only" 60-odd percent voting, or of "fully" or "no less than" 60 percent, have somewhere in their minds a contrasting range of figures.

Perhaps that contrasting range is in the record of the past. In the 1880's and 1890's, more than 75 percent of voting-age eligibles voted—but most women were still excluded from the accounts. In 1920, the first election after national female suffrage, the proportion of eligibles voting dropped below 50 percent. Since then, with the exceptions of 1944, when many males were too busy fighting World War II to vote, and the peculiar 1948 election, the figures show a moderate but fairly regular increasing trend. For hopeful people willing to take the long view, this is an encouraging sign.

But others may read the same figures differently. What must be wrong with a country in which more than a third of the eligible voters do not bother to get to the polls? Why do some other democracies have far higher percentages to report? These questions require a close look at how the "eligible" electorate is defined. As we saw, most figures for the United States are based on the *total population* of voting age, or the civilian or citizen population of voting age. In many comparisons with other countries, these U.S. figures are compared with percentages based on *registered* voters—and some of these countries have compulsory registration and voting laws. This is a bit like comparing voluntary contributions to the U.S. Treasury with income-tax payments. And a close look at that third of the "eligibles" who fail to vote in American Presidential elections shows other sources of misinterpretation.

who "can" vote?

Elmo Roper, the famous pollster, made some informed estimates for 1960 of groups of voters normally counted as eligible, but in fact facing hard barriers to voting.[2] Roper estimated the total

[2]Elmo Roper, "How to Lose Your Vote," *Saturday Review*, March 18, 1961, pp. 14–15. Similar exclusions affected 1968 voting rates. See the Gallup poll for December 10, 1968.

number of citizens of voting age at 104 million in 1960. Of these, 68,832,818 voted, or 66.2 percent, by his calculation. But among those 104 million "eligibles," Roper estimated, were:

8,000,000	mobile adults unable to meet state, county, or precinct residence requirements.
5,000,000	adults kept from the polls by illness at home, in hospitals, nursing homes, homes for the aged, etc.
2,600,000	adults traveling for business, health, vacation, and other reasons, unable to obtain absentee ballots.
1,750,000	adult Negroes in eleven southern states kept from the polls by rigged literacy tests, poll taxes, various social pressures, etc.
800,000	adult illiterates in twenty-five literacy-test states.
500,000	citizens of voting age in the District of Columbia.
215,000	adult prison population.
500,000	U.S. citizens living abroad.
225,000	adult preachers of the Jehovah's Witnesses sect who face a religious disability to voting.

19,590,000 total citizens of voting age unable to vote.

When these citizens are subtracted from the total citizens of voting age, we get 84,410,000 citizens actually eligible to vote in 1960. Now recalculating the percentage voting on this basis, we get not a paltry 66.2 percent, but a rather impressive 81.5 percent! In other words, more than four out of five of the potential voters we might reasonably expect to get to the polls actually did cast their votes in 1960. Were the other 18.5 percent apathetic or alienated? No doubt some were, but we can guess that a good many had realistic reasons for not voting—a snowstorm or car wreck on election day, for example.[3]

Americans move around a lot, and perhaps this is the most significant fact to keep in mind in interpreting real eligibility to vote. Roper's 1960 estimate of 8 million eliminated by residence requirements agrees with that of the President's Commission on Registration and Voting Participation (1963). The Commission estimated that 4 million persons were prevented from voting for the same reason in 1950. So in ten years the number left out be-

[3]William G. Andrews, "American Voting Participation," in William R. Nelson (ed.), *American Government and Political Change* (New York: Oxford University Press, 1970), Chapter 11.

cause they had not lived long enough in one place doubled. The Census Bureau noted that in just one year, 1961, 20 million American adults changed residence.[4] The best prediction is that Americans will continue to move in rapidly increasing numbers.

a politics of places

Now this mobility has important implications. It highlights how politics, in the United States and in most other democracies, is closely tied to geography. The whole structure of states, Congressional districts, countries, cities, and towns is mapped out by definite territorial boundaries, fixed by mountain ranges, rivers, and the surveyor's straight lines. In a complex society, people are linked in many different kinds of groupings, but for most political purposes, it is *where they live* that counts. Only two government officials, the President and Vice President, are elected by all the people (even they depend on cumulating electoral votes state by state); all other elected officials represent constituencies of location, people organized by place of residence. Against this static background, citizens shift from state to state and district to district in massive numbers. They work for corporations and belong to unions whose operations cut across state and district lines. They send their children away to college; many never come home again to stay. They watch national network television and a good many who have never seen New York read the *New York Times*. Their fellow Negroes or whites, Catholics, Jews, or Protestants, Italian-, Irish-, German-, or American-Americans are scattered all over the national lot. But when it comes to participating in politics, the geographical community is the crucial one.

In most American communities, newcomers are at a political disadvantage – not just in voting, but in all types of participation. No law says a Senator or Representative must be a long-time resident of his state or district. (Notice the exact requirements in Article I, Sections 2 and 3, of the Constitution.) And in fact a good many quite short-time residents have been elected to these offices. But the tradition that public offices belong to the area's

[4]Lester W. Milbrath, *Political Participation: How and Why Do People Get Involved in Politics?* (Chicago: Rand McNally, 1965), p. 93.

old-timers or home-town boys dies hard. Similarly it is probably safe to say that the average length of residence of precinct captains, party chairmen, poll watchers, campaign canvassers, and amateur talkers-about-politics is considerably longer than the average for the people they exhort. At least in the election phase of citizen politics, the informal rules of the game favor community stalwarts who have been around awhile or have come back home again.

Whenever we find some political structure (like geographically organized elections) which makes it difficult or impossible for citizens to satisfy certain basic political needs (such as the common interest of Negro minorities in civil rights), then we are likely to find somewhere else on the political landscape another set of structures where participation has more favorable results. In the early twentieth century, when immigrants ran into barriers in getting their needs met by city government officials (mostly Yankees), they turned to political leaders more responsive to their interests—the "bosses" who could deliver food, housing, jobs, and other necessities in return for votes and some help with campaigning at election time. Today many groups that are relatively ineffective in elections have their say at other points in the process of government. Thus civil rights groups, for example, have won their greatest victories not at the polls, but in the courts and, more recently, the Congress. Great corporations, organized on a national basis, play a role in elections, but are particularly active in lobbying. Such interests, often blocked or hampered in geographically organized electoral politics, are often effective in other arenas of participation where geography counts less.

the opportunity to take part

So *opportunity* is a big factor in participation. There are many barriers, some legal, some matters of convenience, such as travel for vacations, arranging for baby sitters, and the like. As a general rule, the first question to ask in analyzing participation is this: What stands in the way of citizen action? What external restraints are there to prevent large numbers of citizens from taking a more significant part? If some type of participation, like voting, is difficult or impossible because of external restraints, we shall be mistaken if we assume lack of participation is due to apathy, alienation, laziness, or some other motivational cause.

Opportunity analysis can get complicated. The barriers are of varying degrees of hardness. After all, a student could cut class to vote if necessary. A union could demand time off for members who want to do campaign work—perhaps at the price of other demands. The tired businessman could spend his evening at a zoning hearing rather than watching television at home. In a good many cases, as we have seen, lack of real opportunity prevents participation; for those in prison or Negroes terrorized by racists, opportunity is the decisive factor. But in other cases, some of which we shall soon examine, other factors must be taken into account along with opportunity.

who participate in what?

In terms of mass participation, a Presidential election is the highpoint of citizen politics. Millions fail to get to the polls even then, but in elections held in non-Presidential years—for Senator, Representative, and especially for local officers—far larger numbers stay at home. Primary elections for choosing candidates are usually even more sparsely attended. And when it comes to other forms of political activities, this is the picture:

> Only about 4 or 5 percent are active in a party, campaign, and attend meetings. About 10 percent make monetary contributions, about 13 percent contact public officials, and about 15 percent display a button or sticker. Around 25 or 30 percent try to proselyte others to vote a certain way, and from 40 to 70 percent perceive political messages and vote in any given election.[5]

In the 1956 campaign and election, four out of ten people (an estimated 44 percent) did nothing in politics but vote.[6] In 1964 only one in twenty did any campaign work.[7] When we move beyond

[5]*Ibid.*, p. 19.

[6]V. O. Key, Jr., *Public Opinion and American Democracy* (New York: Knopf, 1961), p. 184.

[7]William H. Flanigan, *Political Behavior of the American Electorate* (Boston: Allyn and Bacon, 1968), p. 96.

voting in the big, highly publicized Presidential elections, we find a massive fallout of participation, a general desertion from the political ranks. So participation rates in national elections could lead us far astray if we took them as representative of citizen activity.

Only a few do much. The electorate is "stratified," as V. O. Key put it: a thin layer of highly active participants, a thicker layer of those who sporadically do a little campaign work or talk about politics with their neighbors, and an extremely thick layer of those who are politically inert or nearly so.

This layer-cake image of the citizenry is worth keeping in mind because it points up a significant fact. The tendency to participate is structured in a special way: those who participate in the *more active* forms of political activity are also likely to participate in the less active forms. As Robert E. Lane summarizes research on this tendency:

> If a person electioneers he is almost certain to attend party meetings.
> If a person attends party meetings he is almost certain to be among those who contact public officers and other political leaders.
> If a person contacts public officers and leaders he is almost certain to be a member of some politically oriented (though not strictly political) association.
> If a person is a member of such an association he is almost certain to be a voter.[8]

Notice that this is a *one-way* relationship, moving from the more active to the less active. If you reverse the order of these statements, you get a false picture: it is *not* necessarily true that "if a person votes he is almost certain to be a member of an association," for example. This is an ordering of intensities, a kind of scale of activity with a direction sign.

Within these broad levels of participation, activities tend to be generalized rather than specialized, which means a small number of people account for a large proportion of the activity. By and

[8]Robert E. Lane, *Political Life: Why People Get Involved in Politics* (New York: Free Press, Macmillan, 1959), pp. 93–94, summarizing work by Frederick H. Harris, Jr., "A Study of Political Participation in Two North Carolina Counties," *Research Previews*, Vol. 3 (1955), 1–7.

large, we do not have some people concentrating on writing letters to Congressmen and other people writing letters to the President. Odds are that among those who are active beyond voting, the same people are active in a variety of forms of participation. So it makes sense to talk in a general way about a stratified electorate with a minority of activists at the top.

Who are these activists? How are they different from the rest of the lot?

learning and earning

Two factors are powerful determinants: education and occupational level. In general, the more highly educated parts of the population have much higher rates of participation than the less educated, and since year by year the educational level of the average American is on the increase, it makes sense to predict more participation in the future. Today, more than seven million Americans are college students. An idea of what this may mean for politics may be gained from Table 1.3, showing the percentage voting at each educational level in the Presidential elections from 1952 to 1968. Obviously the college-educated turned out in far higher proportions than the grade-school-educated in each of these elections. A basic divider of the politically active from the

TABLE 1.3
Educational Level
and Percentage Voting for President, 1952–1968

	1952	1956	1960	1964	1968
Some college	81%*	89%	92%	81%	83%
High school	70	74	83	73	73
Grade school	56	60	70	62	62

Source: The data utilized in this table, as analyzed by Nathaniel Beck (Political Science Research Library, Yale University), were made available by the Inter-University Consortium for Political Research. The data were originally collected by the University of Michigan Survey Research Center. Neither the Survey Research Center nor the Consortium bear any responsibility for the analyses or interpretations presented here. For 1968, the figures are from *Statistical Abstracts of the United States, 1969*, p. 371.

*These figures are from survey responses and they overstate the percentage voting somewhat because the survey included only persons living in households (not, for example, those in military service) and because some people who did not vote tell the pollster they did.

politically passive, then, is educational background. Postponing for the moment why this is so, we can look at another basic divider, occupational level.

Table 1.4 shows the pattern of voting by citizens at various occupational levels. Here again the figures trend downward, although not so uniformly in the last two elections. In general, those with jobs of higher status and income voted at much higher rates than those with lower status jobs.

TABLE 1.4
Occupational Level
and Percentage Voting for President, 1952–1964

	1952	1956	1960	1964
Professional and managerial*	78%**	85%	92%	80%
Other white-collar	72	79	84	79
Skilled and semi-skilled	68	72	78	69
Farmers	63	73	83	79
Unskilled	55	54	76	64

Source: See source note in Table 1.3.
*Occupation here refers to that of the head of household and not necessarily to that of the respondent.
**See note * in Table 1.3.

Now these simple figures can open up some extraordinarily complex lines of interpretation having to do with relationships between social class and citizen politics, theories of the effects of education, the whole Marxist stream of thought, and so forth. One sensitive analysis of why lower status people participate less points to differences in leisure, economic security, political deprivations and rewards, the visibility of policies, group and individual benefits, social contacts, child-rearing practices, social norms and roles, attitudes of responsibility, cross-pressures, membership in organizations and friendship groups, ability to deal with abstractions, life satisfaction, and interclass mobility.[9] Rarely in political analysis does some simple, common-sense explanation tell the whole story. People behave the way they do in politics for many different, overlapping, mutually supporting reasons, not all

[9]Lane, *op. cit.*, p. 234.

of which they are aware of. The broad outlines are becoming clearer as political scientists build up systematic data and theory, but many of the subtle interconnections are still obscure.

Careful interpretation of the data can overcome some of the obscurity. Take the data in Table 1.4. There we see the "unskilled" category at the bottom of the totem pole, with only 64 percent voting compared with the 80 percent for the "professional and managerial" levels in 1964. Beginners, trying to remember the main thrust of the argument, have a tendency to exaggerate these kinds of differences—at the extreme, fixing in the mind the false notion that almost all professionals and almost no unskilled workers voted.

The trend is in that direction, but it does not go nearly that far. Sixty-four percent of the millions of unskilled workers is a massive political force, one few candidates can afford to ignore. We need to keep in mind that these are *rates* of participation, not absolute amounts. The distinction can be crucial: sons of college presidents are far more likely to go to college than are sons of farmers—but there are a great many more farmers than college presidents. If we are mainly interested in explaining *why* certain categories of citizens participate, it makes sense to concentrate on rates of participation for each group. For assessing the *effects* of participation by various groups on the political system, we would want to notice also the raw numbers in each category.

Participation is related to education and also to occupational level. Why? Of course, one possibility is that a person's occupation reflects his educational training. The highly educated are apt to wind up with high-level jobs. So it might be that it is not one's occupational situation—the people one works with, the income one makes, etc.—that explains differences in participation, but simply the amount of education one has. On the other hand, schooling might be irrelevant, a kind of accidental concomitant of occupation, which is the real reason for the differences. From the evidence we have so far, there is no way to untangle the influence of these two variables. As is so often the case in social science, several different explanations are plausible when we consider possible causes *one at a time,* and we need some more sophisticated way to figure out how the variables *work together.*

resource combinations

One fairly simple way is to break down the categories of participants into smaller groupings, to "control for" the simultaneous influence of several variables. Table 1.5 is an example. First we isolate categories of people with roughly the same educational and occupational levels, such as businessmen with a grade-school education and clerical workers who went to college. Then for each such grouping we see what percentage scored high on an index of political participation—in this case, by voting and performing some other political act. These percentages are shown in Table 1.5.

TABLE 1.5

Education and Occupation Related to Political Participation:
Percentage in Each Group Scoring High in Participation

Occupation of household head	Grade school	High school	College
Professional	*	36%	48%
Businessman	37%	36	50
Clerical worker	16	26	53
Skilled worker	18	32	42
Farmer	18	24	36
Unskilled worker	9	20	*

Source: Derived from V. O. Key, Jr., *Public Opinion and American Democracy* (New York: Knopf, 1961), Table 13.8, p. 330. © Copyright 1961 by V. O. Key, Jr. Reprinted by permission of Alfred A. Knopf, Inc. The entries are percentages of those in each category who voted and reported having engaged in at least one other type of campaign participation. The data are from University of Michigan Survey Research Center 1952 and 1956 election study samples.

*Too few cases for meaningful percentaging.

Reading across this table, we see the effect education has *within* each occupational grouping. For example, within the category of clerical workers, the percentage of high participants rises from 16 to 26 to 53 as we trace from grade school to high school to college level. In fact, within each of the occupational levels (with one exception) this same pattern holds: the more education, the higher the percentage of people who vote and take part in some other political activity. Therefore, we can say with some confidence that education has an influence on political participation and that this influence is largely *independent* of, or holds regardless of, occupational level.

As we read down Table 1.5, the picture is similar if not quite so clear. Within each educational category there is a general decline in participation as we move from professional to unskilled occupational categories. In the grade school category, this is true at the extremes (the contrast between businessmen and unskilled workers is a large one). In the high school and college categories the trend is uneven; actually a slightly higher proportion of clerical college graduates participate than professional college graduates. For occupation, then, we have to make a fudging statement: there is some tendency for higher status occupational groups to participate more than lower status ones, but the relationship is uneven when we control for education.

We saw how opportunity plays a significant role in differentiating active from inactive citizens; among those technically "eligible" to vote, some are really more eligible than others, when the main barriers to voting are taken into account. The findings on education and occupation illustrate a second major factor shaping citizen politics: *resources*. Put briefly, those who *have* more *do* more. A couple of hypothetical cases help make this clear.

the key resources

Suppose we consider an unskilled laborer who quit school after the third grade. After working-hours he has some leisure he could use for political activity, and perhaps he is really interested in getting his views across to the relevant politicians. To do so, he first needs to know who the relevant politicians are. But his limited education has not equipped him with much information on government. Perhaps he is one of the 45 percent who do not know how many Senators each state has.[10] With whom should he get in touch? The divisions of responsibility among federal, state, and local officials, and among legislators, judges, and administrators, are beyond his ken.

In short, he probably lacks one of the key resources for par-

[10]Robert E. Lane and David O. Sears, *Public Opinion* (Englewood Cliffs, N.J.: Prentice-Hall, 1964), p. 61.

ticipation: *knowledge.* A man who does not know where the polling place is will not vote. Neither will one who does not know there is an election going on, as is often the case with primaries, referenda, and local and special elections. The laborer may not realize that the president of his union is a friend of his Congressman and thus might be just the man for him to contact first. More generally, a great many citizens are often unaware that certain decisions with important implications for their lives—such as changes in draft laws, interest rates, housing codes, or medical care systems—are being actively considered at certain times and places. And much useful political knowledge comes from just the sort of interpersonal contacts an unskilled laborer is least likely to have. The whole range of information not usually found in the newspapers—the informal "inside dope"—may not get to him.

A second important resource is *skill.* The laborer with a third-grade education might, by hard study, acquire a good knowledge of the political system and current issues. But on the job he works with his hands; he does not have much experience in persuading people with words, talking in relatively abstract terms, composing letters, and so on. Chances are he has never made a speech. And he is probably much more familiar with machine work than with paperwork. The world of the sports page and family television does not give a man much experience in political persuasion.

A third resource significant for participation is *money;* actually income is more strongly related to participation than occupation is.[11] One form of participation is making campaign contributions. Obviously the rich are more likely to do that than are the poor. Money can buy time—baby sitters, maids, freedom from a second part-time job, two cars, and so on. Money means security, relief from a whole set of worries that might distract one from undertaking an extra activity like politics. In days gone by, a third-grade unskilled laborer might have seen politics as a way of picking up a little extra income, but today, with some exceptions, it costs more than it brings in.

Others farther up the education and occupation ladders have the resources the unskilled worker lacks, so it is little wonder they manage to participate more. The college graduate in an executive

---

[11] V. O. Key, Jr., *Politics, Parties, and Pressure Groups,* 4th ed. (New York: Crowell, 1958), p. 642.

position is far more likely to know who's who and what's going on in politics. Mailing a contribution or writing his Congressmen takes him (or his secretary) a very few minutes. His fellow alumni are used to hearing him sound off about the issues of the day, and in fact his job may require him to attend conferences, plan programs, make speeches. If he needs fifty copies of his thoughts on Viet Nam, he has them Xeroxed or puts an ad in the newspaper. Perhaps most important, his educational experience, reinforced by his experience at work, has equipped him with the personal, social, and intellectual skills useful for a wide variety of political-action purposes.

We have viewed voting eligibility in terms of opportunity to participate, and the influence of education and occupation in terms of resources. These general dimensions – opportunity and resources – bear on any analysis of political participation. Both are necessary for political action. But opportunity plus resources is not enough.

reasons why

In a free society, citizens participate in politics because they want to. If they do not want to, it does not make much difference how many opportunities are available or how large a store of resources they have. Throughout citizen politics there is a very significant element of voluntarism, symbolized in the hundreds of "Volunteers for . . ." organizations that spring up in a Presidential campaign year, but also affecting nearly every aspect of citizen participation throughout every year. The reasons why people choose to take part in politics – their political *motives* – form the third key element in explaining participation.

A focus on motives points up an often neglected choice in politics: indifference. Elections are most often analyzed by the proportion of the vote each candidate got. But of equal importance may be those who for one reason or another were not motivated to vote. A simple example shows this: if Candidate McCartney gets 10,000 votes and Candidate Lennon gets 9,000, obviously McCartney wins. We could say that the margin of 1,000 votes decided the outcome. But suppose there were 2,000 additional eligible voters (really able to vote) who preferred Candidate Lennon but did not get to the polls. Those 2,000 who "voted" to stay home were just as decisive in picking the winner as were those who participated in the election.

Many citizens are indifferent to politics all their lives. Their lack of interest is a significant political fact because it strengthens the power of those who do take part. Many more citizens are *sometimes* motivated to participate. These are the in-and-outers, the people who need some special reason to get to the polls or to make a contribution. Naturally politicians spend a lot of time trying to figure out just what such reasons might be.

Motivating people to take part in politics is not simply a matter of "activating" them, of awakening sleeping citizens. Most people are already active in a wide variety of their own affairs, which may or may not include politics. The problem is to understand why people do *political* things rather than *other* things, why they choose to devote time and energy to politics at the expense of whatever else they may be up to. An interesting and potentially important project for future research would be to explore in detail how citizens make choices among competing alternative uses of their energies.

Later on we shall see how certain short-run features of politics attract citizens to political participation. We have already seen how voting and other forms of political participation tend to cluster—how the politically active part of the electorate is apt to take part in several different forms of participation. To this should be added the time dimension: people who have participated in the past are likely to participate in the present and future. That is, for a great many activists, politics is a habit. Those who have voted in most or all past elections are the ones most likely to vote in the next one.[12] So before turning to some of the interesting short-run exceptions to the rule, we shall explore two main features of political motivation that persist through the years.

what I should do

First, people may want to take part in politics because they feel they ought to. There is a clear and strong relationship between a "sense of citizen duty," as measured by a series of poll questions,

---

[12] Angus Campbell, Philip E. Converse, Warren E. Miller, and Donald E. Stokes, *The American Voter* (New York: Wiley, 1960), p. 93.

and voting. In 1956, 85 percent of those scoring high on this measure voted, while only 13 percent of those with low citizen-duty scores got to the polls.[13] As might be expected, this dutiful attitude is in turn strongly related to education, and there is some independent effect of occupational level on it.[14] Thus knowledge and skill are only two of the results of high-level schooling and job experience. Education in particular is a strong force in developing a feeling of moral responsibility to take part. As Key puts it:

> The characteristic national values and outlooks permeate the entire school curriculum from the kinds of problems posed in arithmetic to the formal instruction in civics. School children acquire some knowledge of American literature, a matter by no means lacking in political significance. Instruction in American history acquaints the child with the great episodes in our past, with our traditional national heroes, and with many of the ideals of the society. History tends to be a sensitive subject; instruction is somewhat selective. The great of the past are elevated into paragons who would scarcely be recognized by their contemporaries; those episodes that redound most to our national glory receive emphasis; and the picture of the past is deficient in cracks and crevices. Courses in civics are explicitly designed to acquaint students with the broad character of the constitutional system and are often billed, somewhat hopefully, as courses in applied citizenship. . . . Whatever the content and whatever the approach, the school system functions as a powerful molder of politically relevant attitudes and as a means of induction into citizenship.[15]

What is the effect of this training on political motives? A peculiar characteristic of this indoctrination is its generality or abstractness. Students are not often taught that they should participate when their interests are at stake in some *specific* contest, or that they should select among alternative opportunities for action such as national vs. state politics, foreign vs. domestic policy areas, or campaign work vs. interelection petitioning. One is exhorted to "participate in politics" — or, more likely, "government" or "public service." Hot issues of the day are seldom dealt with in

---

[13] *Ibid.*, p. 106.

[14] Key, *Public Opinion and American Democracy*, pp. 325–26.

[15] *Ibid.*, pp. 316–17. Copyright © 1961 by V. O. Key, Jr. Reprinted by permission of Alfred A. Knopf, Inc.

any thorough way. (Notice how most American government text-books put the controversial issues at the end.) Most students prob-ably carry away from this experience a rather vague feeling that a conscientious person will do his part, rather than a strong aware-ness of the definite modern problems his participation might help solve.

Vague these feelings may be, but there is evidence that they are effective in moving people to vote. Odds are the sense of citi-zen duty has another component besides the moral command to participate; namely, legitimation. In the course of urging people to activity in this way, educators and others also put a stamp of approval, a kind of moral O.K., on political action. People who feel that politics is tainted with corruption hesitate to get involved; they are likely to see politics as something they ought to stay away from.

Comparative evidence from an important recent study of po-litical attitudes in five nations illustrates the significance of the "obligation to participate." Gabriel A. Almond and Sidney Verba report in *The Civic Culture*[16] how citizens answer this question:

> We know that the ordinary person has many problems that take his time. In view of this, what part do you think the ordi-nary person ought to play in the local affairs of his town or district?[17]

Table 1.6 shows for each country the percentage of the respond-ents who say the ordinary man should be active in his local com-munity, at each educational level.

Education affects this sense of duty in every country; in par-ticular, those with no more than a primary school education are less likely to feel obligated to take part than are those who have gone beyond primary school. This suggests that V. O. Key's assess-ment of American education as "a means of induction into citi-zenship" applies far beyond the borders of the United States. Ap-parently schooling in each of the five nations Almond and Verba analyze is a force for driving home the goodness of community

[16]Gabriel A. Almond and Sidney Verba, *The Civic Culture* (Princeton, N.J.: Princeton University Press, 1963).
[17]*Ibid.*, p. 126.

participation, or at least for reinforcing similar sentiments students bring to school from home.

But there are big differences in Table 1.6 as we move from country to country, differences that hold even within educational categories. More than a third of the American and British subjects whose education ended in grade school think the ordinary man should be active in his local community; less than a fifth of the Italians with some university training share that sentiment. Clearly the sense of obligation to participate is generally highest in the United States, still relatively high in Great Britain, and lowest in Italy, with Germany and Mexico close together in the middle.

TABLE 1.6
Percentage Who Say the Ordinary Man Should Be
Active in His Local Community

Nation	Education		
	Primary or less	Some secondary	Some university
United States	35%	56%	66%
Great Britain	37	42	42
Germany	21	32	38
Italy	7	17	22
Mexico	24	37	38

Source: Gabriel A. Almond and Sidney Verba, *The Civic Culture* (Princeton, N.J.: Princeton University Press, 1963), Table V.3, p. 133. Copyright © 1963 by Princeton University Press. Reprinted by permission of Princeton University Press. Total column and numbers on which percentages based omitted.

There are a great many possible explanations for these findings; political motives develop out of experience, and the experience of the "ordinary man" varies markedly from country to country. Two general categories of reasons for a weak sense of civic obligation are individual and cultural reasons. In every society, some individuals give up on politics. An Italian farmer quoted in another study illustrates this:

> I feel that I just don't count as a person. No one cares one way or the other what happens to me or to my family. We drift along from day to day. All the officials care about is what we can do for them and seeing that they get their taxes. The

Church wants its share. Yet what do we get out of it all? Who cares about us?[18]

On the other hand, certain individuals may have personal reasons for being very active in politics, such as loyalty to a family tradition of public service or ambition for a political career. Individual psychology can be useful in understanding such themes; for example, by exploring how the alienated, the outcast, the politically dispossessed, or the hyperactive, the power-seekers, the superparticipants got that way. Often rooted in special family experiences, these variations of political conscience can give lasting shape to one's attitudes toward politics. Closer to the middle of the range are such moral sentiments as that politics is dirty (so don't touch it—or so clean it up), that service is above self (so pitch in and help—or so do what you're told), and so forth.

But we are dealing here with something more than individual motives. Table 1.6 shows consistent *nation-to-nation* differences. When attitudes about participation are widely shared within a nation, they take on a far more social character. They become part of the national political culture, the collection of beliefs and political habits held in common by very large numbers of people. For example, the feelings the Italian farmer expressed in the quotation above—a sense of being neglected or exploited and thus owing little to the political order—are probably shared by many other Italian citizens, just as the sense of citizen duty is shared by most Americans.

The *sharing* of such beliefs can reinforce each individual's propensities mightily. The American, for example, gets his reverence for the Constitution, for free speech (at least in the abstract), as well as for political activity, from many different sources. His family, neighbors, school-teachers, newspapers, and television—all agree on the main civic virtues. In other countries other common themes are purveyed by these media. Similarly each country develops its own characteristic patterns of political action, so that the obligation to participate gets worked out in special ways. Thus political culture helps shape motives for citizen action.

[18]Hadley Cantril, *Human Nature and Political Systems* (New Brunswick, N.J.: Rutgers University Press, 1961), p. 16.

Looking at patterns of political obligation in other countries breeds caution in elevating common American values to universal truths. For instance, the American emphasis on more participation by more people in more ways perhaps fits our special needs. But as experience in totalitarian countries shows, belief in participation is no guarantee of effective democracy. Without doubt Communist China beats the United States in the frequency and intensity of exhortations to participate, and the voting turnout figures for Nazi and Soviet "elections" have been very high indeed. So it is by no means clear that everywhere and every time more participation in politics is a good thing.

what I can do

As these comparisons show, we need to pay attention to the actual meaning of participation in practice, which leads us to another main dimension of motives for citizen politics. This is the belief that participation will make a difference. Undoubtedly many people in the Soviet Union and in the United States vote without thinking much about the effects of voting. But there is good evidence that a sense of political efficacy—a feeling that the affairs of government can be understood and influenced by individual citizens—encourages voting participation in the United States. In 1956, only 52 percent of those scoring low on an index of political efficacy voted, while 91 percent of those scoring high voted.[19] This sense of efficacy is more than just gratitude for rewards from a beneficent government; it can be interpreted as a feeling that a citizen can *use* the government to improve his life situation, that government is a ready instrument responsive to his instructions.

In their massive survey of five nations, Almond and Verba used a variant of the sense of political efficacy which they call "citizen competence." Citizen competence is measured by several questions resulting in a score for each country, which is the percentage of respondents "who say they can do something about an unjust law on both national and local level." A look at these comparative figures, broken down by nation and education, reveals

[19]Campbell *et al., op. cit.,* pp. 104–5.

some interesting dimensions of this type of political motive. Table 1.7 shows the percentages of respondents in each country and at each educational level who said they could do something about an unjust law on both national and local levels. Here we see roughly the same orders of comparison as in Table 1.6 on the obligation to participate. Probably a good part of these differences in participation rates is due to differences in feelings about the practical possibilities for affecting government action, in addition to the feelings of duty we have already examined. Half the Americans with grade school education feel they can do something about an unjust law, at both the local *and* the national levels. Only one out of five Italians at the same educational level feels that way.

The right-hand column of Table 1.7 shows the difference education makes in civic-competence scores in each nation.

TABLE 1.7
"Citizen Competence" in Five Nations, by Educational Level

Nation	Education		
	(a) Primary or less	*(b) Secondary or above*	*Difference (b − a)*
United States	51%	85%	34
Great Britain	53	64	11
Germany	29	58	29
Italy	20	37	17
Mexico	31	49	18

Source: Gabriel A. Almond and Sidney Verba, *The Civic Culture*, Figure VII.1, p. 173. Copyright © 1963 by Princeton University Press. Reprinted by permission of Princeton University Press. Numbers on which the percentages are based omitted, and "Difference" column added.

Eighty-five percent of those who have been to secondary school in the United States feel they have the power to do something about an unjust law—a leap of 34 percentage points over the figure for those whose education stopped at grade school. In Germany, also, education makes a big difference in how competent citizens feel. In Great Britain, on the other hand, education appears to have less of an impact on this feeling that one can affect his government; Italy and Mexico are intermediate here. Obviously in each country there are many people who are motivated to take part in politics because they think it will do some good. The sense of citizen competence is a culturally supported one. But as Almond and Verba suggest:

> . . . whether or not one believes himself capable of influencing a local or national regulation depends a lot on who he is within his own country. If he has more education, higher status, or is male, he is clearly more likely to consider himself competent. One's self-perceptions of his role as a citizen vary greatly with one's social position within a nation.[20]

As far as education is concerned, this is truer for some countries than for others, as Table 1.7 shows. In some nations, such as the United States and Germany, the more educated and the less educated are widely separated in their sense of civic competence, but in Britain the less educated feel just about as competent as the more educated. To oversimplify: in Britain—generally considered an "artistocratic" nation—members of the educated elite are not much more likely to feel politically powerful than are their ignorant brethren. In the United States—land of equality—those who make it to high school and beyond are much more confident of their political power than are those with only a grade school education.

This rather surprising finding points up the need to look beyond national generalities to group details. Within each country, there are groups not fully sharing in the national pattern. The U.S.A. stands highest among Almond and Verba's five nations on almost every count, but not every American is included. For example:

> The apathy, the aimlessness, the lack of interest in education that characterize the Negro lower classes, and the crisis of identity that afflicts Negroes of all classes, stem from their sense of dependency and powerlessness—their conviction that "Mr. Charlie" controls everything, Negro leaders included, and that he has stacked the cards so that Negroes can never win.[21]

To people who feel they have little or no say in what government does, there would appear to be little use in preachments that they

---

[20]Almond and Verba, *op. cit.*, p. 167. Reprinted by permission of Princeton University Press.

[21]Charles E. Silberman, *Crisis in Black and White* (New York: Random House, 1964), p. 198.

have a duty to participate. Over the long run, the sense of obligation to take part has to be backed up by the sense that one can make good things happen by taking part. Otherwise, frustration and disillusionment sap interest in playing political games.

Many college students who have never personally experienced the oppression of ghetto life share this sense of powerlessness. They feel caught up in a gigantic machine that grinds away their individuality and then plugs them into some fixed slot in the system. They see a society and a political order so dominated by powerful organized forces that there is little use in trying to make progress through politics. There is enough truth in this picture, enough evidence of real suppression of dissent and innovation, and enough clear examples of political stagnation and triviality to discourage even the most hopeful. Perhaps the wonder is that more young people have not yet given up on political action, that so many reject violence or withdrawal and choose instead the tough, slow work of politics.

Clearly, young people who fail to educate themselves for adult political roles are going to lack a key resource for shaping the system. Similarly a person who opts out of politics because he feels powerless is going to wind up powerless. But it is also true that for participation to be meaningful, the system itself must be open enough—and responsive enough—to produce the forward political movement each new generation demands.

motives, opportunities, resources

These three elements fit together to explain citizen participation. They support and reinforce and compensate for one another. Where opportunities are plentiful, only moderately mild motives and a few simple resources may be necessary to trigger participation. People with a generous supply of political resources will not be permanently stopped by scarcity of opportunities; in the long run, they will create them. And the fanatic whose motives are exceptionally strong may find some way to get into the game even if he is relatively resourceless. Here as elsewhere in social science, degrees and quantities and intensities count, and no single element suffices to untangle the web.

chapter ii

Political Action Situations

Any action—including any political action—is a combination of opportunities and resources and motives. For purposes of analysis, we separate them; that is what analysis means. We take something apart to see what makes it go. Synthesis, putting together, is the next step. We turn from the pieces to the whole, from labeling parts to fitting them together in special combinations. Knowing what the parts are helps.

Politics is a series of such combinations, a set of action situations in which motives, opportunities, and resources interact to produce results. In this chapter we shall look at three packages of these factors, three political action situations that illustrate the *interactions* among the basic parts.

To see how these factors work together, consider students in the politics of 1970.[1] That Spring, the invasion of Cambodia and the killings at Kent State and Jackson State Colleges touched off a wave of protest on campuses across the country. Strikes, demonstrations, teach-ins, marches, petitions, and a few violent incidents evidenced the general outrage students felt. Thousands packed off to Washington; thousands more signed up to work in politics for an end to the war.

Rapidly, organizations sprang to life to channel these energies. Professors solicited their colleagues for "a day's pay for peace." Businessmen and mothers and Wall Street lawyers formed new groups, and older labor, civil rights, and ecology groups leaped into the fray. But most national attention focused on the students. The Movement for a New Congress, founded at Princeton, gathered the main forces for practical work in the 1970 Congressional primaries and elections.[2] By June, MNC had chapters on 417 campuses. Excited journalists estimated that as many as 500,000 students would be active in the campaign. Far fewer carried through. Compared with the inflated hopes of May, the performance was a disappointment. Compared with the 1970 activity levels of other age groups, or the past record of student participation, students turned out in impressive numbers. Probably at least 25,000 took some sustained part in the campaign. And these efforts paid off:

> The primary season ended with twenty-five of the thirty candidates who received substantial student aid victorious. These were not easy victories. Five of these doves beat incumbents with from twenty to twenty-eight years of seniority.[3]

[1] William T. Murphy, Jr., "Student Power in the 1970 Election: A Preliminary Assessment," *PS*, Vol. IV, No. 1 (Winter, 1971).

[2] Other groups stressing lobbying (Academic and Professional Alliance, Continuing Presence in Washington), petitioning (National Petition Committee) and fund-raising (Universities' National Anti-War Fund) joined with MNC to form the National Coalition for a Responsible Congress.

[3] *Ibid.*, p. 27.

The main strategy was to turn out voters (identified by a systematic canvass) who favored the antiwar candidate. In the November election, intensive work by MNC volunteers played a critical role in winning at least four Senate and fifteen House races.

Students turned to politics out of a variety of reasons. Undoubtedly, the strongest motive was a hope for peace and a desire to take practical action to that end. Those who worked hard made real sacrifices. Some were turned off by a cool reception from older politicians, some by the drift of Administration policy toward withdrawal from Vietnam, and some by the routine chores expected of volunteers. But in many cases, those who lasted the distance found much satisfaction in the struggle.

Students had several special resources—mainly, time. Several universities gave students time off to campaign. But even without this advantage, a student could find time to devote to politics much more easily than most citizens could. Further, students (especially those living on the campuses of their colleges) were relatively easy to organize because of their receptiveness and familiarity with the skills of campus organization. And by and large, students were—or quickly became—relatively well-informed about the issues.

Most important, 1970 was an election year. In some states and districts where no peace candidates were running, students found nothing to volunteer for. Elsewhere, students were welcomed by candidates who knew from experience that canvassing works—not so much to change people's minds as to find and get the right voters to the polls. Furthermore, it quickly became apparent that Americans, most of whom had no use for "student unrest," thought well of students working door-to-door in political campaigns. Seventy-eight percent of voters polled in one study thought it was a good idea for students to work in campaigns. Actually, many voters did not identify the young person on the doorstep as a "student," but as a regular party worker.[4]

In this case, action—or, better, thousands of actions—developed out of a special set of circumstances, and a particular

[4] *Ibid.*, p. 28.

combination of motives, opportunities and resources. Whether the thrust of student political activism would fade or persevere would depend on sustaining that combination or building new ones.

women in politics

The Almond and Verba five-nation study described in chapter i shows some interesting data on males and females in politics, set forth in Table 2.1.

TABLE 2.1
Percentage of Respondents Who Belong to Some Organization

Nation	Male	Female	Difference
United States	68%	47%	21
Great Britain	66	30	36
Germany	66	24	42
Italy	41	19	22
Mexico	43	15	28

Source: Gabriel A. Almond and Sidney Verba, *The Civic Culture* (Princeton, N.J.: Princeton University Press, 1963), Table X.3, p. 247. Copyright © 1963 by Princeton University Press. Reprinted by permission of Princeton University Press. "Total" column and numbers upon which percentages based omitted.

In every country, men are more likely to belong to an organization than women are, but notice how important an element female participation is: in the top three countries, the United States, Great Britain, and Germany, almost exactly the same proportion of *males* — two-thirds of them — belong to some organization. It is the higher participation rate of *women* in the United States that sets us off from Britain and Germany. Also, notice the "Difference" column. Sex makes less difference in American participation rates than in the British and German rates. Men in the other four countries are two to three times as likely as women to belong to some organization; American women are not nearly that far behind the men. And when it comes to being officers in organizations, the women beat the men by a comfortable margin: 52 percent of female organization members have been officers, compared to only 41 percent of the men.[5]

[5] Gabriel A. Almond and Sidney Verba, *The Civic Culture* (Princeton, N.J.: Princeton University Press, 1963), Table X.8, p. 259.

How to account for these variations in the political role of women? Motives are undoubtedly one important factor. The German *Hausfrau*, the Italian *casalinga*, and, to a lesser extent, their sisters in the United States and Britain tend to view their main role as centered in home and family, and to leave politics to the menfolk. Each culture has its peculiar variations on this theme; German women in particular contrast markedly with German men in organization memberships, and this very probably reflects a strong cultural tradition of male dominance, a tradition most German women probably accept and believe in. In Mexico and Italy these feelings are also widespread, but since the general level of participation — for both males and females — is so low, the contrast between the sexes is not so glaring.

In the United States, the voting rate for women is about 10 percent less than that for men. In the "sense of citizen duty" there is little difference between men and women; in fact, high-school-and college-educated women "are frequently more apt to endorse the common 'oughts' of good citizenship than are men."[6] So women's lesser participation is probably not due to any lack of dutiful feelings. (Although possibly women who score high on citizen duty questions simply mean that their *husbands* ought to be active citizens.) It is the sense of political efficacy — the feeling that one's participation makes a real difference — that separates the men from the women, as Table 2.2 shows. In both areas of the United States and at all educational levels, men appear to feel more confident that they can have an impact on political affairs.[7] This may be changed profoundly in the 1970's as more women, through a growing awareness of their shared problems and interests as women, organize and produce political results.

But of course such motivational differences are not the whole story. Women do have different opportunities for participation than men do. As we saw above, they are more likely to have been officers in their organizations than are men in theirs — perhaps because women's organizations are not so large as men's, on the average, so that women have more chances to serve as officers.

[6]Angus Campbell *et al.*, *The American Voter* (New York: Wiley, 1960), p. 489.

[7]The roots of this contrast go back into childhood. See Fred I. Greenstein, *Children and Politics* (New Haven, Conn.: Yale University Press, 1965), Chapter 6, on sex-related political differences.

TABLE 2.2
Percentage Scoring High on "Sense of Political Efficacy,"
by Sex, Region, and Educational Level, 1956

Region and education	Male	Female	Difference
Non-South			
Grade school	32%	13%	19
High school	47	40	7
College	83	68	15
South			
Grade school	16	3	13
High school	37	31	6
College	78	56	22

Source: Angus Campbell *et al.*, *The American Voter* (New York: Wiley, 1960), Table 17–9, p. 491.

One reason women vote less than men is household demands: across all levels of education, mothers of young children, who find it harder to get out of the house, are less likely to vote than fathers of young children.[8] Much higher proportions of rural women than men fail to vote; in metropolitan areas the male-female vote difference is quite small.[9] Among other elements, this probably reflects the fact that many rural women have difficulty getting to the polls from the farm, while the big-city woman can usually find her polling place just down the street. Numerous other opportunity factors, such as the hours and places political clubs have their meetings, affect sex differences in political participation.

As for resources, the data on educational differences, shown in Table 2.3, are enlightening—and encouraging, for those who think more women should take part. College-educated women are almost as likely to vote as are college men in the United States, and Almond and Verba find that "education reduces the rate of apathy among women in all countries."[10] Sex differences in frequency of political discussion are far smaller among the highly educated than among those who did not complete primary school.[11] Education—here again one of the most powerful variables in the analysis of participation—tends to overcome other

[8] Campbell *et al.*, *op. cit.*, p. 488.
[9] *Ibid.*, p. 487.
[10] Almond and Verba, *op. cit.*, p. 332.
[11] *Ibid.*, p. 327.

sources of difference. Give women the resources to take part in politics and they are apt to find the necessary opportunities and motives.

TABLE 2.3
Percentage Scoring High* in Political Participation,
by Sex and Educational Level, 1956

Education	Male	Female	Difference
Grade school	70%	52%	18
High school	80	71	9
College	91	88	3

Source: V. O. Key, Jr., *Public Opinion and American Democracy* (New York: Knopf, 1961), Table 13.9, p. 331. Copyright © 1961 by V. O. Key, Jr. Reprinted by permission of Alfred A. Knopf, Inc.
  *A score of 3 or 4.

A close look at the life situation of women shows how motives, opportunities, and resources are combined. These analytic categories, useful for systematic thinking about participation, are woven together in the practical circumstances of life. For most women, life centers in the family, so the character of family life in a particular political culture helps to explain the character of female participation. Almond and Verba make this clear in an insightful passage:

> If we consider these data from the point of view of the political system in the five countries, it is evident that we have to revise older theories of the role of women in democracy. These theories have tended to treat the sex differential in the same way that they treat other demographic categories, such as income, occupation, education, and the like. What they have overlooked is the fact that the great majority of adults are married; that they create families, raise children, and help to socialize these children into their adult roles and attitudes. Thus the political characteristics of women affect the family as a unit in the political system and affect the way in which the family performs the political socialization function. In all five countries, of course, the overwhelming majority of politicians, civil servants, and political activists are men. But it makes a great deal of difference whether women tend to live outside the political system in an intramural family existence, which is generally the case in Italy and among the relatively uneducated German and Mexican women, or within the political system, which tends to be the case in the United States and Britain. Duverger's com-

ment that women ". . . have the mentality of minors in many fields and, particularly in politics, they usually accept paternalism on the part of men. The man—husband, fiancé, lover, or myth—is the mediator between them and the political world" is an essentially continental European comment, and even here Duverger may be commenting more on the past and present than on the future.[12]

Attitudes linked with something as fundamental as sex are not likely to change radically in a short time. But over the years, as more women obtain advanced education, as the number of young children per family declines, as more families move from farms to urban suburbs, and as "American" attitudes about relationships in the family take root in other parts of the world, we can expect a general and accelerating growth in the participation of citizens who are also women.

the Goldwater nomination

Rarely in American political history has there been a Presidential election as offbeat as that of 1964. Lyndon Johnson got nearly 16 million more votes than Barry Goldwater. If, as has so often been said, national party conventions aim to nominate a winner, to pick the one candidate who has the best chance of capturing the Presidency for his party, the Republican National Convention made an immense mistake in 1964. A careful and fascinating analysis of the 1964 election by Philip E. Converse, Aage R. Clausen, and Warren E. Miller of the University of Michigan gives some clues to what happened.[13]

All through the 1940's and 1950's the conservative wing of the Republican party had been arguing that a great many "real" Republicans did not bother to vote because the party's Presidential candidates were too middle-of-the-road in ideology. "Nominate a true Republican rather than a Tweedledee, the theory went,

[12] *Ibid.*, pp. 333–34. Reprinted by permission of Princeton University Press. The internal quotation is from Maurice Duverger, *The Political Role of Women* (Paris, 1955), p. 129.

[13] Philip E. Converse, Aage R. Clausen, and Warren E. Miller, "Electoral Myth and Reality: The 1964 Election," *American Political Science Review*, Vol. 59, No. 2 (June, 1965), 321–36.

and enough of these stay at homes would return to the polls to put him in the White House."[14] This theory persisted despite the steady accumulation of evidence to refute it. In fact:

- From at least 1944 on, Republicans have had higher rates of voting than Democrats, even though Republican nominees in these years were never selected from the party's conservative wing.
- Republicans with strong feelings of commitment to the party ("real" Republicans?) and highly developed ideological beliefs had remarkably high turnout rates during this period, on the order of 96 and 98 percent.
- In 1952, Republicans who preferred the conservative Robert A. Taft as their candidate actually turned out to vote for Eisenhower in much higher proportions than did Republicans who preferred Eisenhower—and this by a significant margin, 94 percent to 84 percent!

Despite these facts, the theory of a large stay-at-home Republican vote, waiting to leap forth into the electorate as soon as a conservative candidate appeared, continues to be heard. As Converse, Clausen, and Miller note,

> It is less of a wonder that the theory was generated, particularly before sample survey data took on much scope or stature in the 1940's, than that it persisted with greater or lesser vigor into the 1960's in the face of repetitive contradictory evidence readily available to any proponents with an edge of interest as to what the facts actually were.[15]

Why *has* this theory persisted in conservative Republican circles? Converse and his associates put forth an intriguing tentative explanation. For a number of reasons, Goldwater and those around him seem to have distrusted public opinion polls and to have felt they knew better from other sources how the voters were thinking. One such source may have been the opinions of a small but very vocal segment of the electorate: those who write letters to public officials or to newspapers and magazines. In the Survey

[14] *Ibid.*, p. 322.
[15] *Ibid.*, p. 323.

Research Center national polls, only about 15 percent of the adult population reports ever having written to a public official, and two-thirds of the letters were written by about 3 percent of the population. Letters to newspapers or magazines were written by about 3 percent of the people, and two-thirds of these were written by fewer than one-half of 1 percent of the people.

Now suppose the conservatives were basing their estimates of the electorate's mind on the letters their colleagues in government received and those that appeared in the press—the way many estimates of public opinion were made before systematic polling was common. To get a picture of how the public's sentiment would look by that method, Converse, Clausen, and Miller scored each person who had written one or more letters to officials or the press by giving him one "vote" for every such letter he had written in the preceding four years. In other words, a person who favors Goldwater and has written six letters to the editor scores six for Goldwater, a person who favors Johnson and has written three letters scores three for Johnson, and so forth. These figures might give some indication of national political opinion as it would appear to an analyst relying on what he reads in the mail and the letters columns.

This "letter opinion" turns out to be strikingly out of line with the poll results. For example, in early 1964 samplings of vote intention, a national opinion poll showed Johnson leading Goldwater by nearly 3 to 1—but the "letter opinion" had Goldwater leading Johnson by a wide and comfortable margin! Similarly, far more Republicans and independents polled at the time of the Republican convention preferred some other Republican nominee than preferred Goldwater—but the "letter opinion" showed Goldwater out-distancing all other candidates combined. Voters who felt the federal government was getting too strong, who opposed negotiation with Communists, and who had relatively elaborate conservative ideologies stood out far more clearly in the "letter opinion" than in the national sample surveys.[16] Similarly in 1967, letter writers were far more likely (63 percent) to favor intensifying the war in Vietnam than was the general public

---

[16]Sidney Verba and Richard A. Brody, "Participation, Preferences and the War in Vietnam," *Public Opinion Quarterly* (Fall, 1970).

(49 percent). Only 12.5 percent of those who participated in demonstrations wanted to accelerate the war.[17]

This special case of the 1964 election drives home three lessons for the student of political participation. One is that any theory predicting massive changes in participation under certain conditions must deal with a few key questions: Who are the citizens who will change their behavior? What is their present level of participation? And what might lead large numbers to become more active or less active? Often the problem for analysis disappears rapidly as soon as a few facts are held up against the theory. In this case, since there were in fact relatively few conservatively oriented citizens outside the active electorate, pondering how to bring large numbers of them in would be a fruitless exercise.

Second, the disparities between "letter opinion" and survey opinion remind us of the marked discontinuities in various forms of participation. We can be sure that an extremely high percentage of those who write letters also vote. But only a small fraction of those who vote write letters. And most significant: the people who engage in the more active forms of participation (such as letter writing) may be not at all representative of the general population.

Third, this case cautions against neglecting any one of our three basic factors. The Goldwater champions could easily have learned that most Americans are not practiced in writing letters on political matters, that most lack the desire to write them, and that editors are inclined to select which few to print of the many they receive. If these statements had been strongly contradicted by evidence in 1964, Goldwaterites could rationally have taken some encouragement. But in all three respects—in motives, opportunity, and resources—the letter writers were atypical.

the Negro in New Haven

If one way to be misled about citizen participation is to scan only the most visible evidence, another is to rely on one factor alone to explain the participation. Take politically relevant resources,

[17]Sidney Verba and Philip E. Converse, *Vietnam and the Silent Majority* (New York: Harper & Row, 1970), p. 33.

for example. We have seen how economic status is an important political resource. Across the board, nationally, those with more money and better jobs are more likely than their opposites to take part in politics. Finding such a persistent regularity, the analyst is tempted to make it the touchstone of an economic interpretation of politics, to simplify the matter by a radical excision of other factors.

That resources give us only part of the picture, and that explanations based wholly on political resource analysis can be vastly misleading, is evident from some data in Robert A. Dahl's *Who Governs?*[18] Negro citizens in New Haven, Connecticut, have clearly been disadvantaged in economic terms. The Negro ward in New Haven, Dahl found, was near the bottom of the list in median income and the proportion of the labor force in white-collar jobs. Surely, someone who sees economic relationships as the basis for politics would predict very low levels of voting, campaigning, and officeholding for this group compared with those better off. Indeed, this kind of prediction appeared to hold *in general* for New Haven: the lower the income, the less participation in local political affairs.

But for Negroes the evidence was markedly out of line. Only one out of ten of the registered voters was a Negro—but one out of four of those who participated most in campaign and election activities was Negro. Forty-four percent of the Negroes were among Dahl's "high" and "highest" campaign participants, compared with only 20 percent of the whites. New Haven Negroes were far more likely than whites to prefer a job with the city government to one with a private firm. In other words, Negroes participated in New Haven politics far more than a strictly economic-resources explanation would lead one to expect.

To explain these strange findings we need to look beyond money and job status to other factors. In the first place, New Haven Negroes were not completely bereft of politically relevant resources: in education the main Negro ward, with a median of 8.8 school years completed, was only slightly below the median for the whole city, 9.1 years. Negro income and job levels were markedly lower than those for whites, but the contrast was not

[18]Robert A. Dahl, *Who Governs? Democracy and Power in an American City* (New Haven, Conn.: Yale University Press, 1961).

nearly so stark as in many other communities throughout the nation. The minimal resources for political action were there.

But more significant were opportunity and motivation factors. Opportunities for political participation by Negroes were far more readily available than opportunities in other arenas of enterprise. Negroes met high barriers in nonpolitical arenas. There was much discrimination in housing and in hiring for private enterprise throughout the New Haven area. But as Dahl points out, the Negro got a *relatively* better break in politics:

> In contrast to the situation the Negro faces in the private socioeconomic sphere, in local politics and government the barriers are comparatively slight. There is no discrimination against Negroes who wish to vote; they have participated in elections for generations. Though they are a relatively small minority, both parties compete vigorously for their support. Partly because of their votes, Negroes are not discriminated against in city employment; they have only to meet the qualifications required of white applicants to become policemen, firemen, school teachers, clerks, stenographers. Negroes also share in city patronage, city contracts, and other favors. Because both parties nominate a Negro to run as alderman from the Nineteenth Ward, the Board of Aldermen always contains one Negro. Both parties nominate a Negro to one city-wide elective office. In 1954 Mayor Lee appointed a Negro as corporation counsel, in 1960 he appointed a Negro to the Board of Education.[19]

Given this special set of opportunities *in politics,* Negroes spent their relatively meager resources for *political* action at a much higher rate than the economic determinist might suppose. The implication is clear; where barriers are low, modest resources will suffice to overcome them.

Provided, however, there is sufficient motivation. In the case of the New Haven Negroes, two kinds of motives were probably most important. Personal motives were linked with politics. A Negro could get a job with the city. He could take a significant role in party activities. Politics was a path to patronage and other welfare benefits for many Negroes. So the Negro looking out for his family and his own career might well turn to political action. More broadly, though still linked with personal motives, were

[19] *Ibid.,* p. 294.

policy motives. The Lee administration, while certainly not perfect in these regards, had driven through policies in urban development, job training, and education which promised to distribute important benefits to the Negro community. Mayor Lee's remarkable effectiveness in marshaling Negro support and action was due in no small measure to these policy proposals. Negroes were motivated to take advantage of their special political opportunities because they thought they stood to gain, individually and collectively, a better life through government action.[20]

situations and situations

These examples do more than tell stories. They are meant to illustrate, concretely, how basic factors come together to produce action. Along with information, you should be picking up some ways of thinking that will be useful in figuring out other situations.

The idea of abstraction should come across. Every situation is unique; life is very complicated. Politics in particular is a tangle of complexity. We get at what it means and how it works by abstracting from the morass of detail the factors of key importance, those powerful causes and effects that show up in many different situations.

[20]Only later did it become apparent to the Negro community that urban development could leave them even worse off in terms of housing and show little improvement in their employment rates.

chapter iii

Political Thinking

In 1971, the eighteen- to twenty-year-olds got the vote. Millions of young people were added to the eligible electorate for 1972. No one could foresee the results, but the decision required Congress, the courts and state legislatures to make some interesting guesses.

Nearly every time Americans debate adding voters, the same arguments about facts come up, arguments similar in many ways to those that have surrounded nearly every historical debate about extending the franchise — to the propertyless, women, soldiers, southern Negroes in America, as to the common man in England. One set of arguments centers in the minds and hearts of the potential citizens in question. Do they know enough

43

to vote wisely? Do they understand and believe in the democratic process? Do they have the good judgment to take part in important decisions? Information, beliefs, and judgment—these are the individual qualities on which the issue has often turned.

Then there are some questions of social relations that go beyond the individual. Will the new voters form a bloc, a tight-knit cluster capable of swinging elections their way? Will they simply follow their leaders—the wives their husbands, the students their professors? These are questions of fact or of prediction about what will actually happen if . . . Of course, much of the argument has also focused on questions of moral principle, questions of the *right* to vote as distinguished from the practical effects of expanding the suffrage. The broad answer on the latter is in, at least for the United States. We have opened the gates of political participation and the foundations of free government remain solid.

But the broad answers fuzz over some difficult questions about how democracies manage to perform effectively. For democracy to work, what is required of the citizens? What qualities of thought, what mental states foster or impede democratic politics? In this advanced democracy, what is the condition of the citizen's "political mind?"

knowing

Supposedly a citizen would need to know what the government is and does before he could make a rational judgment about political questions. This knowing, in the sense of simply having information, would seem to be about as primitive a test of citizen rationality as we could get. We have seen that a high proportion of eligible voters makes political decisions at the polls. In public opinion surveys, it is rare to find more than a quarter of the respondents with "no opinion." What is the information base for these actions and opinions?

To understand the game, we might think, one should know who the players are. Here is some evidence from a dramatic election year in which the first Republican in twenty years was elected in a massive landslide:

> . . . In June 1952, two months before he was nominated for President, Adlai Stevenson was unknown to 66 percent of

the public. In August of that year, just after the conventions, with their attendant publicity, 55 percent of the public did not know the name of the Republican vice-presidential candidate, Richard Nixon, and 68 percent did not know the name of the Democratic vice-presidential candidate, John Sparkman.[1]

Some famous men fared better, but some worse: in 1955 only 33 percent knew who Karl Marx was, 10 percent of Americans could not identify Christopher Columbus, and only 22 percent had ever heard of Sigmund Freud.[2] When we move down from the national level, the picture is even worse. Typically less than half the people know who their Congressman is, and only a bare majority can name one of their Senators. Far fewer are able to identify those who conduct local governments.[3]

Leaders change, but institutions endure. What of the public's notions of the basics of our constitutional system? In 1945, a cross-section of the nation was asked, "What do you know about the Bill of Rights? Do you know anything it says?" Nearly four out of five voters failed to give a correct answer. That same year responses to the question "How many Senators are there in Washington from your state?" were only 55 percent correct. Ten years later only 35 percent knew what the electoral college is, and in 1954 only 19 percent could give a correct answer to: "Will you tell me what the three branches of the Federal Government are called?"[4]

Issues? Often fairly large proportions of the public — in the 70 and 80 percents — claim to have some awareness of major issues. But this tells us little of their actual information on such issues. Even on the softer criterion of "awareness," we fall short on many significant questions. In 1961, only 22 percent said they had heard or read anything about the Common Market.[5] In repeated

[1] Robert E. Lane and David O. Sears, *Public Opinion* (Englewood Cliffs, N.J.: Prentice-Hall, 1964), p. 58.

[2] Hazel G. Erskine, "The Polls: The Informed Public," *Public Opinion Quarterly*, Vol. 26 (1962), 669–77, as cited in David O. Sears, "Political Behavior," in G. Lindzey and E. Aaronson (eds.), *Handbook of Social Psychology*, rev. ed. (Reading, Mass.: Addison-Wesley, 1968).

[3] *Ibid.*

[4] Lane and Sears, *op. cit.*, p. 61.

[5] Erskine, *op. cit.*; Erskine, "The Polls: Exposure to Domestic Information," *Public Opinion Quarterly*, Vol. 27 (1963), 491–500; Erskine, "The Polls: Exposure to International Information," *Public Opinion Quarterly*, Vol. 27 (1963), 658–62, as cited in Sears, *op. cit.*

polls only about half gave some reasonably accurate description of the "cold war."[6] Nearly everyone claimed to have read or heard about it when one of our U-2 planes was shot down, but only about a fifth to a fourth of the public had heard or read about the term "bipartisan foreign policy," the Americans for Democratic Action, President Truman's Point Four Program, or the Bricker Amendment.[7]

On the information score, then, the public looks pretty bad. Most readers of this book can make a quick confirmation of this point. As college students, you are probably well above the national average in education and intelligence and attention to public affairs. Therefore we would expect a considerably higher level of political knowledge from you than from the average person, a level commensurate with the role of the active, attentive citizen concerned with local, national, and international affairs. Perhaps it would not be unreasonable to expect you to know:

—the names of several leaders just below the top in the Soviet Union, the name of the minority party leader in the House of Representatives who would become speaker if his party won a majority, and the names of several of the leading members of your local legislative body;

—about half the provisions of the Bill of Rights, the main requirements in the Constitution for eligibility for election as Senator and as Representative, the procedure for selecting a President in case no candidate gets a majority of the electoral votes, and how chairmen of Congressional committees are chosen;

—what a reciprocal trade agreement is, the population of India (within 20 million), what the Office of Economic Opportunity does, and why "a man's home is his castle" and "neighborhood schools" often have reflected anti-Negro feelings.

Odds are this self-survey reveals some gaps. A great many people who have to make judgments about candidates—and that is the main judgment citizens are called upon to make—seem to lack the rudiments of knowledge of the system in which these candidates will work. Take Congress, for example. A great deal of political science work has gone into analyzing the groupings

[6] Lane and Sears, *op. cit.*, p. 59.
[7] Sears, *op. cit.*

of Congressional votes, stability and change in Congressional blocs, the ins and outs of Congressional strategies. For most of the public, this is like a foreign language. Not even half the public knows which party controls Congress,[8] much less what the members of Congress do. At one off-year election time, only about a quarter of the public had heard or read *anything* about both candidates for the House of Representatives from their districts, and for 46 percent the whole affair was a blank, since they knew nothing about either candidate.[9]

What shall we make of these findings? The numbers themselves are neutral; as in the case of evaluating participation rates, the facts alone cannot tell us whether these levels of political knowledge are high or low or middling. The optimist can find comfort in some comparisons: Americans today probably know more about politics and public affairs than ever before in our history. More of us are better educated and have access to much larger stores of information from the mass media than our grandfathers had. Also Americans are better informed, on the average, than the citizens of nearly all other countries in the world.[10] The pessimist, on the other hand, can argue that in a time when the United States confronts problems of immense complexity and fatefulness for the welfare of the world, most of the public lacks even the rudiments of political understanding.

But our task here is to become not optimists or pessimists, but realists. The facts show the need to readjust our expectations about what the public knows. We need to fix in our minds the idea that democracy survives in this country in a context of general ignorance about government. And we need to try to account for both the ignorance and the survival. This requires some reexamination of our premises.

What is it realistic to expect the general public to know about

[8]Lane and Sears, *op. cit.*, p. 61.

[9]Warren E. Miller and Donald E. Stokes, "Constituency Influence in Congress," in Angus Campbell *et al.* (eds.), *Elections and the Political Order* (New York: Wiley, 1966), p. 367. In polls taken in 1957 and 1958, only about half as many people (37 percent) could identify the famous person who said, "The only thing we have to fear is fear itself," as could identify who said "Hi-ho, Silver!" (71 percent). *Public Opinion Quarterly*, Vol. 27, No. 1 (Spring, 1963).

[10]Gabriel A. Almond and Sidney Verba, *The Civic Culture* (Princeton, N.J.: Princeton University Press, 1963), p. 58. Canadians may do a little better. See Lane and Sears, *op. cit.*, p. 58.

politics and government? Most people acquire knowledge and retain knowledge when they have a need for it, the ability to take it in and hold it, and the chance to get and keep it without excessive cost. In other words, the acquisition and retention of political information is an act of participation, and can be analyzed as we analyzed other forms of political participation in chapter i. Take first the opportunity factor. It would seem that Americans suffer from no lack of opportunities to acquire political information. Newspapers, television, schools, libraries are all full of facts about politics. The problem is not the quantity of information available; there is plenty for all. The opportunity problem is its lack of organization. Every student knows how much easier it is to put facts into his head when he can organize them into some coherent framework, some set of relationships that "makes sense" out of a mass of detail. Bits and pieces of fact get lost quickly unless they are glued together in a larger picture. But much political information as it reaches the average citizen consists of just such unglued bits. He is bombarded with stimuli on many topics, from many directions, presented in many contexts. Much of it is "news," which by definition is something different from, some departure from, the information he had before. The cost of sorting all this out may be very high indeed, requiring considerable time and skill (resources) and/or considerable desire (motives).

Public skill levels for these tasks are probably on the rise, with rising education, even though much schoolwork is poor preparation for independent analysis and synthesis. Motivational levels are probably also increasing. People are motivated to learn when they can see some payoff for learning, and the growth of government, with its increasing involvement in many facets of life, gives more people more reasons for trying to learn what they need to know to cope with it. Despite this, however, as you will recall from chapter i, only a thin layer of the public participates in political activities beyond voting. The average citizen has little occasion to amass political knowledge. Most of the time he has little use for it, and there are other, more pressing demands on his senses and memory. Around election time he will pay more attention because he will soon have to vote; he feels some knowledge will make it easier for him to decide which way to vote. *When he needs something* from the government—a driver's license, a job, help on the income tax, a draft deferment—*he will* make some effort to *find out* about the situation. Otherwise, it is never very clear to him why, for his own benefit, he should trouble himself with the technics of government.

If things are going well, what does he care about the electoral college?

categorizing

Suppose a citizen has some motive for political learning, perhaps because he has to make some decision involving the political order. (Of course, sometimes citizens will learn for the love of learning—particularly the political buff, who follows politics as some others follow baseball—but this situation is rare enough for us to put it aside.) A prime tool in his political learning, as in all learning, will be categorizing—step one in the process of organized thinking. Language itself is a form of categorizing. A child learns to read by grasping the association between certain symbols and certain objects. He learns the names of things, names that are abstract symbols for classes or sets of individual items sharing certain characteristics. This process of categorization is perhaps the one most powerful tool for thinking.

In their pioneering work *A Study of Thinking*, the psychologists Bruner, Goodnow, and Austin[11] spell out systematically why categorizing is so useful, indeed essential, for thinking. The effort involved in categorizing is considerable; the achievement of categories is worth it because:

- *Categories reduce the complexity of the environment;*
- *Categories enable us to identify (or place) the objects in the world around us;*
- *Categories reduce the necessity for constant learning;*
- *Categories provide direction for purposeful activity; and*
- *Categories make it possible for us to order and relate classes of events (not just individual items).*

These points may seem obvious, but their importance to citizen thinking about politics can hardly be overemphasized. Take,

[11] Jerome Bruner, Jacqueline J. Goodnow, and George A. Austin, *A Study of Thinking* (New York: Wiley, 1956), pp. 12ff.

for example, an item from the news, such as "HHH Blasts Admin Viet Stand; Calls for UN Force." This is an extremely complex statement, pure gibberish to the politically illiterate. To grasp its meaning the citizen must first know what the words mean; that is, he must relate the concepts to concrete people and events. "HHH" is not just another voice in the wilderness, but a particular politician who has been heard from before. The citizen trying to make sense of this headline may be able to put "HHH" in his place, so to speak, to identify him as a familiar political object rather than a complete mystery. Henceforth whenever he sees that symbol he can call up what he has learned about "HHH" before; he need not figure it all out again every time the symbol comes along. He may have reached a further step in this categorization: assessing the implications of the statement for his own action. In this stage, the citizen views this piece of news in a context of what he may do about it. Perhaps he has been compiling reasons (perhaps semiconsciously) for and against voting for Hubert Humphrey, and adds this item to that collection in a way that helps him make up his mind. And, finally, he can put this item in a much wider context, that of his *system* of concepts. He can see the statement as it is related to his larger picture of, for example, the unity of the Democratic party, the role of the United Nations in peacekeeping, the whole complex of categories implicit in the word "Viet."

When we speak of a citizen as trying to make sense of politics, trying to figure out what it means, trying to get the idea of it all, trying to know what to do about it, trying to get a clear picture of the situation—all these familiar phrases refer in part to problems of categorization.

What does political categorizing have to do with rational thinking about politics? It is easier to point out the extremes of irrationality here than to say just what a politically rational citizen does. A main dimension is rigidity vs. disorganization of thought. Our age has had plenty of examples of the rigid mind in politics. The doctrinaire communist and the doctrinaire anticommunist often share the rigid approach to politics. This is the closed mind, the mind that consists of *fixed* categories that experience is incapable of altering. Such a mind is a static structure, not a machine for thinking. It understands everything, in the sense that it fits every item it perceives quickly and easily into a few simple and definite boxes. It sidesteps all the difficulties of dealing with a sloppy, contradictory, clouded political world. Its world is neat and clean and false. Superficially logical, such a mind is often the prisoner of strong and deep emotional tides, of a basic desire to get away from the anxieties of realistic political calculation.

If the closed, rigid mind is irrational in the sense of being incapable of inventing new categories to suit new problems, the thoroughly open mind also has its irrational possibilities. Some people are so open-minded that they cannot sustain any useful categories for political analysis. They perceive disconnected events, bits and pieces of information, without being able to make anything of them. The style of thought is the "stream of consciousness." One perception follows another with no continuity or consistency. Such people are especially vulnerable to the fads of politics. They are easy to persuade, but it is not worth much to persuade them because they are unlikely to stay persuaded. The main defect here is a lack of the mental organization that enables one to make some sense of the complexities of politics.

Of course, most of us fall between these extremes. We have some capacity for categorization, but do not elevate our categories into fixed ideas. We are able to make decisions and take action even though we are never quite certain that our choices are the best ones. Most important, we can use information from the real world with some effectiveness, both because we have some mental constructs to help us interpret facts and because we can alter those constructs as we gain more experience and knowledge. Few of us do these things very well, but at least we are not locked into a jailhouse of fixed ideas or wandering around in a swamp of disconnected thoughts.

using political categories

We are viewing political categories as tools for political thinking. How does the public use these tools? There are at least three ways we might suppose that citizens would use political categories:

1. To put like phenomena together in the same category. Here we usually think of such dimensions as liberal vs. conservative. The citizen would make sense of the political world—of leaders,

groups, issues, etc. — by arranging them along a liberal-conservative scale. The model for this kind of conceptualizing is: A is like B, or at least, A shares certain important characteristics with B.

2. To link general categories with specific events. For example, we try to deduce from certain principles of democracy how we should act in particular cases. The model is: A is a special case of B, the general category. In logical terms, A follows from or is deducible from B.

3. To make predictions about the course of events. In making our political decisions we may be specially interested in projecting the effects of various policies. For instance, what effects would follow from a guaranteed annual wage for every American? Which among many plausible policies will best further the cause of international peace? The model for predictive categorizing is: If A happens, B will follow.

liberals and conservatives

Suppose we look first at the simplest of these types of uses: A and B belong together because they are alike, as exemplified in the concepts "liberal" and "conservative." How useful are these broad categories for citizen thinking?

In the first place, it is clear that these terms, familiar enough to most college students, do not enter heavily into the calculations of many citizens. To be sure, about half the population appears to have some idea of what liberal and conservative mean in American politics.[12] But when it comes to linking concepts with political choices, such as choosing one candidate for President over the other, only a thin slice of the electorate refers to this ideological dimension. In 1956, according to the University of Michigan Survey Research Center, only about 3.5 percent of the voters made fairly systematic use of a liberal-conservative dimension to order their thinking. This does not mean that even these voters were applying a worked-out philosophy, but only that they seemed to be clustering various facets of politics around a rough idea of liberalism vs. conservatism. Here is a sample of this type of response, coded in the highest category of ideological sophistication:

[12] Philip E. Converse, "The Nature of Belief Systems in Mass Publics," in David E. Apter (ed.), *Ideology and Discontent* (New York: Free Press, Macmillan, 1964), pp. 206–61.

(Like about Democrats?) No. (Is there anything at all you like about the Democratic Party?) No, nothing at all.

(Dislike about Democrats?) From being raised in a notoriously Republican section—a small town downstate—there were things I didn't like. There was family influence that way. (What in particular was there you didn't like about the Democratic Party?) Well, the Democratic Party tends to favor socialized medicine—and I'm being influenced in that because I came from a doctor's family.

(Like about Republicans?) Well, I think they're more middle-of-the-road—more conservative. (How do you mean, "conservative"?) They are not so subject to radical change. (Is there anything else in particular that you like about the Republican Party?) Oh, I like their foreign policy—and the segregation business, that's a middle-of-the-road policy. You can't push it too fast. You can instigate things, but you have to let them take their course slowly. (Is there anything else?) I don't like Mr. Hodge. (Is there anything else?) The labor unions telling workers how to vote—they know which side their bread is buttered on so they have to vote the way they are told to!

(Dislike about Republicans?) Mr. Hodge! (Is there anything else?) I can't think of anything.[13]

That is hardly to be considered an ideological reply, but it is nearer to being one than the great majority of responses. Another 12 percent made some use of liberal-conservative labels, but with even less content or consistency. As might be expected, education makes a big difference here: the highly educated are far more likely to think in these clusters, to have some coherent left-right way of perceiving the political environment.

But our concern here is less with labels than with substance. Even though most people do not use a liberal-conservative line, possibly they work out other ways of clustering or combining opinions on different topics. Sometimes people are logical without realizing it. How does the public stack up in relation to this much looser criterion?

The evidence available does not produce a picture of clear, consistent categories. For example, we might think that there would be a strong relationship between liberal positions on

[13]Campbell *et al.* (eds.), *op. cit.*, pp. 228–29.

domestic issues and internationalism—that those who think the national government should play a more positive role inside the country would also think the government should take a more active part in the world's affairs. Not so. Or at least not so in the Eisenhower years, for which we have the most detailed data. For example, in 1956 half of those who were "low" in liberalism were "high" in internationalism. Fifty-eight percent of those "high" in liberalism were also "high" in internationalism. In other words, an internationalist was just about as likely to be a conservative as to be a liberal.[14] There are many other such inconsistencies. For instance, there is not a strong relationship between (a) answers indicating that more ought to be done internationally (in foreign aid, military policy, etc.) and (b) answers indicating opposition to tax cuts. Similarly there are large numbers of voters who want the government to do more at home but at the same time cut taxes. In fact, as V. O. Key reported, "Taxation to finance welfare programs meets opposition among those who favor welfare programs even more frequently than among those who oppose them"[15]—a strange pattern. Conservatives on the issue of medical care for the aged were about as likely as liberals on this issue to favor school integration. Conservatives on a range of domestic issues were *more* likely than liberals to oppose the idea of firing "any government worker who is accused of being a communist even though they don't prove it."[16] Even in 1964, an election year in which there was much talk of ideology, there were only weak connections among issues for most voters.[17]

By and large, then, we do not have a picture of the American electorate as systematically clustering specific issues around a liberal-conservative ideological dimension.

"Consistency," after all, is in the eye of the beholder. To me, your opinions may be inconsistent if they

   (a) point toward actions that conflict with one another, or

   (b) derive from conflicting principles, or

   (c) refer to conflicting expectations of the future.

But to you, your "inconsistent" opinions may represent

---

[14]V. O. Key, Jr., *Public Opinion and American Democracy* (New York: Knopf, 1961), p. 158.

[15]*Ibid.*, p. 168.

[16]*Ibid.*, p. 171.

[17]Sears, *op. cit.*, p. 30.

(*a*) actions that are different but not mutually exclusive, or
(*b*) applications of principles to differing circumstances, or
(*c*) differing possibilities for a very uncertain future.
Furthermore, consistency may not be very high on your list of
fundamental values. For a great many citizens, the need for bringing their opinions into some consistent order comes up very
rarely, if at all. The question "Is opinion A like opinion B?" has to
take into account not just the bare words of the opinions, but also
their implications, the conditions under which they operate, and
the probability that their apparent likenesses or differences will
become significant.

principles and implications

Possibly we have been taking too close a look, focusing too immediately on contemporary issues. Political categories may exist
at a higher level of generality—that of principles of government,
for example—which can be seen only when we step back a way
from medicare, foreign aid, integration, etc.

Certainly there is an immense consensus in the United States
at the level of general political principles. As Robert A. Dahl notes,
"It is very nearly impossible to find an American who says that he
is opposed to democracy or favors some alternative. . . ."[18] In this
sense, we are all democrats. In surveys in the 1950's and 1960's,
only a very few respondents failed to agree with such statements
as "Democracy is the best form of government," "Public officials
should be chosen by majority vote," "The minority should be free
to criticize majority decisions," and "I believe in free speech for
all no matter what their views might be."[19] There is probably more
reverence for our form of government, at least in its broad constitutional outline, than in any other country.

But translating these principles into practice is another matter. How does the second type of categorizing—linking general-

[18]Robert A. Dahl, *Pluralist Democracy in the United States: Conflict and
Consent* (Chicago: Rand McNally, 1967), p. 330.

[19]James W. Prothro and C. W. Grigg, "Fundamental Principles of Democracy:
Bases of Agreement and Disagreement," *Journal of Politics,* Vol. 22 (1960),
276–94; and Herbert McClosky, "Consensus and Ideology in American Politics,"
American Political Science Review, Vol. 58 (1964), 361–82.

ities with specifics—work in regard to democratic principles? It is obvious that there *are* violations of civil rights and liberties in the United States from time to time, violations that sometimes involve whole communities, not just isolated individuals. A great many Americans are ready to support specific actions that contradict their democratic principles. Table 3.1 shows the proportions

TABLE 3.1
Percentage Supporting Specific Applications of Civil Liberties

	General public	*Community leaders*
Freedom of Speech		
If a man wanted to make a speech in your community favoring government ownership of all the railroads and big industries, should he be allowed to speak, or not?	58%	84%
Consider a man whose loyalty has been questioned before a Congressional Committee, but who swears under oath he has never been a Communist. Should he be allowed to make a speech in your community, or not?	70	87
Suppose an admitted Communist wants to make a speech in your community. Should he be allowed to speak, or not?	27	51
Civil Liberties for Atheists		
If a person wanted to make a speech in your community against churches and religion, should he be allowed to speak, or not?	37	64
If some people in your community suggested that a book he wrote against churches and religion should be taken out of your public library, would you favor removing the book, or not?	35	64
Should such a person be allowed to teach in a college or university, or not?	12	25

Source: Samuel A. Stouffer, *Communism, Conformity, and Civil Liberties* (New York: Doubleday, 1955), pp. 29, 33, 36, 41. Copyright © 1955 by Samuel A. Stouffer. Reprinted by permission of Doubleday & Company, Inc.

of the public willing to support free speech in specific cases, as determined by one nationwide study.

Community leaders are readier to allow Communists or atheists to have their say (perhaps because this is one way of exposing the inadequacies of their arguments), but even at the leadership level there is a weakening of support compared with the support general principles get. Only a minority of the general public comes to the defense of free speech for these radicals.

In 1970, a CBS News poll asked this question: "As long as there appears to be no clear danger of violence, do you think any group, no matter how extreme, should be allowed to organize protests against the government?" Three-fourths said no.[20]

Thus rationality in the sense of a tight deductive logic does not describe the links between principle and practice—or at least practical beliefs—in America. It is probably true that our collection of democratic beliefs acts as a restraint to some degree, that democratic principles pull us over toward more libertarian practices than would be the case if we had other beliefs. But the linkage is weak. Winning the minds of men over to general beliefs in democracy will not necessarily change the behavior of men over to practical support for freedom. In citizen politics, logic is a sometime thing.

future implications

The third form of thinking, predictive categorizing, appears much more prevalent among Americans as a method for dealing with political choices. As we saw above, this does not necessarily imply consistency. The use of predictive styles of thought may not be accurate, but it is evidently widespread.

A great many voters who lack a clear or logically applied political philosophy substitute for that a strong sense of the good and bad *effects* of government for themselves and their groups. About two out of three voters questioned by the Survey Research Center in 1956 referred to such benefits and harms in evaluating parties and candidates.[21] Most voters in this category simply saw one

[20]Hazel Erskine, "The Polls: Freedom of Speech," *Public Opinion Quarterly*, Vol. 34, No. 3 (Fall, 1970), p. 493.

[21]Campbell *et al.* (eds.), *op. cit.*, p. 249.

party or candidate as being "for" or "against" their group, as when one said, "I like the Democratic Party because I know they are more for the poorer people."[22]

Future orientation is clearly demonstrated in the following comment by a mother to her daughter the night before election day, 1968:

> I hope your father never finds out what I do tomorrow but in my heart and in my true conscience I have to vote for Humphrey. He sounds like he'll do more for peace. I can't vote for Nixon, not with a son in the service. Nixon hasn't ruled out a military victory, you know.
>
> I've been listening to Humphrey more and more this week, and he sounds so sincere. Nixon's so ambiguous. He answers questions, but when he's finished you don't know what he meant. At least Humphrey says I *will* do this.[23]

There is at least a little calculation in this response. The mother is trying to predict, from what she sees and hears, which candidate is the kind of man who can be counted on to stop the war. Her attention is focused on the days to come. There is little to go on—neither scholars nor citizens have been very successful in predicting what Presidents will do—but she tries, as she must, given our election system. She uses rough categories drawn from experience to assess the future.

individual and social rationality

We have been focusing on individuals and how they *think* about politics. Many citizens make many political decisions without much thought. As we shall see later in this book, political opinions are very often shaped and sustained by tradition, particularly a traditional choice of party, and many political opinions serve personal needs other than the need to think effectively. But there is more to the process of political thinking in a democracy than the information and categories individuals have and use.

Citizen thought about politics goes on in a social context. In

---

[22] *Ibid.*, p. 238.

[23] Samuel Lubell, *The Hidden Crisis in American Politics* (New York: Norton, 1971), p. 59.

many ways, we think together. Notice the elaborate arrangements
we have to make for secret voting — the screened booth, the voting
machine, the poll watchers to ensure that no one interferes. This
picture highlights the rarity of isolated, individual choice in politics. Nearly all the time we are operating in a web of human relationships. Is there a rationality of a different kind, a social or
cooperative rationality, involved in our joint efforts to think
effectively about politics? As individual citizens we may have to
rely on scanty knowledge and crude categories. As a *citizenry,* we
may be able to relate to one another in ways that produce, collectively, a more nearly adequate set of guidelines for our common
choices.

One angle of social rationality should spring to mind quickly
for those readers who have grasped the idea of a politically stratified citizenry. The minority in this country who take an active part
in politics — who vote, attend meetings, read and watch political
news, and so on — are not disconnected from the rest of the population. This minority is pretty small. V. O. Key concluded that "Day
in and day out the odds are that less than 10 percent of the adult
population could be regarded as careful readers of the political
news."[24] To be sure, television and the other media put out a good
deal of information about politics, but, given the public's inattention, "The flow of the messages of the mass media is rather like
dropping a handful of confetti from the rim of the Grand Canyon
with the object of striking a man astride a burro on the canyon
floor."[25] Nevertheless, the media messages that *do* hit someone
tend to get passed on. They enter into a network of social communication, are passed on by word of mouth from the more attentive to the less attentive. This "two-step flow" — step one: from
the media to the attentive public; step two: from the attentive
public to the inattentive public — has been confirmed by numerous
studies.[26] It points up the fact that the public's relation to the
media is not that of a passive, faceless mass audience to an all-
powerful broadcaster. In between is a layer of the active and informed, mediating between Walter Cronkite and the man in the
street. More about this later.

Here two features need to be noted about these mediators or

[24] Key, *op. cit.,* p. 353.
[25] *Ibid.,* p. 357.
[26] *Ibid.,* Chapter 14.

middlemen. First, they are scattered throughout the social structure. At every level of income and education there are significant numbers of citizens who keep up with politics and pass the word on to their neighbors. So we do not have a layer of rich Ph.D.'s on top of a mass of ignorant workers. The evidence is clear on this. One survey found that although the rich at economic level A were more likely to be active than those at lower economic levels, level A contributed only 13 percent of the "very active," while level C contributed 54 percent of those in that category.[27] There are political talkers—relatively well-informed ones—in lumber camps and corporation boardrooms, in college seminars and pool halls, in the Mississippi Delta and on Wall Street.

Second, those who think and read and watch and talk most about politics tend to be those who already have their minds made up. They are partisans. They are far more likely than the average citizen to be strongly committed to a party, and to that party's cluster of candidates and issues. The celebrated "independent voter" who enters each election campaign period with an open mind, studies the candidates and issues carefully, and votes according to his objective analysis of the situation is a very rare bird indeed. The fact is that the great majority of "independent voters," in the sense of those who are not committed to a party and who tend to switch their votes from election to election, are political outsiders. There are exceptions, but by and large these are the people who neither care much nor know much about politics. The filtering of information in the two-step flow, then, is done mainly by committed partisans who reinforce their strong opinions by drawing on the media and pass on those opinions and facts to the less committed.

A moment's thought will make clear what this means: that the main immediate effects of increases in the flow of political communication (such as takes place in a Presidential election year) are to increase political polarization *between* the parties and to increase unity *within* each party. More messages, of more significance, are filtered through larger numbers of the more partisan.

[27] J. L. Woodward and Elmo Roper, "Political Activity of American Citizens," *American Political Science Review,* Vol. 64 (1950), 870–85, as cited in Key, *op. cit.*

toward a more realistic model
of citizen political thinking

By now it should be fairly clear that few citizens think like computers or like philosophers or even come close to the canons of scientific method (which few flesh-and-blood scientists adhere to). The citizen is not an angel genius who follows a course of:

1. Philosophical reflection to produce clearly defined goals;
2. Survey of all available means to reach those goals, and selection of the most appropriate means;
3. Intense activity to achieve goals by applying means.

In practice, of course, goals and means and actions are all mixed up. As we saw in chapter i regarding participation, there are no neat sequences from motives to opportunities to resources to action. Similarly for the citizen's intellectual processes. He often decides what he thinks by what he knows, what he wants by what he can get, what he should do by what he has to do it with.

Not only are the main elements of political thinking scrambled in practice, but the whole scope of political thinking is restricted by restraints on attention. A man holding down a full-time job and raising a family can spend only so much time and effort perceiving and thinking about political matters. Therefore, he *must* simplify his thinking, and the way he goes about that—multiplied by many millions of citizens—has profound effects in shaping the political system. We have seen some ways by which citizens simplify politics. We turn now to the one set of categories which appears to have the most powerful effects on the political thinking of Americans.

partisan political thinking

One of the real mysteries of American politics is why so many citizens consider themselves Republicans or Democrats. As the

authors of the most extensive study of voting behavior to date
note:

> A general observation about the political behavior of Ameri-
> cans is that their partisan preferences show great stability
> between elections. Key speaks of the "standing decision" to
> support one party or the other, and the same phenomenon
> soon catches the eye of any student of electoral behavior.
> Its mark is readily seen in aggregate election statistics. For
> virtually any collection of states, counties, wards, precincts,
> or other political units one may care to examine, the correla-
> tion of the party division of the vote in successive elections is
> likely to be high. Often a change of candidates and a broad
> alteration in the nature of the issues disturb very little the
> relative partisanship of a set of electoral units, which sug-
> gests that great numbers of voters have party attachments
> that persist through time.
>
> The fact that attachments of this sort are widely held is
> confirmed by survey data on individual people. In a survey
> interview most of our citizens freely classify themselves as
> Republicans or Democrats and indicate that these loyalties
> have persisted through a number of elections. Few factors
> are of greater importance for our national elections than the
> lasting attachment of tens of millions of Americans to one of
> the parties. These loyalties establish a basic division of
> electoral strength within which the competition of particular
> campaigns takes place. And they are an important factor in
> insuring the stability of the party system itself.[28]

But why? The parties themselves would not seem to be very
likely rallying points for citizen loyalties. In fact, a keen observer
would be hard put to say exactly what he means by the Republican
or Democratic party in this country. Each is a disparate conglom-
eration of candidates and organizations loosely strung together
across the landscape. Only at the height of a Presidential campaign can it be said that our political parties are organized in the
same way that a corporation or labor union is organized. In many

---

[28]Angus Campbell *et al.*, *The American Voter* (New York: Wiley, 1960),
pp. 120–21. On the long-range historical import of party identifications, see
Charles Sellers, "The Equilibrium Cycle in Two Party Politics," *Public Opinion
Quarterly*, Vol. 29, No. 1 (Spring, 1968), 16–38. On party identifications and perceptions of the Supreme Court, see Kenneth M. Dolbeare and Phillip E. Hammond,
"The Political Party Basis of Attitudes toward the Supreme Court," *Public Opinion Quarterly*, Vol. 32, No. 1 (Spring, 1968), 16–30.

places, party organizations virtually cease to exist as active forces between elections.

When we move from the activists to the citizen level, it is even harder to understand these loyalties. There are many millions of citizens who think of themselves all their lives as Republicans or Democrats without ever having attended a party meeting or having been asked to do anything more for the party than to cast a vote now and then. Contrast that connection, that kind of "membership," with the citizen's continuing activities in his work, his church, or his family. How can we explain the meaning of party loyalties among a citizenry with no party membership cards, no dues, no flags, no oaths, no secrets?

Part of the answer is that people think of themselves as Democrats or Republicans because this helps them think about politics. We want to consider here the parties as categories that help people make sense of an extremely complex political environment. At the moment we shall not be concerned with the question of the correctness of such political perceptions, but only with their organization.

Party identification is the term political scientists use to specify these loyalties. It is measured by the responses citizens make to a series of questions: "Generally speaking, do you think of yourself as a Republican, a Democrat, an independent, or what?" Then those who classify themselves as Republicans or Democrats are asked, "Would you call yourself a strong (Republican, Democrat) or a not very strong (Republican, Democrat)?" Independents are asked, "Do you think of yourself as closer to the Republican or Democratic party?"[29] So we are concerned here—and this is important to keep in mind—not with facts such as votes or formal memberships, but with perceptions. We take the respondent's word for it. We are interested in the way *he* sees the truth. Party identification, then, is the citizen's own sense of where he belongs in the party spectrum. In this way, he "identifies" himself as a party member (or independent) even though he may have no formal or active connection with a party.

That party identification is a strong shaper of much political thinking is clear from a long series of studies which show that:

• Almost all voters, around 90 percent of them, admit to some

---

[29]Campbell *et al., The American Voter,* p. 122n.

degree of identification as Republicans or Democrats when asked the above questions.

- About a fifth think of themselves as strong Democrats; about one eighth think of themselves as strong Republicans.[30]
- There is a strong relationship between strength of party identification and voting. Strong identifiers are more likely to vote—and to vote consistently for the same party over a period of time—than weak identifiers, who, in turn, are more likely to vote and to vote consistently than independents. The thrust of this finding is the same regarding other forms of political participation: the stronger the identification, the more active and consistent the political action.
- In general, party identifications are consistent with attitudes on political issues, although this is not as strong a relationship as that with voting, and the relationship may be weakening in contemporary elections. But especially for the strong identifiers, if we know which party he feels himself to be associated with, we can make a pretty good stab at his position on a considerable range of issues on such matters as social welfare policy. (Foreign policy attitudes seem to be the least predictable by party identification.)
- Similarly, attitudes toward candidates are profoundly affected by party identification, as are attitudes toward the implications of government policies for one's own groups.[31]

Across the board of political perceptions and evaluations and actions, party identification stands out as one of the most powerful political predictors. To some extent this may be an American peculiarity. In France, for example, partisanship is far less clearly defined, and many voters do not appear to have a definite sense of belonging to a party.[32] Of course, this does not mean that other identifications, such as with class, region, or religious groups, do not also have strong influences on political behavior, but only that

---

[30] *Ibid.*, Table 6–1, p. 124.

[31] Key, *op. cit.*, Chapter 17, and Campbell *et al.* (eds.), *Elections and the Political Order*, Chapter 6.

[32] Philip E. Converse and Georges Dupeux, "Politicization of the Electorate in France and the United States," in Campbell *et al.* (eds.), *Elections and the Political Order*, Chapter 14.

party is stronger. Party identification is important mainly, almost solely, in the *political* realm. When people are asked which of all their groups are important to them, only a relative few mention a political party, in contrast to the very large numbers who refer to religious, occupational, or nationality groupings.[33] So what we are dealing with is a specialized kind of identification, one invoked for particular purposes in a particular context to decide particular questions.

There are important exceptions to the linkage between identifying with a party and voting for that party. In the American South in recent decades, there has been a marked upswing of voting for Republican candidates. In South Carolina, for example, Republicans got only 5 percent of the Presidential vote in 1944; in 1960 they got 49 percent.[34] However, the Republicans appear to have gained very little in the way of new Republican *identifiers*.[35] One study shows that in 1960 in the South, 50 percent of the Negroes who called themselves strong Republicans were actually registered with the Democratic party.[36]

Furthermore, the mix of party identification and other loyalties is not absolutely constant from election to election. In the 1960 Kennedy-Nixon contest, for example, religious loyalties added a special dimension to the main flow of the vote channeled by party identifications. The force of party identification is strongest when the various short-term forces—issues and candidates—are confused or nearly evenly balanced between the two parties.[37] It is in the more low-key, routine elections, such as midterm Congressional voting, that party identification has its strongest shaping influence. Even so, it is hard to find elections in which any other factor outweighs party identification. Even when there are elections without party labels—nonpartisan elections—voters tend to line up as if there *were* parties.[38]

[33] Robert E. Lane, *Political Life: Why People Get Involved in Politics* (New York: Free Press, Macmillan, 1959), p. 300.

[34] Robert E. Lane, James D. Barber, and Fred I. Greenstein, *An Introduction to Political Analysis*, 3rd ed. (Englewood Cliffs, N.J.: Prentice-Hall, 1962), p. 45.

[35] Donald R. Matthews and James W. Prothro, in M. Kent Jennings and L. Harmon Zeigler (eds.), *The Electoral Process* (Englewood Cliffs, N.J.: Prentice-Hall, 1966), p. 166.

[36] *Ibid.*, p. 147.

[37] Campbell *et al.* (eds.), *Elections and the Political Order*, Chapters 5 and 6.

[38] Heinz Eulau, Betty H. Zisk, and Kenneth Prewitt, "Latent Partisanship in Non-Partisan Elections: Effects of Political Milieu and Mobilization," in Jennings and Zeigler (eds.), *op. cit.*, Chapter 10.

How can we account for this special force of party identification? Part of the answer lies in where the identifications came from in the citizen's past—his life experiences, and particularly the politics he learned as a child. Similarly, it is clear that party loyalties are related to the social context—to the community of friends and fellow workers in which the individual finds himself.

But our interest here is in how party identification fits in with citizen thinking about politics. What model of political cognition helps us most to understand this strange loyalty to such an indefinite object as a party? The data suggest at least the following:

In the first place, the citizen's party identification *places the citizen himself in a category along with political phenomena.* That is, he puts himself in the picture. Unlike other categories by which a citizen tries to make sense of the political environment—as something he observes, something separate and distinct from him—party identification links him with politics in a direct and personal way. It is the difference between "they-thinking" and "I-thinking." It is one thing to say, even with some feeling, that Asians are killing Asians in South Vietnam, and another thing to say, as an American, that *Americans* are killing Asians. In much the same way, it is a different thing to say, as a spectator, "The Democrats are for civil rights," than it is to say, "I am a Democrat." Party identification is a concept bridging the gap between the citizen and politics.

A second feature of the party identification model is its specialization. Party identification refers to a narrow slice of the citizen's life. In terms of political thinking, party loyalties are *highly salient for politics only.* The precise meaning, the content, the detailed implications of party "membership" in this sense do not spill over much into other arenas of life. This feature of the party identification model reminds us that political thinking does not take place in a vacuum. We cannot assume that because a person has this or that personal characteristic he will always or even typically act on or think with that part of his makeup. We always want to ask, regarding the significance of any political characteristic, "With respect to what?" Apparently, party identification affects a wide range of political thinking and behavior. But political thinking and behavior are a minor part of the citizen's life. When he needs it—that is, when he needs to make a political decision—party identification is there for him to call upon.

two parties and many other identifications

Party identification links citizens to the world of politics. But why only two parties? Given all the many shades of opinion on hundreds of more or less important issues, why do we, nearly all of us, wind up as Republicans or Democrats? One way of answering that question is to delve into our collective history and into the history of each of us individually to uncover the roots of these simple identifications. If we made such an investigation, we would see how our electoral system, based on the single-member district and majority rule, would probably have some long-term effect in pushing us toward a two-party choice.[39] We would see how the historically developing major party organizations have swamped out the small parties during the course of our history.

Here we pose the question a little differently: What is the effect of two parties on political thinking? Beyond that, how does party identification relate to all the other kinds of identifications we have that are relevant to political thinking?

The key relation between two parties and political thinking is in the matter of *choice.* Somehow or other, our electoral system has to wind up producing one winner per contest. That means that we are forced to move in our minds from a host of scattered images and preferences and sentiments to a definite, final choice.

Offhand, a choice between two parties may not seem like much of an opportunity to use your head. I may not like either of the two Presidential candidates. I may wish I could choose to vote for another man who lost out at the national convention. I may feel that my group rarely gets one of its own on the ballot. (Who was the last college professor elected President?) The two-party contest may not even take up for debate the issues that seem to me to be the crucial ones. Or if they do take them up, I may find neither party position just right. In other words, the two-party system may seem to be about the last rational mechanism for helping me choose among a reasonable array of candidates and issues.

The upshot of that line of thought might well be a preference

[39] But see John G. Grumm, "Theories of Electoral Systems," *Midwest Journal of Political Science,* Vol. 2 (1958), 357–76.

for a multiparty system. Robert A. Dahl carries out the logical implications of that preference as follows:

> Yet, if four parties are better than two, are eight parties better than four? And sixteen parties better than eight? Or, for that matter, why not a separate candidate for every point of view held by any citizen in the country? But suppose the voter were confronted with the choice among twenty parties and twenty candidates. Might he not then reason as follows: there are too many alternatives; I cannot possibly appraise them all. Anyway, what do I gain if the man I vote for wins? If there are twenty parties in the parliament, my representative and all the others will have to make many compromises by the time they reach the final decision. How do I know what compromises they will make? Would it not be much better if most of the compromises had been made already, so that I could then choose between two possible coalitions, knowing roughly the direction in which each would go if it won a majority of seats . . . ?[40]

In other words, rational choice demands *both* a reasonable array of possibilities *and* a reasonable way of actually reaching choices among these possibilities. Every party system in a democracy is somewhere in between the utter confusion of a party for every point of view and the utter confinement of choice to Tweedledee or Tweedledum. Dahl suggests that our system is not really all that simple. A lot of choosing goes on at times other than election day. Before the election, there is a long and complicated series of nominating choices, the primaries, the state conventions, the public opinion polls, the slow accumulation of millions of conversations. With the advent of public opinion polling, election day has become in many cases something of an anticlimax; similarly, in some cases the party nominations for President are foreseen in the results of national surveys, so that the national party convention becomes a show with a program known in advance. As more and more citizens perceive these developments, those who want to get in on the real choices will more and more have to take part in the complicated game of prenominating politics.

Also there are many more than two choices in politics *following* the election. The election itself gives a definite answer about

[40] Dahl, *op. cit.,* p. 251.

who wins and who loses, but it gives a very indefinite answer about policies. This indefiniteness leaves much room for maneuver and choice even after the voting machines have been put back in storage. The shaping of proposals to Congress, the choice of top advisers, the selection of agencies to carry out policy—in short, the whole complex process of policy-making—all this is effected by postelection choices. And citizens, through their direct and indirect representatives, make choices in that arena, even if the choice is to do nothing.

This view puts the two-party contest into the perspective of the larger picture. What we have been looking at as a one-time choice now appears as one slice of time in an ongoing series of choices, a kind of one-shot answer to a simple question that has taken a lot of time and effort to define and which still leaves open a great many matters of implementation.

There is a general point here. In all our models of citizen thinking about politics, we should keep in mind at least three features or dimensions of the situation affecting choice:

1. The *size* of the collection of possible choices.
2. The *structure* of relationships among those choice possibilities.
3. The *process*—over time—by which choice is achieved.

In many ways party identifications represent standing choices by the electorate of one broad direction of government over another. And we have seen how party identification links the citizen into the political system and how it relates to political choice. But of course, party identifications do not exist in isolation from our other identifications with groups. We do not have minds divided up into watertight compartments, one for politics and one for each of the other kinds of choices we face. Party identifications are strong in part because they build upon other identifications. Some quotations from voter surveys make that clear:

> A semiskilled California worker: (Like about the Democratic party?) "So far, the Democrats are always interested in farmers. I was a farmer, my folks still are. The Republicans promise they will help farmers and then never do. We have no trouble with the sale of farm products and poor people have a better chance with the Democrats and the workingman does have, too, with Democrats."

A Texas janitor: (Like about the Democratic party?) "I think Democrats are more for the workingman; give more help to the laboring class." (Dislike about the Republican party?) "That party has always been for moneyed men. I don't like them. They are for the big man; people with money."

Waiter in San Francisco: (Like about the Democratic party?) "I like the Democrats because they fulfill what they promise. With the Democrats I always had a job and with the Republicans I was in the breadlines. (What else?) I feel the Democrats are for the small businessman and the poor people."

Retired Boston wholesaler: (Like about Republicans?) "The Democrats is all right but it's not a money party. I like to string along with big business and big money. Well, I'll also tell you under the Republicans the country has prospered."

California doctor: (Like about the Republican party?) "A more stable and dignified party, a party able to handle all affairs at home and abroad. The party has clear vision. Serious-minded people in office."

Pennsylvania farmer: (Like about the Republican party?) "Yes, they do more for the country and clean up Washington —never any drinking down there when the Republicans are in."[41]

These quotes show how voters weave together party and other identifications in their political thinking. A Democrat may be for his party because he thinks his party is for his occupational group or for his region or for his class. He may be against the Republicans because he sees that party as favoring groups opposed to his own.[42]

Most of the time, for most people, there will be a rough consistency among their identifications. That is, party loyalties and loyalties to other groups will reinforce one another in the citizen's mind rather than conflict with one another. But notice carefully

---

[41] Key, *op. cit.*, pp. 435–38. Copyright © 1961 by V. O. Key, Jr. Reprinted by permission of Alfred A. Knopf, Inc.

[42] It is interesting that there is a clear difference between Republican and Democratic voters in the degree to which they refer to groups in evaluating the parties. Republicans are far less likely than Democrats to refer to group affiliations in evaluating parties. As V. O. Key, Jr., explains, "The popular image of the group affiliates of the Republican party is, on balance, negative. On the whole, people have other types of good things to say about the party" (*ibid.*, p. 437).

what we mean when we say that identifications are in conflict or congruence. What we do *not* mean can be represented in a far too simple picture, as shown in Figure 3.1.

FIGURE 3.1

The Citizen

Party
Identification
↓

↑
Group
Identification

This picture would suppose that identifications are in conflict or in harmony only *inside* the mind of the citizen, within the circle of his collection of identifications. But a moment's reflection will make clear how inadequate that model is. Think of your own present party choice. Now think of several of your other group identifications. Is there conflict or harmony between your party identification and your group identifications? Think about it.

Notice that in your thinking you found it necessary to refer to objects and events in the world external to your collection of identifications. You were forced to raise the question "Conflict or harmony with respect to what?" There is, for example, no *inherent* contradiction between an identification as an intellectual and an identification as a Republican. To decide whether the identifications are in conflict or harmony, you have to move your attention outside yourself to the political implications. So the model is more complicated, something like Figure 3.2.

This picture shows more accurately how we make judgments when our identifications conflict. The point is much the same as the one we argued in a different context in chapter i. There we saw how political action had to be analyzed, not in terms of motives or resources or opportunities, but in terms of mixtures of these elements. In much the same way, a citizen trying to think

FIGURE 3.2

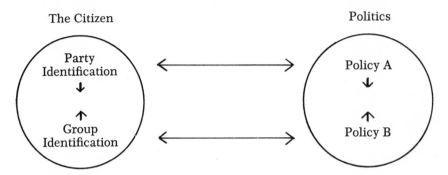

his way through politics by referring to his party and group identifications does not confront the problem of resolving *all* the possible conflicts among these identifications at each election. This
fact has big implications for the ability of citizens to make political
calculations, because the task is limited to those conflicts that are
salient or important in the politics of the day.

You can see this in your own life. Suppose a student is very
strongly interested in political science and is also a rabid skier. He
wants to study and he wants to go skiing. For him that's a problem in December but not in June. If he is attending a college in
Texas, it's not much of a problem at all. Or if he's in a school
where there is lots of skiing and very little political science, the
problem is not going to worry him much. The point is: *most
people, most of the time, are not pressed to bring their various
identifications into a consistent order.* Most people, most of the
time, can live with a good deal of inconsistency.

We all go along most of our lives with a pretty miscellaneous
bag of identifications, some of which occasionally become highly
relevant when we face particular kinds of choices imposed by the
environment.

Recent elections show this. In 1960 religious identifications —
a factor that up to then had seemed on the way out as a significant
political category, at least at the Presidential level — played a large
part in many voter choices. The basic shape of the voting was consistent with long-term configurations of party identification and
turnout levels. But the election was so close that even very slight
influences from other factors in the short run were extremely

important. And the religious factor was not small. Of the voters who switched from Stevenson in 1956 to Nixon in 1960, 90 percent were Protestants. Of the people who voted for Eisenhower in 1956 and for Kennedy in 1960, close to 60 percent were Catholics.[43] Catholics who attended church regularly and had strong identifications with the Catholic community were more likely to switch to Kennedy.[44] (There is even some evidence that *Irish* Catholics switched to Kennedy in larger proportions than did non-Irish Catholics.)[45] Similarly, Protestant voters with high rates of church attendance and strong identification with the Protestant community were far more likely than other Protestants to switch to Nixon in 1960.[46]

In other words, when the first Catholic Presidential candidate appeared and when his opponent was not a Catholic, many voters suddenly felt a new tension, a new problem of political choice to figure out. A special feature of the political situation aroused a conflict that had been dormant in modern elections up till that time. We would be making a mistake to think that long periods in which racial, ethnic, and religious identifications are asleep mean that they cannot be aroused by special political circumstances. Despite the American melting pot, these group identifications crop up again and again in American politics. This is especially so when there is a clear *difference* in the group identifications of competing candidates. In New Haven, for example, the voting behavior of Italian-American citizens did not change much as long as the choice was between one Yankee and another Yankee. But when Italian-Americans began to appear as candidates, Italian voters gave them massive support.[47]

The effect is normally not so strong as regards issues, although there are striking exceptions. In 1964, virtually all the Negro voters in the United States voted for Lyndon Johnson—or against Barry Goldwater. This picture of conflicting identifications might incline us toward thinking that there is a fine tuning be-

[43] Campbell *et al.* (eds.), *Elections and the Political Order*, p. 84.

[44] *Ibid.*, p. 108.

[45] *Ibid.*, p. 105.

[46] *Ibid.*, pp. 89, 119. The findings on Protestants appeared to hold for southern voters and for clerical or blue-collar voters in the North, but not for professional or business voters in the North. See *ibid.*, Table 6–6, p. 119.

[47] Raymond E. Wolfinger, "The Politics of Progress" (unpublished Ph.D. dissertation, Yale University, 1961).

tween the citizen's identifications and events in the political environment. But of course we have seen how rarely that is the case.[48] In fact, we know that most voters are poorly informed about their political environment, that there is a great deal of slack and sloppiness in most political perceptions. So a model that has the set of identifications tightly tied to the set of political events is obviously a misleading one. Political thinking goes on inside the skulls of citizens, so it only has to deal with stimuli that, by one route or another, pierce that bony barrier. Certain facilitating circumstances can make that more likely and, furthermore, can press the voter toward resolving conflicts among his identifications.

A very simple facilitator is exposure. Exposure means the communication to voters of the external political situation. Putting the exposure factor into our model would make it look something like Figure 3.3.

FIGURE 3.3

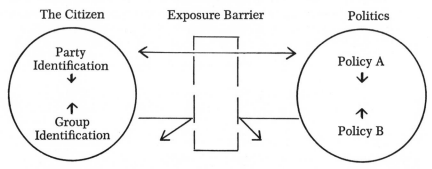

| The Citizen | Exposure Barrier | Politics |

Consider how the exposure barrier works. The kind of tension and confusion that can arise in conflicts of identification are clear in the following two quotes from interviews with voters in 1960:

> I'm so confused this election year. (How is that?) I'm a Republican and a Catholic, and religion and politics are important to me. I'll have to make a decision, looks like I'll have to go against my church. (Is there anything you like about the Democratic Party?) Well, no . . . it is just like religion. (How do you mean?) Politics is something wide and deep—no end to it—you get it in your system so deep.

[48]See above, p. 71.

> (Is there anything you like about the Democrats?) No, there
> isn't. I am Republican committeewoman for this district. (Is
> there anything about Kennedy that might make you want to
> vote for him?) No, there is not. The only thing he is a Demo-
> crat. I could not vote for him for that reason. I *couldn't*. On
> the other hand he is a Catholic — Oh, dear! Why does it have
> to be that way?[49]

These voters had been exposed to the fact that Kennedy was a
Catholic. Only then did they experience conflict between their
political and religious identifications. For many voters, this was a
gradual process:

> There is strong reason to believe . . . that most of the public
> had no idea who Kennedy was until the spring of 1960, and
> that a very large portion first learned of his existence when
> he was nominated for the Presidency. The initial reactions
> of Protestant Democrats were particularly interesting, as
> best we can piece them together from our early interview
> materials. One subset of Protestant Democrats learned that
> Kennedy was a nominee without learning that he was a
> Catholic. These respondents were often well along in the
> time-honored process of taking the unknown candidate of
> one's own party to the bosom before word of the Catholic
> background reached them; the reaction was one of betrayal.
> Other Protestant Democrats learned at the outset that their
> party had nominated a Catholic and were in high dudgeon
> at the fact. Word of Kennedy's Catholicism travelled fast
> enough so that by mid-September most Protestant Democrats
> "knew" and were in considerable torment.[50]

So exposure obviously made a difference. It made a difference
in *generating* conflict among identifications.

But as Converse points out in his interesting account, there
was more exposure to come, and the main effect was probably to
dampen the conflict among identifications. The television debates
and other mass-media messages did much to modify anti-Catholic
stereotypes regarding Kennedy. Protestant Democrats probably
came to see him more and more as a Democrat rather than as a
Catholic, and also to see him as a human being who did not fit very
well with anti-Catholic prejudices.

So in this case, as in many others, exposure gave rise to con-

[49] Campbell *et al.* (eds.), *Elections and the Political Order,* p. 96.
[50] *Ibid.,* pp. 123–24.

flict among identifications and exposure provided the means for *resolving* that conflict.[51]

These contradictory possibilities of exposure as both creating and dispelling conflict among identifications are brought out nicely in some research by Samuel J. Eldersveld on Detroit voters.[52] This research focused on party contact; voters were categorized according to how much or how little exposure they had had to the political parties in terms of attending political clubs, going to party people for advice or help, personal acquaintance with precinct leaders, being personally contacted by party representatives and the like.[53] Eldersveld then relates this kind of exposure to political "rationality" in the sense of consistency among the citizen's political ideology, perceptions, and identifications, and the vote. His main finding is that this kind of exposure is related to this kind of rationality in an odd and contradictory way: party contact seems to lead to both more rationality *and* more irrationality. For example, of the Democrats highly exposed to the party, 21 percent voted Republican, while only 10 percent of the Democrats who had had no such exposure made this "mistake"! On the other hand, 67 percent of the highly exposed Democrats voted consistently with their party identifications, compared with 45 percent of the Democrats who were not exposed to party contact.[54] So for some people, it appears, a conversation on the doorstep with a party worker helps to clear up contradictions. But in other cases the canvasser may be creating doubts and tensions where none existed before. Clearly exposure was an important factor in both processes. The model is complicated by introducing this new factor, but it is more accurate as a representation of reality.

which way do the arrows go?

In the model pictured in Figure 3.3, the arrows have heads at both ends. This indicates that, as far as we know, influences are operating in both directions. Candidates and issues affect the vot-

---

[51] *Ibid.*, p. 124.
[52] Samuel J. Eldersveld, *Political Parties: A Behavioral Analysis* (Chicago: Rand McNally, 1964).
[53] *Ibid.*, p. 442.
[54] *Ibid.*, Table 19.6, p. 489.

er's identifications and these in turn affect the candidates and issues. Obviously it would be helpful to know not only that there is some influence in both directions, but also how much. At least it would be helpful to find out for each arrow which is the *predominant* direction of influence. An example can help to clarify this problem.

In much of our analysis so far, we have been talking about issues and candidates as they exist in the voter's mind as somehow derivative from this more basic party and group identifications. We have been reflecting the main thrust of research on voting and political attitudes, which takes this tack. The image is one of the citizen possessing certain basic loyalties that guide and channel and distort and make consistent his choices of issues and candidates and his voting behavior. Some observers would see this approach as putting the cart before the horse. Candidates, issues, and party loyalties go together, the evidence says. But which comes first in citizen thinking?

This question of the direction of causality is one we ought to raise whenever we see evidence that two political factors are related to each other. If we find that Republicans are conservative, is it that they are conservative because they are Republicans or that they are Republicans because they are conservative? Simply posing the question in this way shows how the answer is likely to be a mix. But a useful model ought at least to make a try at estimating whether the recipe calls for a ton of flour and a pinch of salt or a ton of salt and a pinch of flour. At the general level of models, the level we are dealing with here, we are not going to be able to answer that kind of question very specifically. But an example from recent research shows how significant the question is.

In *The Responsible Electorate*,[55] V. O. Key, Jr., raises the question dramatically:

> The perverse and unorthodox argument of this little book is that voters are not fools. To be sure, many individual voters act in odd ways indeed; yet in the large the electorate behaves about as rationally and responsibly as we should expect, given the clarity of the alternatives presented to it and the character of the information available to it. In American

[55] V. O. Key, Jr., *The Responsible Electorate* (Cambridge, Mass.: Belknap Press, Harvard University Press, 1966).

presidential campaigns of recent decades the portrait of the
American electorate that develops from the data is not one
of an electorate straight-jacketed by social determinants or
moved by subconscious urges triggered by devilishly skillful
propagandists. It is rather one of an electorate moved by concern about central and relevant questions of public policy,
of governmental performance, and of executive personality.
Propositions so uncompromisingly stated inevitably represent over-statements. Yet to the extent that they can be
shown to resemble the reality they are propositions of basic
importance for both the theory and the practice of democracy.[56]

On the one hand, then, we have a picture of voting choices as
resulting from more or less fixed characteristics of voters. In this
view, a citizen's vote, like his opinions and conversations about
politics, springs from his group and party identifications. Votes
and opinions are thus reflections, the frosting on a cake of custom
and habit. In extreme form, this argument would virtually eliminate political thinking. Voters would be responders, not thinkers.
They would march like automatons to the polls, like human machines pulling levers on voting machines to produce a mechan-
ically determined outcome.

Few political scientists who have looked into the matter seriously have come to that kind of extreme conclusion. But in some
studies, there has been a tendency to think first of the arrows of
causality shot out from basic identifications as the main thrust of
causation of political action, and to pay less attention to the idea
that there are arrows being shot in the opposite direction. Much
of this is simply a matter of scholarly attention. Not many scholars
are liars, and those who make important silly mistakes usually
get corrected. Distortions in social analysis far more frequently
result from inattention, from a failure to see the forest for the trees
or to see that it is trees that make up a forest.

Key's argument is complicated but it centers in the analysis of
voters who switch from a vote for one party to a vote for the other
party. The analysis of the data from the days of the New Deal on is
consistent with the idea that switchers have reasons for changing
their votes from one party to another between two Presidential
elections. That is, if we know how a switcher feels about the

[56] *Ibid.*, pp. 7–8.

policy issues of the day, we can make a pretty good guess as to which way he will vote. Key points out that most such judgments of issues refer to what has already happened:

> The patterns of flow of the major streams of shifting voters graphically reflect the electorate in its great, and perhaps principal, role as an appraiser of past events, past performance, and past actions. It judges retrospectively; it commands prospectively only insofar as it expresses either approval or disapproval of that which has happened before. Voters may reject what they have known; or they may approve what they have known. They are not likely to be attracted in great numbers by promises of the novel or unknown. Once innovation has occurred they may embrace it, even though they would have, earlier, hesitated to venture forth to welcome it.[57]

For these particular categories of voters, then — that is, for the switchers — one line of explanation is that issues cause votes. The arrows moving toward the left of our diagram above would be strong and dark for these voters. And in some elections a great many voters make this kind of switch. For instance, for 1960 Key gives as estimates within "shouting distance of the realities" of 10.3 million voters switching to Kennedy and 2.7 million switching to Nixon.[58]

Key builds a reasonable case for the idea that switchers take issues into account in their political thinking. There are at least two difficulties with the argument viewed more broadly. One is how to account for all of those voters who do *not* switch. Another is to explain the fact that switching occurs in *both* directions — from a Republican to a Democratic vote and from a Democratic to a Republican vote.

This is but one intriguing example of the direction-of-causality problem. There are cases where that is no problem. Sex affects participation rates, but one doubts it works the other way. But in many other political thinking phenomena, the query "Which way are the arrows stronger?" is a real one.

---

[57] *Ibid.*, p. 61.

[58] The reader who has accustomed himself to keeping one eye on the nature of evidence and inference will not need to be reminded that the fact that a great many people share common characteristics or move in common directions does not at all imply that for *any one* of these people, the characteristic is very important or the movement very far.

beyond political thinking

Citizens think about politics. And the ways they think are not random. Nor are people thinking machines, programmed to reach conclusions through a set form of logic. Few of us are political philosophers; few of us can comprehend a great many facts about politics. We move in a complex, shifting, ambiguous, uncertain, and risky political world. Yet we must make choices, even when we choose not to choose.

We have explored some of the main outlines of political thinking as suggested by modern research. At the same time, we ourselves have practiced a style of political science thinking. We have tried our hand at making models, at setting up outlines and frameworks and categories and pictures, all of which we note to be gross simplifications of a complicated reality. But this is one way in which our own rational process as students of politics acquires system and a certain kind of freedom for the imagination. As political scientists, we work in a data-saturated environment. It is very easy to get lost. We can learn to tinker with the itsy-bitsies of politics. Another escape is to retreat from the data entirely, to lapse back into the comfort of armchair scholarship in which one's speculations are limited only by one's vocabulary. As you have seen, we have been working in the middle, trying to think through some main ideas without losing touch with the facts of life.

chapter iv

The Debating Model

Shortly before he was shot to death in 1968, Robert F. Kennedy appeared on television with Eugene McCarthy to discuss campaign issues. Try as they did, the reporters who questioned the candidates had a hard time generating disagreements. At least on questions of the major directions of national policy, the Senators found little to fight about. They did disagree on several significant points of emphasis and interpretation. But in a brief show with three newsmen, there was not much chance to develop them. Was this a debate?

Lawyers in court argue their cases before a jury. Their traditional "adversary proceeding" requires them to prosecute or defend vigorously, with all their skill, defendants whom both sides may know to be guilty—or innocent. Is that a debate?

A Senator stands before his colleagues and reads recipes late into the night. What sort of debate is that?

The question is important. Our political system is a means of managing conflict to produce choice. The *form* of that conflict can make a great deal of difference to the substance of the choice. From the political philosophy of our Founding Fathers to modern political science, much observation and discussion has focused on constructing systems—not to eliminate conflict (which is probably impossible and surely very costly to other values) but to channel conflict in such a way as to produce rational choice. Behind the apparent artificiality of the many rules governing political conduct—for example in Congress—lies a conviction that democracy is not a free-for-all but a hard-won, long-tested process for moving from argument to action.

From the citizen's viewpoint, a political campaign is a debate and he is the judge. In the American judicial system, courts generally consider only cases—specific conflicts in which there is a genuine difference of opinion. This process focuses the attention of the judges. They can ignore all aspects of the situation that are irrelevant and consider only those that are relevant to the issues about which the parties are fighting. Similarly, the citizen who is short on political information and attentiveness tries to perceive *differences* between the candidates in a campaign. As we shall see, even this is a difficult task, given the many ways politicians can evade a stand on controversial issues. Yet we keep reaching for techniques for better political thinking, realizing all the while that perfection is beyond us.

From the citizen's viewpoint, a political campaign as a whole is a kind of debate and he is the judge. It is a contest for his affections, but also for his thinking. We have considered citizen thinking about politics as an individual enterprise. In this chapter we shall consider some of the external conditions which foster and impede political thought.

The pure debate with all its rules and procedures is a rare event in politics. The point of examining this peculiar form of political ballet is not to describe a common reality, but to pose an abstract scheme—a model—which will help us think more systematically about the realities. No living cell is precisely like the biologist's model; no bridge is an exact geometric form. In both cases, and in political models, we use the theoretical pictures as a way of separating the essential from the accidental, and of discerning, in the differences between ideal and reality, where the important problems are likely to lie.

social rationality and debates

The essential argument for debates goes beyond the idea that two heads are better than one. The classic statement is John Stuart Mill's:

> The only way in which a human being can make some approach to knowing the whole of a subject is by hearing what can be said about it by persons of every variety of opinion, and studying all modes in which it can be looked at by every character of mind. No wise man ever acquired his wisdom in any mode but this; nor is it in the nature of human intellect to become wise in any other manner.[1]

A very simple model of Mill's idea is: people can get information from a variety of sources, not just one. Some primitive nations and some totalitarian nations come close to restricting access to information to one or a very few sources. Even there people can usually talk to their neighbors and families to get some information different from what the officials put out. But fear can be a powerful deterrent and life can be made very difficult for dissenters. In a democracy, a kind of minimum requirement would be that there is more than one way to get the "facts."

In the United States there are a lot of different sources of information. Obviously the press and other mass media are not tools of the government in any direct sense of control. They keep up a continual drumfire of criticism of government. Nor is there a secret conspiracy among the mass-media managers to shape their messages in a common direction. We have some 1,750 daily English-language newspapers in this country;[2] it would be a tremendous task for some behind-the-scenes group to control that

[1] John Stuart Mill, "On Liberty," in Edwin A. Burtt (ed.), *The English Philosophers from Bacon to Mill* (New York: Random House, 1939), p. 964. Quoted in Stanley Kelley, Jr., *Political Campaigning: Problems in Creating an Informed Electorate* (Washington, D.C.: Brookings Institution, 1960), p. 11.

[2] V. O. Key, Jr., *Public Opinion and American Democracy* (New York: Knopf, 1961), p. 371.

medium alone. It is true that a growing number of communities, especially smaller ones, have only one newspaper. In 1920, about four out of ten cities with daily newspapers had more than one of them; by 1967, this was true of only 3 percent of such communities.[3] But the rise of radio and television makes this decline less significant. Nowadays more people say they get most of their news from television than from any other medium. And people— especially young people—trust television as a source of news more than they trust the other media.[4] Again the picture is mixed: much TV news actually comes from the newspaper wire services; strongly radical views often have a hard time getting a serious hearing, and there is less attention to public affairs in the media than many would like. Much of what comes across is celebration of the status quo, a tradition-bound pointing with pride and viewing with alarm. But at least there are available to the interested citizen several different ways to find out what is going on in politics.

By the test of this very simple model—the availability of information from a variety of sources—perhaps we do all right.

In a matter this complex, "very simple models" may not take us far. In interpreting this one, we need to recall that *opportunity* is only one factor in the citizen's situation. We need to remember that only about one person in ten, if that many, follows the day-to-day news carefully. Social rationality affecting such small numbers may not meet some stiffer criteria for democracy. A harder set of tests, centering in the main features of political debates, may make clearer how an electorate composed, by and large, of politically irrational *individuals* might yet make up a politically rational *citizenry* when the system of political communication is shaped in certain ways.

The audience for the first of the famous Kennedy-Nixon television debates in 1960 included about 70 million of the 107 million U.S. adults and probably 10 to 15 million younger people.[5]

[3] *Ibid.,* p. 372 (1920 data); Raymond B. Nixon, "Trends in U.S. Newspaper Ownership," *American Newspaper Publishers Association,* 1969 (1967 data).

[4] Elmo Roper and Associates, "The Public's View of Television and Other Media: 1959–64," in Edward C. Dreyer and Walter A. Rosenbaum (eds.), *Political Opinion and Electoral Behavior: Essays and Studies* (Belmont, Calif.: Wadsworth, 1966), pp. 309–17.

[5] Elihu Katz and Jacob J. Feldman, "The Debates in the Light of Research: A Survey of Surveys," in Sidney Kraus (ed.), *The Great Debates* (Bloomington: Indiana University Press, 1962), p. 190.

Fifty-seven percent of the voters thought the debates had influenced their decisions about Kennedy and Nixon, according to a Roper poll. For this event, at least, the general pattern of avoidance and apathy was broken. Shortly we will look at some of the effects of these debates, but first it will be useful to think theoretically about what a debate is and how debates can contribute to social rationality.

Ordinary political campaigns are often called great debates, but few are that, except in a very indirect sense. In almost all campaign situations, a candidate addresses an audience made up of people already predisposed in his direction (that is why they tuned him in). He exhorts them, tries to inspire them. His purpose is seldom to change their minds, but rather to energize them—basically to get them to the polls on election day. A great deal of campaigning is stuck at the level of simple propaganda, such as this Eisenhower spot TV announcement in 1952:[6]

> VOICE: Mr. Eisenhower, what about the high cost of living?
> EISENHOWER: My wife, Mamie, worries about the same thing. I tell her it's our job to change that on November 4.

Modern-day political advertisers help the candidates enlighten the public—insofar as that is consistent with winning the election. The flood of balderdash is meant to sweep voters to the polls, usually by working on their feelings more than their thoughts. How might the campaign be structured to counteract tendencies toward hokum and tomfoolery? Given that few voters are really well-informed or attentive and that few candidates are above such appeals as "In your heart you know he's right!" how nevertheless could the campaign *situation* be modified to improve social rationality?

conditions for debate

We might focus on the debate as a model. In other words, a debate does not require an audience of political geniuses. It does require, in its classic form, certain definite arrangements for rational argument. For example, a debate requires that both contenders perform before the same audience. If Republicans hear only Republican candidates and Democrats hear only Democrats, there

[6] Kelley, *op. cit.*, p. 62.

is no debate. So a *common audience* is the first and most obvious feature differentiating a debate from a campaign rally. J. Jeffrey Auer has set forth several additional requirements, drawn from numerous works on debating:

> A debate is (1) a confrontation, (2) in equal and adequate time, (3) of matched contestants, (4) on a stated proposition, (5) to gain an audience decision.[7]

This formula bears pondering. Read it again. A few moments' thought makes clear how each of these elements is meant to raise the chances that a debate will encourage rational decision-making.

1. "... a confrontation ..." Frequently on television specials around election time we see a kind of pseudo-debate: films are cut in such a way as to show first Candidate A speaking to his audience and then Candidate B speaking to a different audience. For example, Edmund Muskie addressing the Mothers of Maine and then George McGovern addressing the Friends of Peace, perhaps both on the same general topic but at different times and places. This can be informative, but it lacks an enlightening feature of debate: the fact that *the contenders are forced to respond to one another.* The idea is that we are more likely to get at the truth if Mr. A's assertions are made in Mr. B's presence, and Mr. B has a chance (and uses it) to challenge Mr. A's viewpoint. Much as lawyers in a courtroom, practicing their "adversary proceeding," supposedly argue truth into a jury's mind, so the candidates, by debate, will clarify the strong and weak points in their positions.

2. "... in equal and adequate time ..." More specifically, a debate is an attempt to equalize the conditions, including time, under which the contestants must operate. At least two kinds of problem arise here. One is: How many contestants are there? The classic debate is a two-man contest. But the "equal time" provisions of campaigning laws have pointed up the difficulty, in politics, of determining where to draw the line between serious candidates who have a chance of winning, and, it is concluded, thus deserve equal treatment, and a host of other "candidates" who want to be heard. Include them all and you have a marathon session no one will listen to (not to mention the cost of television

---

[7] J. Jeffrey Auer, "The Counterfeit Debates," in Kraus (ed.), *op. cit.*, p. 146.

time). Exclude important ones and you muffle voices of dissent and innovation it might be good for the citizenry to hear. The practical consequence has usually been to focus on the major candidates, those of the Democratic and Republican parties.

A second equality problem regarding debates refers back to some ancient controversies about the meaning of equality, but can be expressed more simply here. Equal time is taken to mean the same amount of time. As rough justice, that may do. But again we need to be aware of the complexities of equality: for example, effective attack in debate may need less time than effective defense. The attacker has to find a hole in his opponent's position. Often the defender has to respond by defending his *complete* position, which takes more time to do effectively. As in the story of "The Emperor's New Clothes," the "attacker" has only to yell, "Look!" The Emperor's explanation takes longer. More broadly, it is obvious that there is no logical or necessary relationship between the time it takes to lay out one argument and the time it takes to lay out an alternative. With the complexities of calculating such subtleties and the difficulties of getting both parties to agree on them, the usual solution has been the simplest rule: equal time means the same amount of time.

What of "adequate time"? Lincoln and Douglas had seven debates of three hours each. Nixon and Kennedy had three minutes to answer each question and then one minute for refutation.[8] All sorts of practical restrictions, such as cost, audience patience, and so forth, affect judgments about how much time is adequate. Obviously the particular topics debated affect how much time is "adequate." But even at the theoretical level the problem is not simple. You can prove that to yourself by trying to put down *types* of questions requiring extended debate vs. those requiring much less time. For example, in political controversy, does a debate on "national goals" need longer than one on "foreign policy," which in turn needs more time than "U.S.-Thailand relations" or "the choice of a U.S. ambassador to Bangkok"? On the face of it, a general proposition might seem to require more time than a specific one. A moment's reflection will call to mind many exceptions to that rule.

3. "... of matched contestants ..." You do not have a real

---

[8] *Ibid.,* p. 147.

debate between, say, a Presidential candidate and his Vice Presidential running mate. They are not "contestants"; they are collaborators and one is subordinate to the other. You do not have a real debate between a professor of economics and the man who runs the corner candy store. (That might be interesting, but probably not too enlightening; the two are experts in very different things.) Nor is an effective debate on foreign policy likely to take place between the Secretary of State and the Secretary of the Interior. "Matched contestants" means, therefore, at least that the two are (*a*) relatively independent of one another, but (*b*) share a common area of primary concern, and (*c*) are roughly equal in competence to discuss the issue.

In debates between major candidates for the same office, their equality as matched contestants is assumed, or perhaps derived from the fact that they have been nominated by the major parties. A problem in even arranging debates is often that of persuading the front-runner or incumbent to take part. Why should the President debate with his challenger? In 1960 this question did not arise, because neither Kennedy nor Nixon was President. But we all know that a first-term incumbent President usually has an excellent chance of being reelected to a second term. He is much more visible to the public than is his opponent. It would seem that he has nothing to gain and everything to lose by giving his adversary a chance to appear as his equal; not only does he risk being bested on the merits of argument, but also he risks making some silly slip damaging to his reputation.

Possibly this problem will be overcome as debates between Presidential candidates become traditional, so that the risk of refusing to debate is raised for the incumbent. The odds are that only some such mechanism will bring about a sense that matched contenders at the Presidential level are "matched" not only in their general abilities, but also in the risks they bear in the debating situation.

4. ". . . a stated proposition . . ." As all of us know from our experiences in conversation and in classroom discussion, there is a big difference between a fragmented series of quips and a connected discourse on a single subject. Much of the "debate" that goes on in political campaigns is not much more than a rain of little slogans. Candidate A scores a point on civil rights; Candidate B counterattacks with a charge on foreign policy; Candidate

A comes back with a statistic on unemployment. There is a lack of development, of cumulation, of argument in which the speakers and the audience grow in understanding of an issue as the argument proceeds. The result is not a reasoned position, but a confused collection of items that helps us little in making up our minds.

An old principle of propaganda says: "Never answer your opponents' charges unless you have to." In other words, don't call attention to your own weak points by trying to prove that they are not so weak after all. Don't let the other guy control the agenda. Better yet, make him spend his time answering *your* charges.

Obviously, this kind of charge and countercharge process militates against connected debate. The strategy has its limits, though. In a national Presidential campaign, a candidate accused of selling out to the Chinese Communists could hardly avoid making some kind of response. Furthermore, at any given time, the agenda of major issues before the electorate is a fairly short one. For instance, in 1968 neither major-party Presidential candidate could get by without discussing Vietnam and the crisis of the cities. So there is likely to be some continuity to the campaign discussion even though neither candidate may want it. In a formal debate, this control is even more severe; there is one proposition stated in advance, and a moderator to see that the issue gets dealt with.

Another way debate can get off the track of a stated proposition is for it to turn into a quiz show. We can see how this happens by referring back to our own bull-session experiences, in class and out. Suppose the proposition is: "The United States should withdraw its forces immediately from Vietnam." The negative speaker cites the distance from Saigon to Manila. The positive speaker comes back with current casualty figures. Negative points out the provisions of a treaty. Positive shows the tonnage of bombs dropped on North Vietnam in the past year. And so on. All these facts are more or less relevant to the larger proposition, but the relevance is neither specified nor explored in depth. A genuine discourse uses facts in a context. Facts are not just ping-ponged across the table. Real discourse deals in clusters of facts significantly related to one another through their relationship to a larger proposition. Perhaps the quiz-show format of the Kennedy-Nixon debates was their worst feature, not at all untypical of the statistic-ridden speeches candidates make as they go their separate ways.

5. ". . . to gain an audience decision." The classic debate winds up with a verdict on the proposition, either from the audience or from a panel of judges. Of course, it is a rare debate that really lays a question to rest. (Has anyone ever heard the losers confess that they have seen the light and now endorse the position of their adversaries?) But the discourse does end with some kind of judgment by a third party that on balance one side has made a stronger case than the other.

Now of course the anticipation of a final decision affects the way in which the participants conduct the debate. It presses them to marshal their arguments around the central proposition. They are more likely than otherwise to organize their statements to emphasize their strongest arguments—to use cannonballs rather than buckshot—and to aim at the enemy's most vulnerable target. Much as we arrange our thoughts more systematically in anticipation of a focused seminar than of a kaffeeklatsch, so a debater facing a decision is less likely to drift off into irrelevancies in the hope of creating a vague favorable impression.

Political campaigns do end with a major decision—defeat or victory at the polls—anyone can see how the anticipation of that big decision affects the campaigners' thinking and rhetoric. But in many ways the election decision does not meet the criterion for debate. The decision is too big, so big that it is difficult to say with any precision what issues have been decided how. The decision says, "You win and you lose," not "Issue X is decided this way, Issue Y is decided that way." Think back to 1964 for a clear example of the difficulty. Most of the time in most of our elections the outcome is perfectly clear regarding people and disturbingly obscure regarding issues.

approaching reality

The purpose of presenting an overall model of the debate situation is not to suggest that any real debate in politics is likely to meet each criterion. Rather we are trying to see just how—and how far—real political situations deviate from a simple, abstract model of the classic debate. This is one way to systematize our own perceptions and thoughts about the political process. Like the citizen trying to understand current issues and events through simplifying categories, we are trying to see our way through political thinking by posing systematically statements we know are only crude approximations of the facts but which have the virtue of clarity.

A student interested in seeing how reality and the classic debate model relate to one another in one context should look at *The Great Debates,* edited by Sidney Kraus. This is a series of articles on, and the full texts of, the Kennedy-Nixon debates of 1960. There he would find some interesting facts:

1. More than half the adult population watched or listened to all four of the debates, and four-fifths saw or heard at least one of them. The audience was split about equally between Nixon and Kennedy supporters.

2. "Independent voters" were much less likely to watch the debates than were partisans. About half the people talked about the debates with others the next day.

3. Most people felt that the clash of personalities, rather than the issues or facts, was most interesting. There was a tendency to see one's own candidate as the winner (although there was no formal decision). Surprisingly, there was no clear tendency for Democratic voters to remember more what Kennedy had said than what Nixon had said, or vice versa. Apparently the main impacts of the debates on issues were to make some stand out as important, to clarify the candidates' stands, but to make few changes in issue opinions.

The longer range impacts of the Kennedy-Nixon debates are hard to assess. They may have enlightened a good many voters regarding several continuing issues, but more importantly they may have helped to set a slightly different standard for subsequent political controversy at the national level. We may well see a repetition of these events, particularly when the Presidential contest is between two nonincumbents. And for the national audience, perhaps it is realistic to hope for fewer responses of the type one woman reported when she said that she would vote against one of the candidates because she "didn't like the look in his eyes, especially the left one."

chapter v

Political Feelings

Perhaps no other political thinker had more effect on the American Revolution than did John Locke. The authors of the Declaration of Independence found in Locke's words a new way of looking at political society. Theoretically, at least, the Declaration includes everybody—"all men"—as potential participants. From that time to this, and throughout the world, the idea of a political order in which every man has his part to play has spread with revolutionary rapidity. Citizen participation has escalated so rapidly in so many different parts of the world that we have come to take it for granted. Perhaps that revolution in participation is the most profound change, the most fundamental development, in the entire history of political life.

We forget how long it took before the average man was brought into the circle of those who had to do with government in any way except as a passive object of control. The very idea of mass citizenship is as ancient as politics in theory and as new as America in practice.

Around the world millions of citizens are voting, debating, taking part in political parties, serving on juries, in numbers beyond the dreams of the most ardent democrats of only a few centuries ago.

But there is another revolution. It too has roots in John Locke's work. It is the revolution of political legitimacy. Locke shows its meaning in the preface to his main work:

> To establish the throne of our great restorer, our present King, William; to make good his title in the consent of the people; which being the only one of lawful governments he has more fully than any other prince in Christendom; and to justify to the world the people in England whose love of their just and national rights with their resolution to preserve them, saved the nation when it was on the brink of slavery and ruin.[1]

"To make good his title in the consent of the people"—that is the fundamental change. For most of the world's history and for the great mass of the people, rulers were simply there. The idea that their rule had to be justified at all, that they had to be legitimate rulers of the nation, seldom came to mind. Or if it did, the argument was very simple: as James I put it, "Kings are breathing images of God on earth," and since "it is atheism and blasphemy to dispute what God can do . . . so it is presumption and high contempt in a subject to dispute what a king can do." King James proclaimed that "a wicked king is sent by God for a curse to his people and a plague for their sins. . . . Patience, earnest prayers to God and amendment of their lives are the only lawful means to move God to relieve them of their heavy curse." But in the last analysis, the legitimacy of kings was not something to be argued about: "that which concerns the mystery of the king's power is not lawful to be disputed; for that is to wade into

[1] Quoted in John H. Hallowell, *Main Currents of Modern Political Thought* (New York: Holt, 1950), p. 102.

the weakness of princes and to take away the mystical reverence that belongs to them that sit in the throne of God."[2]

Those days are gone forever. Today all governments, totalitarian or democratic, justify their existence on the basis of the consent of the governed. This is the revolution of legitimacy, a movement from the idea of government as something imposed on a people by God and nature, to be accepted without question, to the idea of government as an instrument subject to the will of the whole society.

Probably no one would be more surprised than Jefferson, were he to return to life today, to see this idea at work in India, in the new Japan, and even in the drab conformity of modern Communist "people's republics."

Practical politicians have long understood the necessity for consent. At least in democratic politics (and to a degree and in a different way in totalitarian politics), government cannot be made to work without consent. Force is a weak weapon, a last resort, which, if used too often, undercuts political power. As Karl Deutsch has argued, force in politics is like gold in economics. Most of the operation of government is done on a kind of political credit; when a politician has to use force he is already in the kind of trouble that an economy is in when it has to use gold.[3] And we see clearly in Nazism how even a ruthless political genius like Hitler, who had no qualms about the uses of torture and murder, took great pains to win the allegiance of the German people, and was able to embark on his foreign ventures only when he had achieved that allegiance on a massive scale.[4]

Never more than today have political leaders had to concern themselves with these fundamental feelings not only in the United States, but around the world. In new nations that have cast off colonial rule, new grounds for legitimacy must be found and fostered. Unless the *nation* can emerge as the focus of loyalty, all the competing loyalties—to regions, tribes, classes, and

[2]*Ibid.*, p. 71.

[3]Karl W. Deutsch, *The Nerves of Government* (New York: Free Press, Macmillan, 1963).

[4]For a fascinating account of how the Nazis managed this, see William S. Allen, *The Nazi Seizure of Power: The Experience of a Single German Town 1930–1935* (Chicago: Quadrangle Books, 1965).

sects, for example – can divert and confuse the thrust for unity.[5]

What kind of loyalty, what feelings of political legitimacy and allegiance will foster democratic progress? What kinds will lead down the track toward the swamp of totalitarianism? More broadly, what role is played by feelings like loyalty and consent in democratic politics?

devotion, alienation, allegiance

Suppose we begin by staking out some of the outlines of these feelings. Obviously, there is one kind of feeling about government that we can call devotion, a kind of religious faith in a ruler or set of rulers. At the extreme is the fanaticism of the true believer. Politics can offer a substitute for religion, a source of great hope for the future among people hopeless or threatened in the present.

> To those impoverished of life's joys, there is great comfort in giving up the individual struggle and in following leaders who promise a glorious future. To embrace a leader and his cause is one way to give meaning to an empty life. To be free of decision-making is to be free of care. Life is good because life is active. Life is meaningful because ends are determined that are defined as desirable and necessary. Life is happy because one derives joy from service. Life is full because the state leaves no moment undirected.[6]

The focus on the future is very significant in these beliefs, in part because it removes the restraints of present reality. We can see that in the comments of a French Communist when he says:

> When the future society of Communism arrives it will be so wonderful – we have no doubts about it. We hardly dare believe it. There will be no more exploitation. There will be no more conflicts. Mankind will be able to get more culture. There will be no more reason to fight each other. I am very confident. I believe it will be like that.[7]

[5] Seymour M. Lipset, *The First New Nation* (New York: Basic Books, 1963), p. 16.

[6] Morton Grodzins, *The Loyal and the Disloyal* (Chicago: University of Chicago Press, 1956), p. 85.

[7] Hadley Cantril, *The Politics of Despair* (New York: Basic Books, 1958), p. 94.

We notice here the intensity of beliefs of a religious or pseudo-religious nature. The man thinks that communism will bring heaven on earth.

Historically in the worship of Stalin and of Hitler, and currently in the devotion of millions of Chinese to Mao, these feelings are focused on a single national leader as political messiah. But there is also a dimension of this feeling which focuses on "the movement," the bundle of symbols, group activities, hopes and fears that the believers share collectively. As we might expect, it is difficult to maintain such intense feelings about something as amorphous as a movement, and therefore there is almost always a strong tendency to focus them on a single person at the top. When, as in the case of Stalin, the person and the movement diverge and the leader becomes an outcast, there is a strain in the fabric of belief which individuals find problematical. From what we thought about in chapter iii, we can imagine some of the ways in which such conflicts are resolved. But the nature of this kind of belief is clear: it focuses on the leader. It views him in highly positive terms. And, compared with other beliefs, this devotion is intense.

One form of alienation is the mirror image of devotion. This is the alienation of hate, of deep and fundamental antagonism toward the powerful in a society. Like the devotee, the political hater feels intensely and derives from his hatred similar personal rewards. As Eric Hoffer has written, for such people hatred

> pulls and whirls the individual away from his own self, makes him oblivious of his weal and future, frees him of jealousies and self-seeking. He becomes an anonymous particle quivering with the craving to fuse and coalesce with his like into one flaming mass. . . . Common hatred unites the most heterogeneous elements.[8]

Political haters usually require a personal devil, an individual or group thought to be at the root of all the hateful things one perceives in politics. For a small and not insignificant minority of the politically alienated in this world, hatred of the regime becomes a style of life, a dominating theme of the personality in all its relationships.

[8] Eric Hoffer, *The True Believer* (New York: New American Library, 1951), pp. 85–86.

Numerically, the devotees and the haters are not very many. A far more extensive form of political feeling than love or hate is withdrawal, a turning away from government or politics or both as something alien, or foreign, to the person. We have already seen a mild form of this alienation in the millions of people who take no part in something that after all is their own — the work of government. For most people this means not much more than neglect. But for another sizable minority it goes beyond neglect to rejection.

The fundamental feeling in this form of alienation is that one is dependent upon the political order but cannot share in its life. Robert E. Lane adds up the meaning of political alienation as encompassing three fundamental attitudes:

> 1. I am the object, not the subject of political life — I have no influence and do not participate. Politically, I speak in the passive voice.
> 2. The government is not run in my interest; they do not care about me; in this sense it is not my government.
> 3. I do not approve the way decisions are made; the rules of the game are unfair, loaded, illegitimate; the Constitution is, in some sense, fraudulent.[9]

There is the feeling, as one of Lane's respondents says about government, that "they've never bothered with me and I've never bothered with them. . . . I have nothing to do with the government; no, I've never had anything at all to do with them."[10] For the broad range of citizens in this category, the government and the political order are seen as not particularly helpful, not particularly harmful, something one might as well stay away from. The object of the feeling is diffuse, not focused, as political love and hate usually are, on a single individual. Nor is it intense; this is a low-key emotion at the edge of attention.

Political allegiance, as it is most usually found, is similarly low-key. This is what we mean when we think of the feeling widespread among Americans of respect for the Constitution and the Bill of Rights (often accompanied with very little knowledge of either). When Lane's respondents "think of 'government,' they think of a positive, supportive, nurturant organization."[11] And as

[9] Robert E. Lane, *Political Ideology: Why the American Common Man Believes What He Does* (New York: Free Press, Macmillan, 1962), p. 162.
[10] *Ibid.*, p. 172.
[11] *Ibid.*, p. 171.

Geoffrey Gorer noted, "For the vast majority of Americans the term 'democracy' has no connotations beyond 'political forms after the American fashion.'"[12] These are familiar, indeed almost natural feelings in our rich, old democracy. In many of the world's poor new nations, alienated feelings are much more prevalent. In our own society, there are millions of the poor and the black for whom the government seems to belong to someone else. For most people there is a mixture of positive and negative feelings about this or that aspect of government and politics, a mixture that changes and fluctuates over time within a range on the generally positive side of the scale.

This range of devoted, alienated, and allegiant feelings shows variants we will be returning to in more detail. But already we see three features of political feelings that will be helpful to keep in mind:

1. *Intensity*. Political feelings run the gamut from the fanatical to the apathetic. We need to notice where any expression of political feeling is along this scale of intensity. The most usual mistake is to think that widely shared feelings are necessarily intense ones.

2. *Direction*. Feelings may be for the political order, against it, or away from it (in the sense of withdrawal). Obviously, it makes a difference for a society whether the political feelings of its citizens balance out on the pro or con side, and also the numbers and proportions of citizens whose feelings make them political dropouts.

3. *Focus*. Political feelings may be focused on a single leader, a set of institutions, a political movement, myths and symbols, and any number of other facets of an amorphous political order. Feelings of loyalty or distrust acquire special implications for political action when they are sharply focused.

what difference does it make?

In this chapter we shall be asking this question again and again, for one of our purposes is to get a grip on an instrument of political analysis which has proven to be extremely useful: the idea of

[12] Geoffrey Gorer, *The American People* (New York: Norton, 1948), p. 222.

function. Fundamentally, this is an extremely simple idea or question. It means that whenever we observe an important political phenomenon, we ask not only is it good or bad, strong or weak, new or old, unique or general, but also *who benefits* from it, how, and why?

This seems simple enough, but there is much thought about politics that fails to reach this question. Yet without it, what goes on in politics is mysterious. How can we understand a constitutional anachronism like the electoral college? In part by understanding how certain political forces — those in the large urban states — benefit from this feature of Presidential politics. How can we understand the persistence of the old-time boss-led political machines in America, with all their corruption and inefficiency? In part by understanding how they have helped, albeit in a crude and often unjust way, great masses of strangers in America who had no place else to turn. How can we understand the rise of totalitarianism in the "civilized" world? Partly by understanding what this kind of perverted patriotism offers to a society smarter than it is wise. If we are to understand before we judge, these are just the kinds of questions we need to raise. Few political arrangements or attitudes last long unless they benefit somebody, and in a large and democratic nation, only those institutions and feelings that benefit *many* people will persist.

We saw part of this picture of the idea of function in the last chapter. Party identification helps people with a tough task: making sense out of politics. Here we shall be looking at a variety of ways in which political feelings benefit the citizen who not only thinks but also sympathizes and distrusts.

Much of what we shall be looking into will concern ways people use politics in managing their feelings. All of us, to varying degrees, have to cope with problematic environments. We are a striving race; we live on our hearts and stomachs as well as in our brains. We are never neutral about things that are important to us. We react emotionally, most of the time, *before* we get around to thinking about a situation. In all these ways and others, citizens have need of help in managing their feelings as well as in coping with the objective, calculable aspects of their environments. And politics — that shifting cloud of images and voices — offers all sorts of opportunities for emotional expression.

So what? What difference does it really make to the welfare of humanity how people feel about politics? Why get into "soul stuff" when we're supposed to be trying to figure out political reality and not personal sentiment? Why not stick to what people objectively have and know and want, rather than delving into the psyche of the citizen?

why citizen feelings count

Increasingly, popular sentiments about politics are known to, and are taken into account by, decision-makers. This is direct influence; the responsible public official finds out how people are feeling about various issues and enters this information as one important item in his political calculations. It is easy to overemphasize this kind of direct influence. Despite the revolutionary development of public opinion polling, there is still room for a great deal of uncertainty as to what the public is thinking and feeling about particular issues at any given time.

For example, one public opinion poll in 1966 showed that a majority of the public supported the President's handling of the Vietnam situation *and* a majority also approved the policy of deescalating the war effort.[13] Parallel surveys of Congressmen and their constituents show that on many important issues Congressmen are quite ill informed about their constituents' feelings.[14] Yet Congressmen are constantly taking actions based on some picture of what their constituents think.

On certain simple dimensions, such as a favorable or unfavorable view of the President, we now have reliable knowledge and can see how these feelings fluctuate over time. From the days of Presidents Kennedy and Johnson onward, no President will be able to ignore these direct expressions of popular sentiment.

From the beginnings of the United States, sentiments about our leaders have counted heavily in political decisions. For example, odds are there would never have been a United States without the popularity of George Washington. "The early American Republic," writes Seymour M. Lipset, "like many of the new nations,

[13] Leo Bogart, "No Opinion, Don't Know and Maybe No Answer," *Public Opinion Quarterly,* Vol. 31 (Fall, 1967), 336.

[14] Warren E. Miller and Donald Stokes, "Constituency Influence in Congress," in Campbell *et al.* (eds.), *Elections and the Political Order* (New York: Wiley, 1966), pp. 351–72.

was legitimized by *charisma*. We tend to forget today that, in his time, George Washington was idolized as much as many of the contemporary leaders of new states."[15] Washington's biographer Marcus Cunliffe says:

> In the well-worn phrase of Henry Lee, he was *first in war, first in peace, and first in the hearts of his countrymen* . . . he was the prime native hero, a necessary creation for a new country . . . hence . . . the comment . . . made by the European traveler Paul Svinin, as early as 1815: "Every American considers it his sacred duty to have a likeness of Washington in his home, just as we have the images of God's saints." For America, he was originator and vindicator, both patron saint *and* defender of the faith, in a curiously timeless fashion, as if he were Charlemagne, Saint Joan and Napolean Bonaparte telescoped into one person. . . .[16]

Washington had his critics, but the main effects of his overwhelming popularity are clear. He gave the new nation — really a scattered collection of isolated communities — *time* to find itself. Fortunately Washington did not retire after one term in office, as he devoutly wished to do. By staying on, he provided a focus for national loyalties while a system of political parties developed to manage conflict through peaceful competition and compromise.

This is but one of the ways citizen sentiment supports the political system. We see all around us in the teeming instability of many of the world's nations, new and old, how popular feelings about leaders play crucial roles in building or destroying democracy.

Often leaders do not know how their followers feel. But how leaders *think* people feel is immensely important to the leadership. The endless speculation, often quite ill informed, in Washington about the tides and eddies of public opinion has a profound effect on elected officials. Faced with an amorphous and uncertain public opinion — in which, for example, "the lower-status groups and the least educated, even though they have the most to gain from social change, are least in favor of it"[17] — nevertheless politicians try continually to guess what is on the "public mind."

[15] Lipset, *op. cit.*, p. 18.

[16] Marcus Cunliffe, *George Washington: Man and Monument* (New York: Mentor Books, 1958), pp. 20–21.

[17] Lane, *op. cit.*, p. 441.

But there is much more to the meaning of citizen sentiments for the political system than specific, focused feelings about particular leaders or issues. There are at least three fundamental political feelings that function to support the system.

e pluribus unum

First is *community.* "A house divided against itself cannot stand." It cost the American Republic 600,000 lives to learn that lesson. Around the globe today, we see nations torn apart by racial and class and religious and ethnic stresses in the social fabric; in the late 1960's Americans were warned that our own nation was on the verge of division into a black community and a white community. In part national community is a matter of interest and calculation; there is a realization that cooperation pays off. But a large dimension of community is a matter of feeling, a matter of trust. To what degree do people feel affection for one another? Or if not affection, acceptance? Or if not acceptance, tolerance? These are obviously critical questions, not only for leaders trying to build nations and maintain them, but also for political scientists trying to understand them. At the one extreme is a "nation" like the Congo, torn apart by group hatreds. At the other extreme is the dull conformity of an East Germany or a Portugal, in which the very thought of conflict seems to have been washed out of the national consciousness. Somewhere in the middle, democracies like the United States and France and England engage in continual testings of their ability to stick together without becoming stuck in some static, frozen pattern. From the viewpoint of the individual citizen, the question is one of the degree to which he can maintain a sense that others are like him—that they share his fundamental humanity and his basic political attitudes—and yet different enough to make discussion and peaceful competition worthwhile.

faith in the system

A second major set of political sentiments that have fundamental functional importance for the operation of the political system refer to *faith,* not in the particular personalities who occupy the seats of power, but *in the system* of power itself. In a remarkable study of one French village, Laurence Wylie tells of the typical villager's feeling toward the political system:

> Theoretically Government may be an alter ego of la Patrie but in point of fact it is made of men — weak, stupid, selfish, ambitious men. It is the duty of the citizen *not* to cooperate with these men as the civics books would have people do, but rather to hinder them, to prevent them in every possible way from increasing their power over individuals and over families.
>
> This is a point on which everyone in Peyrane would agree: a man with power over you is essentially evil. They readily admit that a man may be virtuous when he goes into politics, but they would deny that he can remain virtuous if he attains power. Except for a few supporters of the MRP, the voters of Peyrane say that the heads of their parties, and of all other political parties, are "a pile of bandits."[18]

Peyranians may stick together, may form a community of some solidarity, but they do not extend that trust to the political system. For them, the government is one more thing run by strangers against their interests. There is a basic distrust of the legal order, which appears to the citizen as a "paralyzing network of official laws and regulations" imposed upon a different system of "human relationships where with resourcefulness one may move freely to accomplish what may be legally unobtainable."[19] Similarly the right to vote is seen not as an opportunity to change government for the better or to use government to improve one's welfare, but rather as a means of protest against the order of things by saying "leave me alone" to those who hold the reins of power.[20]

Such feelings can have profound effects on the operation of the political system itself. To a large degree, a successful democracy depends on agreement as to how the system is to be used, on the "rules of the game." When government itself is seen as fundamentally corrupt and unfair, people are inclined either to avoid it as much as possible or to use the machinery of government itself

---

[18] Laurence Wylie, *Village in the Vaucluse* (Cambridge, Mass.: Harvard University Press, 1964), pp. 207–8. Wylie returned to Peyrane a decade later and noted marked changes, especially in the peoples' sense of solidarity with other French farmers.

[19] *Ibid.*, p. 335.

[20] *Ibid.*, p. 330.

as a way of expressing their negative feelings rather than as a way of solving problems. Part of the revolution of legitimacy has been the spreading sense that government owes its very existence to the consent of the governed. When that consensus breaks down, it is very probable that the government will break down either by becoming a stable but unresponsive structure of repression or by becoming a disordered flux of accidental alternations between complete ineffectiveness and personalized tyrannies.

It is tempting to contrast Peyrane with America. In the United States, there is a strong theme of respect and allegiance to the system and its leaders. Later we shall see some of the contradictions and ambiguities in that theme, but it is true that Americans rank top public offices very highly, with U.S. Supreme Court justices in first place.[21] There is a consensus on principles of democracy abstractly expressed. As we have seen, these broad principles are given some very mixed interpretations in practice, when such specific questions as the right of an atheist or Communist to speak in one's community are posed. Nevertheless, it is probable that adherance to the principle has some constraining influence on practice.

A survey in 1964 showed that nine out of ten Americans agree that "I usually have confidence that the government will do what is right."[22] Only very small minorities — on the order of 3 to 5 percent — in the main Western democracies (United States, United Kingdom, Germany, and Italy) say of their national governments that they would be "better off without it."[23] Even shortly after the riots in the Watts district of Los Angeles in 1965, two-thirds of a mixed sample of whites and Negroes answered yes to the question: "Do you think elected officials can generally be trusted?"[24] In a 1964 survey in Wisconsin about two out of three citizens agreed that "people who work for parties during political campaigns do our nation a great service," that "democracy works best where competition between parties is strong," and disagree with the

[21] Wendell Bell, Richard J. Hill, and Charles R. Wright, *Public Leadership* (San Francisco: Chandler, 1961), pp. 132–33.

[22] Herbert McClosky, "Consensus and Ideology in American Politics," *American Political Science Review*, Vol. 58 (1964), 361–82.

[23] Gabriel A. Almond and Sidney Verba, *The Civic Culture* (Princeton, N.J.: Princeton University Press, 1963), pp. 80, 82.

[24] David O. Sears, "Political Behavior," in G. Lindzey and E. Aaronson (eds.), *Handbook of Social Psychology*, rev. ed. (Reading, Mass.: Addison-Wesley, 1968).

statement that "it would be better if, in all elections, we put no party labels on the ballot."[25]

The evidence is thus clear that most Americans adhere to some generally favorable views of the political system. These sentiments are more widespread regarding "government" than regarding "politics," but the party system does receive a fairly clear vote of confidence at this general level. Furthermore, most Americans feel that they can do something effective about unjust or harmful laws, both at the local level (77 percent) and at the national level (75 percent).[26] Most of the working-class subjects Robert E. Lane interviewed felt that their votes have real influence on the way the government operates, a feeling vividly expressed by one factory worker for whom voting is just about the only form of participation:

> To me, voting is the thing, the right to put in the guy you want—that's the big thing. I mean, I know that over there they don't have that and they have a lot of trouble. The kid that was born to Princess Elizabeth—he is going to be the king some day. That's all there is to it. Nobody else is gonna run it, know what I mean? . . . Here, there is always a contest against each other trying to serve the people the best way they could to stay in power. And that's a good thing.[27]

Lane's comment on this passage clarifies the significance of these feelings:

> In this way the election transmutes the subject . . . into a citizen. It is a symbolic act of enormous importance in leading men to speak of their relationship to government in the active voice, however confusing it may be in detail, however difficult to specify the nature of the control it represents, however inflated the claims made in the name of popular government. After all, voting for and against officials is what you do to government in an exchange where it does much to you.[28]

[25] J. Dennis, "Support for the Party System by the Mass Public," *American Political Science Review*, Vol. 60 (1966), 600–15.

[26] Almond and Verba, *op. cit.*, p. 142. In Great Britain, 78 percent of citizens thought they could do something about a local regulation and 62 percent believed they could take effective action regarding a national regulation. The contrasting figures for Mexico are 52 percent and 38 percent, and for Italy 51 percent and 28 percent.

[27] Lane, *op. cit.*, p. 166.

[28] *Ibid.*, p. 166.

Thus despite the complaints and ambiguities, the American political system has about it, for most citizens, an aura of legitimacy and acceptance. And the theme is a very old one, as sentiments about government go. It traces back to the beginnings of our national history. Perhaps the most critical turning point in our national history was the election of 1800, marked by a crucial nonevent; as Lipset points out, this was "the first occasion in modern politics in which an incumbent political party suffered an electoral defeat and simply turned over power to its opponents."[29] National unity was far from securely established at that time. But it was of profound importance that a pattern of faith in the system was established. The idea that the defeated parties could go on, could endure defeat and yet neither withdraw from the system nor create a revolution, set a pattern that has lasted to this day.

what citizens want and expect from government

A basic allegiance to the system, a sense that — somehow or other — the system works for the citizen, seems necessary for a democracy to work. When citizens feel that *the government produces* for them, they are probably more likely to develop that sense of allegiance on which stable democracy depends. And this sense of satisfaction is not just a matter of feeling; there is evidence to back it up. After all, the American system

> . . . has evolved and survived from aristocracy to mass democracy, through slavery, civil war, the tentative uneasy reconciliation of North and South, the repression of Negroes and their halting liberation; through two great wars of worldwide scope, mobilization, far-flung military enterprise, and return to hazardous peace; through numerous periods of economic instability and one prolonged depression with mass unemployment, farm "holidays," "veterans'" marches, tear gas, and even bullets; through two periods of post-war cynicism, demogogic excesses, invasions of traditional liberties, and the groping, awkward, often savage, attempt to cope with problems of subversion, fear and civil tension.[30]

[29] Lipset, *op. cit.*, p. 44. Italics omitted.
[30] Robert A. Dahl, *A Preface to Democratic Theory* (Chicago: University of Chicago Press, 1956), pp. 150–51.

It is not entirely clear how much of this happy outcome is due to the political system and how much is due to various accidents of history, such as our geographic position and scope and the rich profusion of natural resources on which our economic prosperity developed. Probably the attitude of most Americans is one of mild and tentative gratitude. Loyalty is widespread but not very intense.

Loyalty looks to the past; *expectations* look to the future. Certainly a key factor in making democracy work is the wants people have and the time in which they expect them to be gratified. The apathetic citizen who has given up on government, thoroughly disillusioned, expects little and hopes for even less. His view of the future is pessimistic; things are likely to get worse and there is not much he can do about it. At the other end of the scale is the political fanatic who wants and expects utopia tomorrow. Living on logic, he can see no reason why the political system should not be transformed immediately into perfection, into a political heaven on earth. If the apathetic lacks hope, the fanatic lacks a sense of history, of the ways the human organism grows stage by stage.

Obviously most Americans fall in between these extremes. As we have already seen, there is a good deal of indifference to the political system. Not all our hopes are wrapped up in what the government may or may not do. We have other places to turn. The strain of skepticism about politics and politicians helps to protect Americans against massive disillusionment. Politicians who promise everything at once lose their audiences. Out of the exaggerations of election time, we read the *directions* the different candidates would likely take if elected, the ways they differ from one another in the goals they would pursue. But we typically pay less heed to the *extent* of their promises. When we hear "a chicken in every pot," we think "maybe some more chickens in some more pots." The attitude is moderate progressivism, the essential characteristic of which is a willingness to take action — to participate — without the hope of complete success right now.

The sense of *time* is crucial to an understanding of what people expect from government. Often it is a main factor dividing the pragmatist from the fanatic. In their heyday, the Stalinists were able to gather much support among moderate progressives by appearing as "fellow progressives in a hurry," sharing the same goals as the others but wanting to reach them much faster.[31]

Every political movement—indeed every culture—has its peculiar sense of time. Some want to stop the clock; others want to turn it backward. The evidence is sketchy here, but most Americans seem to focus their political feelings on a kind of intermediate-range future, on the day after tomorrow. They think of what will happen just after the next step: "When we save up enough money, we will. . . ." "When I finish my training, I will. . . ." "We are sending John to parochial school to prepare him for. . . ." "When I retire we will move to. . . ."[32] Undoubtedly these culturally supported hopes affect people's political feelings. There is a sense that the political system has made a qualified promise to make the day after tomorrow somewhat brighter than today. There is an acceptance of the necessity to delay gratification, an acceptance that buys time for the system to show what it can do.

the key political feelings

At least these three feelings are functional for the sustenance of democracy:

1. *A sense of community.*   People share a common identity as fellow citizens, at the core of which is trust. Democracy requires that confidence in others, that mutual respect which makes debate natural and violence unacceptable.

2. *Faith in the system.*   People focus their patriotism on political fair play. The government is seen as an instrument of the nation, not an alien rulership. Political feelings support the rules of the game (known and unknown) in the Constitution.

3. *Moderate hope for the future.*   People expect the political system to meet their present and future needs—not all at once, but with "reasonable" speed and impact. The pace and scope of government action is measured against the record of the past, on the one hand, and the emerging needs of the future, on the other.

[31] Irving Howe and Lewis Coser, "Totalitarianism as Ideology," in Edgar Litt (ed.), *The Political Imagination* (Glenview, Ill.: Scott, Foresman, 1966), p. 113.
[32] Lane, *op. cit.*, p. 286.

These political feelings are *functional* for democracy. They provide a reservoir of sentiment for leaders to draw upon. In specific action circumstances, these sentiments have to be interpreted and applied to make the system work. Like the gap between theory and practice, the gap between political feelings and political actions is a large one. But the feelings are far from irrelevant. Without them—or with their opposites—we would confront a very different kind of politics in the United States.

Why do citizens adhere to their political feelings? In what ways is it rewarding—or punishing—to a person for him to feel loyal to the nation, for example? The positive functions that opinions serve for people are illustrated in chapter vi. But not all the functions are positive; the negative functions—or, to jargonize, dysfunctions—are important also, because they show how democratic sentiments can conflict with other feelings citizens experience, in ways that can dampen or divert their force.

"the fear of equality"

Surely part of the cutting edge of progressivism in the United States has been the idea of equality. We started off saying that "all men are created equal." and we have interpreted that as an ideal, a goal toward which the whole society should move. The fact is, of course, that we have a long way to go before there is real equality—of wealth, of opportunity, of status, of respect—in this country. But time and again political movements and their leaders have been able to call upon equality as a rallying cry for progress. Surely we would expect that the pressure for equality would be strong among those at or near the bottom of the ladder, such as Lane's working-class subjects.[33]

Most of them did see equality as an important feature of American life, at least in terms of opportunity. But they had to struggle with a difficult psychological problem: if this is the land of equal opportunity, what are they doing at the bottom of the ladder? The tension between their own feeling that they were the equal of any man, that this is truly the land of opportunity, and their sense that they themselves had not made the most of their

[33] *Ibid.*, Chapter 4.

opportunities was painful and led them to seek a variety of ways to reduce that tension.

> When something is painful to examine, people look away, or, if they look at it, they see only the parts they want to see. They deny that it is an important something. So is it often with a person's class status when the reference is upward, when people must account not for the strength of their position, but for its weakness.[34]

One way is to push the problem aside. A person may deny the relevance of the problem, as when one says:

> I think a lot of people place a lot of stress on the importance of social classes, [but] I feel that I have a job to do, I have my own little unit to take care of. If I can do it to the best ability that is instilled in me at birth or progress through the years, I feel that I rightly deserve the highest classification you can get. I don't particularly like the headings, "upper, middle, working, and lower."

Or, as another puts it:

> I don't think it [social class] is important. I mean, whenever I went and asked for a job, the boss never asked me what class I was in. They just wanted to know if I knew my business. Oh, yes, and I don't think in politics it makes any difference.

Or one can give up, resign himself to the place he is in:

> It's hard, very hard. We seem to be struggling along now, as it is, right here, to try and get above our level, to get out of the rut, as you might say, that we're probably in right now. . . . [But] After you get to a certain age, there, you stop—and you say, "Well, I can't go any farther," I think I've gotten to that point now.

Obviously these thoughts help a person make peace with the feeling that he is now as equal as he would like to be. Some of Lane's respondents went beyond this to the thought that a radical rise in their position would not represent an increase in happiness.

[34]*Ibid.,* pp. 62–63.

Here are some of their responses to the question: "Are the rich happier than people who are just average?"

> I think lots of times they're never happy, because one thing is, the majority of them that are rich have got more worries. You see a lot more of them sick than you do, I think, the average. I think a lot of your mental strain is a lot greater in the higher class—in the rich class—than in the other.

> . . . the majority of these big men—I don't think they devote as much time and get a thrill out of the little things in life that the average guy gets, which I think is a lot of thrills.

Besides, the upper class is not, for many of these citizens, an all-powerful minority elite running the country. "The biggest part of the people in this country are working class," and through their votes "they've got a big part to do with running this country." The whole economy is seen as depending on the workers, the millions of people who can bear the strain of hardship better than those who, in the depression, for example, "lived so high that they couldn't stand it any more when they went broke, and they committed a lot of suicides there. But we were used to living that way, it didn't bother us." Furthermore, it is money, not status, that makes the difference; one subject finds comfort in that:

> I certainly would hate like hell to be a while-collar worker in the middle class and making the money that the white-collar worker does. I would rather be a worker in the lower class, and making their money, see?[35]

Lane's working-class subjects came up with many other explanations for their relatively lower positions. Unequal in wealth, they felt themselves equal in moral value—"just as good as anybody else"—as a person, as a human being. Rather than resenting their positions, they felt that many in the upper class deserved to be better off, as a reward for greater effort, higher ability, or just good luck. As workers, some of them felt a considerable disdain for "a lot of people who . . . will go on living on that welfare—they're happier than hell."

What would happen if, all of a sudden, all men *were* equal?

[35] *Ibid.*, pp. 63–67.

How would they feel about that? Some felt they would be uncomfortable among the better off:

> I think it's hard. Let's say—let's take me, for instance. Supposing I came into a lot of money and I moved into a nice neighborhood—class—maybe I wouldn't know how to act then. I think it's very hard, because people know that you just—word gets around that you . . . never had it before you got it now. Well, maybe they wouldn't like you . . . maybe you don't know how to act.[36]

But the main theme was that equality would cut the ground out from under an order of society that justified effort:

> I think it would be a dull thing, because life would be accepted—or it would—rather we'd go stale. There would be no initiative to be a little different, or go ahead.[37]

All their own work would be for nothing and society would grind to a halt. As Lane concludes, in part, "The greater the emphasis in a society upon the availability of 'equal opportunity for all,' the greater the need for members of that society to develop an acceptable rationalization for their own social status."[38]

These feelings about equality are but one example of how citizens can restrict their wants and expectations in ways that protect their self-respect. Erich Fromm, in his book *Escape from Freedom,* paints a similar picture regarding the ideal of liberty. Most people, most of the time, would find complete equality or liberty discomforting, if not threatening. From the citizen's viewpoint, a degree of inequality and control in the system is functional. He would, he senses, lose something if they disappeared.

where political feelings come from

Deep feelings have deep roots in personal experience. We shall see more of how some of those feelings relate to the situation a person finds himself in—the cluster of other people with whom

[36] *Ibid.,* pp. 73–74.
[37] *Ibid.,* p. 76.
[38] *Ibid.,* p. 79.

he is most closely related, his identifications with various groups (the labels he attaches to himself), the problems he has in understanding the contemporary world. These factors bring out a picture of political feelings as part of a much broader map or pattern of feelings associated with family, work, and social life. So when we view the current pattern of political feelings, we should always be aware of the connections they have with a wide range of other feelings. Part of the strength of these political sentiments is derived from their reinforcement by related feelings toward other objects in a person's psychological life-space.

Their strength also derives from the experience of a personal history.

The roots of deep political feelings run back into the past of the citizen. Research on political socialization shows that even in early childhood we can find evidence of political sentiments. Long before the child *knows* much of anything about his country or its government, he thinks both of them are great. Virtually all grade school children surveyed agreed with such statements as "The American flag is the best flag in the world" and "America is the best country in the world."[39] This primitive patriotism has a strong religious flavor: "Not only do many children associate the sanctity and awe of religion with the political community, but to ages nine or ten, they sometimes have considerable difficulty in disentangling God and country."[40] Young children think of America as simply good and Russia as simply bad. Only slowly do they learn that it is legitimate to criticize the government. In one survey only 15 percent of the fourth-grade students agreed that "you can say things against the government." By the eighth grade 54 percent agreed that criticism is all right.

These early positive feelings are focused not only on the country and its symbols, but also on the government. The same study found that 90 percent of the third-grade students felt that "what goes on in the government is all for the best." From 80 to 90 percent at all grade levels agreed that "the United States government knows what is best for the people."[41] Seventy percent of the

[39] Robert Hess and Judith V. Torney, *The Development of Political Attitudes in Children* (Chicago: Aldine, 1967), pp. 69–73.

[40] David Easton and Robert Hess, "The Child's Political World," *Midwest Journal of Political Science*, Vol. 6 (1962), 238.

[41] Hess and Torney, *op. cit.*, p. 121.

third-grade students recalled that Nixon and Kennedy had never "said anything bad about each other."[42]

These same sentiments are also focused on top political leaders, especially the President. As we might expect, many of the simpler and earlier political feelings are personalized, concentrated on highly visible and understandable personalities. Almost every schoolchild can tell you the President's name. In the child's consciousness, the President is first on the scene; later he adds the other players in supporting parts. For example, three-fourths of the second-grade students surveyed thought that the President makes the laws. By the eighth grade, only one out of twenty students made that mistake.[43] So in terms of attention – the focus of feelings – the President starts off with an immense advantage. Far fewer students (and adults!) know who their Congressmen and local officials are.

Not only is the President better known earlier, but he is also very favorably perceived, at least by northern urban children. Large proportions of students in early grade school years think of the President as "about the best person in the world," one who "cares a lot what you think if you write to him," who "would always help me if I needed it."[44] The President emerges as, in Fred I. Greenstein's telling phrase, "a benevolent leader."[45] With age there is a falling off in these naïve expressions of support. Party identifications are also formed in the early years, again without much basis on information, and there is a tendency for these early identifications to carry over into adult life. The relationships are not overwhelmingly strong, however. It is rare to find shifts from one end of the party spectrum to the other, but there is much middleground movement over a lifetime. Thus a child who grows up in a Democratic home is relatively unlikely to become a Re-

[42] *Ibid.,* p. 145.

[43] David Easton and J. Dennis, "The Child's Image of Government," *Annals of the American Academy of Political and Social Science,* Vol. 361 (1965), 40–57.

[44] Hess and Torney, *op. cit.,* pp. 86–90. Opinions of the President by rural, isolated, poor children may be much less positive. See Dean Jaros, Herbert Hirsch, and Frederic J. Fleron, Jr., "The Malevolent Leader," *American Political Science Review,* Vol. 62, No. 2 (June, 1968). Black children in Pennsylvania were also found to have less favorable attitudes toward the President. See Edward S. Greenberg, "Black Children and the Political System," *Public Opinion Quarterly,* Vol. 34, No. 3 (Fall 1970).

[45] Fred I. Greenstein, *Children and Politics* (New Haven, Conn.: Yale University Press, 1965), Chapter 3.

publican, but he may become an independent or retreat into apathy.

Adolescent rebellion is much overrated as an explanation for political change. Unless politics is a very important thing to his parents, a "rebellious youth" is more likely to kick up his heels about matters pertaining to dates and cars and bedtime than about Presidents and elections.[46]

Many factors tend to sustain these feelings over a lifetime. In school a person learns that he is supposed to have opinions and is told pretty much what those opinions ought to be. Higher education tends to loosen up the earlier attitudes, but then the individual is most likely to go on to an occupational life at about the same level as his father, so that there is a tendency to reinforce the old feelings all over again. As V. O. Key, Jr., summarizes:

> In the largest sense the educational system is a great mechanism for conserving the values, the institutions, the practices of the political order, as it inculcates from the primary school even through college the memories, the unities, and the norms of the system. Yet the educational process does not completely embalm the political system. From it there come the political innovators as well as the conservers.[47]

What difference does it make that the earliest political feelings are (a) highly positive, (b) almost completely without an informational basis, and (c) strongly focused on top political leaders, especially the President? The answers to that question are not yet entirely clear in the research; as they are developed, they will probably provide a key to understanding the role of *sequences* in the development of political feelings. It seems probable, for example, that such early feelings, if firmly established, would affect all later learning, perceptions, and sentiments. That is, a child starts out with the feeling that his government is good. When new messages come in to the effect that the government is bad, they have to deal with that preestablished sentiment. The child who has learned the earlier lesson thoroughly is unlikely to give it up on the basis of a few negative experiences or facts. It is psy-

[46] Robert E. Lane and David O. Sears, *Public Opinion* (Englewood Cliffs, N.J.: Prentice-Hall, 1964), pp. 23–24.

[47] V. O. Key, Jr., *Public Opinion and American Democracy* (New York: Knopf, 1961), p. 343. Copyright © 1961 by V. O. Key, Jr. Reprinted by permission of Alfred A. Knopf, Inc.

chologically plausible that in cases of conflict between an earlier and a later acquired feeling, the earlier one will win out. Conflict has a tendency to engender regression, a psychological moving back in time to some earlier position. However that may work, it seems likely that the highly favorable sentiments of young children come to color all of their later feelings and provide a basis for a strong underlying sense of trust and affection for government. In this way, approval of the government is functional for the person, as it leaves his established sentiments undisturbed.

The fact that these feelings are established *before much information* is brought into play is probably quite important in understanding political learning. We all know that our feelings affect our learning, that we learn better those things we are excited about or can see some use for. So it makes sense to suppose that much of the bad side of government and politics and politicans tends to be screened out by citizens who long ago came to feel that their government was friendly and worthy of respect. Students of the history of municipal government and politics know how difficult it has typically been to reform corrupt regimes, even when there is a great deal of information to support the charges of corruption. Perhaps one part of the reason it is so hard to mobilize citizens for reform is that something in their minds, something that has been there for a long time, makes them doubt that things are as bad as they have been painted.

The fact that the President appears as the first major actor on the political scene for children undoubtedly complicates the political feelings of adults. It seems probable that the disillusionment trend, by which a new President receives very high levels of support from the public and then progressively declines in its favor, springs in part from some effects of this early learning. Great things are expected of the President, and when he is unable to deliver, a process of disappointment sets in, a sense that the President has not done what he could and should do, given all of that favorable feeling. The exaggerated expectations about a man who is, after all, one major actor in a complex system make the subsequent disillusionment all the stronger.

The early establishment of the President's position probably also makes political conflict seem partially illegitimate in the eyes of many voters. The fights the President inevitably has with Congress may seem wrong, a kind of revolt against the chief by his helpers, rather than a normal part of the system.

These are speculations. More research is needed to give us more solid knowledge of the ways political feelings grow. Yet it is undoubtedly true that the school of life has two curricula. One teaches our minds, the other teaches our hearts. In the curriculum of the mind, logical sequences—as in the programmed learning of mathematics—are appropriate. We accept as a matter of course that such sequences are necessary and important in shaping and refining our intellectual equipment. Plato designed a lifelong course of study with close attention to the order of learning, the steps from opinion to knowledge. These days the social studies curriculum in the schools is continually under review to discover, among other things, the sequence in which students should be introduced to various facets of the social and political world. Much more remains to be done along these lines.

Knowledge about sequences in political learning should enlighten us about the ways children and teen-agers and adults and oldsters acquire and develop those deeper sentiments upon which the fundamental structure of democratic institutions rest. And the implications of such studies go to the heart of a basic question of the theory of political science, namely, how *time* enters into the character of political phenomena. Political scientists are constantly inferring time sequences from relationships among facts. In our puzzlement over the direction of causality, we have too rarely brought evidence to bear over a sufficient period of time so that we can see which of the related phenomena occurred earlier and is thus most likely to deserve the label "cause."

For example, consider how sequences of development may help explain Table 5.1, showing the percentage of respondents

TABLE 5.1
Percent Opposed to Protest Demonstrations
(by Education and 1968 Candidate Preference)

| Education | *Preferred* | | |
	Humphrey	*Nixon*	*Wallace*
Some college	43%	66%	79%
High School or less	79	83	91

Source: Seymour Martin Lipset and Earl Raab, *The Politics of Unreason: Right-Wing Extremism in America, 1790–1970* (New York, Harper & Row, 1970), p. 405. The figures are the percentage saying they tended to disapprove of protest demonstrations. Southern respondents were excluded from this table. Numbers of respondents omitted.

(excluding those from the South) who were opposed to protest demonstrations.

Apparently, college-educated people are more tolerant of demonstrations than are the less educated. In terms of candidate preference, Wallaceites are most opposed to demonstrations, Nixonites next, and Humphreyites least. Here we have three factors: one refers to the past (that is, educational experience), one to the future (preferences for a future President), and one to the current social scene (demonstrations). How might they have combined? What in the college experience strengthened tolerance for this form of dissent? How did attitudes toward protest affect candidate selection? Or was the sequence the other way round— first the respondent selected a candidate and then came to agree with his views on protest demonstrations? By carefully tracing the political development of citizens over time, research might reveal the critical sequences.

The long-run significance of such studies can hardly be exaggerated, because they would show us not only what we are at a given time, but also how we got that way—and thus, possibly, how we as a citizenry might change. We would also find it easier to discover the functions served by changes in politics. For neither the system nor the individual citizen can benefit forever from more of the same.

chapter vi

How Opinions Help People

Opinions are not just items isolated from the rest of a person's life in some separate little compartment of the mind. They are linked with a wide variety of personal needs and wants and goals. In other words, people *use* opinions to help them get along through life. The "reason why" behind many political opinions includes more than objective evidence and logic. It includes the functions opinions serve for citizens. To understand how this functioning works, we need be aware of the whole man, the personality into which opinions are fitted. People are not computers. Their feelings affect their thoughts as well as their actions.

An image might make this point clear. Consider a student driving across the country. He has a *purpose:* to get from here to there. That purpose is an organizer of activity, shaping all the lesser decisions about which way to go. As he drives, he watches for road signs and other hints and cues to guide him to his objective. In other words his mind is working out a map—a psychological *construct*—which will help him find his way. This is the positive side of the student's thought process. Suppose the route is strange to him. As he passes through unknown territory he becomes wary, alert to possible threats and dangers. His head is then full of cautions. He relies on certain patterns of response—psychological *defenses*—to protect him from surprise and accident. This is the negative side, the use of defenses to prevent harm.

The traveler is not responding just to the immediate cues he sees and hears. He is also responding to an *inner environment*. He brings to the new situation habits of action, techniques that have helped him before. He has driven long distances before, met other dangers, and now he calls upon those *lessons of experience*.

The driver is not completely aware, in his conscious mind, of all those lessons. Some he has learned so well he has forgotten where they came from. But his thoughts and feelings are not just a teeming mass of chaotic and uncoordinated sentiments. He is a person, he has a *personality*. There is a kind of organization, a psychological (not always logical) *structure* that relates his sentiments one to another. In most ways, he arrives at his destination the same person he was when he set forth. Not only are the elements of his personality related to one another, they are also ordered: some are more important than others. For example, his survival on the road may be more important to him than cutting an hour off his travel time.

Suppose the traveler stops along the way for coffee and talks with the waitress. She is new to him, but he tends to respond to her in part on the basis of the way he has responded to similar people (women, waitresses, friendly humans) he has known before. This is part of the *continuity* of personality as a set of growing and enduring ways of relating to other people. The man's social environment affects him; his feelings and thoughts in conversation with the waitress represent an interplay between his older habits of responding to and eliciting responses from people, on the one hand, and the new situation he finds himself in, on the other.

Now to generalize the traveling student's experience to that of the citizen in politics. Political opinions are also purposeful and defensive. They have a history in the life of the individual. They are interrelated and, to a degree, organized around a few dominant attitudes. They exist and are expressed in a social environment and are affected by the character of other people with their own purposes and defenses and habits of thought.

In crude terms, that is what the machinery is like. What makes it go? What are the uses of opinion, the functions opinions serve for citizens? Research indicates that there are at least three important types of functions that opinions serve.[1]

making sense of the political world

Confusion is uncomfortable. Most of the time most people are somewhat confused. We learn to live with a certain amount of confusion, particularly in politics. Furthermore, confusion bothers some people more than it does others. And intellectuals (who are probably bothered more by confusion than are most citizens) are often amazed to discover that people can hold many obviously contradictory opinions without feeling in the least confused.

But once we have said that, it is still true that a major function of political opinions is to make sense of the confusing world. In their excellent study of *Opinions and Personality,* Smith, Bruner, and White quote from one case study that makes this clear. A subject called John Chatwell had long had a strong need to figure out in some rational and consistent way what in the world was going on and what it meant for him. He felt lost as a student in Harvard College. He was full of questions:

> Where in the world am I? I need complete reorientation; I don't know where I stand. Should I be in college? How shall I fit myself for what I want to do? What do I want to do? I live entirely in the present and do not face the future. I don't seem to have any guts and I don't seem to care.[2]

[1] This and the following three sections rely heavily upon M. Brewster Smith, Jerome S. Bruner, and Robert W. White, *Opinions and Personality* (New York: Wiley, 1956), pp. 41–47.

[2] *Ibid.,* p. 71.

Chatwell became a lawyer. He retained his thirst for understanding the world long after college, as is evident in these answers to questions about Russia (the year is 1947):

> E: So we might start out by my asking you to tell us more or less how you feel about Russia. . . .
>
> S: When you say, "Russia," you mean Russia or the Russians?
>
> E: Well, if you want to make that distinction, that's something you can do.
>
> S: All right. Ah . . . I don't know very many Russians. I've met a few. I know a good many Asiatics of other sorts and Europeans. And my general feeling about the Russians themselves is that I would have no more quarrel with Ivan than I would with John Smith if Ivan lived next door to me.
>
> E: You think Russians are pretty much like anybody else?
>
> S: Well, I wouldn't say that. I . . . I . . . it depends on what you mean by "anybody else." I'd say they are certainly more like Americans than the Chinese are like Americans, for example, but . . . I certainly have no emotional bias for or against the Russian people as individuals, I . . . do feel, however, that as nearly as I can determine, and I don't know this, Russia is in effect a police state, and in a police state, the individual . . . ah . . . characteristics, or the characteristics of individuals, are not the effective factors, in affairs by and large. My general feeling, even so, and granted that Russia is a police state, I don't have any feeling even toward the Russian government, because it's my own observation that whatever steps Russia has taken, inimical as they may have been to our interests, they have clearly been in the interest of Russia. I don't think it lies in our mouths to criticize a man who does what he thinks is right for Russia because it isn't the best for us. Ah . . . however, I do think that . . . that they may be wrong about it and the fact . . . that Russia's national, in the sense of governmental, policies have developed as they have is an unfortunate thing for international relations.[3]

Here we see how a man with strong needs for making sense of his own *personal* world also used the same style of thinking to make sense of the *political* world. Notice how he is categorizing and defining various aspects of the Russian political system. Behind this objective, intellectual purpose is another one: relating

[3] *Ibid.*, p. 77.

himself to Russia, figuring out his own stance toward the Russians, individually, collectively, governmentally. As Smith, Bruner, and White put it, he is ". . . classifying for action the objects of the environment."[4]

Clearly this is one way we use opinions: to reduce an uncertain and changing political world to an image we can understand and use to guide our actions and feelings.

getting along with others

Usually when we think of "getting along with others," we mean "agreeing with others," but this is only part of the picture. In fact, the fellow who always agrees with everyone is not likely to win much respect or affection from others. The social-adjustment functions of opinions have a broader focus: they include all those ways in which holding and expressing opinions help a person maintain and advance the kind of relationships with others he prefers. That may mean fighting with others or ignoring others as well as agreeing with them.

The distinction between holding an opinion and expressing an opinion is important here. Most people, most of the time, refrain from saying everything they think. They acquire habits of selection and emphasis by which they translate what is in their minds into a form appropriate to the social environment. If our humanity is defined by the fact that we think (as in *Homo sapiens*), according to Aristotle our political character is defined by the fact that we speak. There are many complicated ways in which speech affects thought and thought affects speech; we know that there are people who think as if they were speaking to others and those who speak as if they were thinking aloud. But for most of us the distinction is a real one; we select from our thoughts certain themes to tell others about.

Getting along with others may include avoiding or neglecting them, but political scientists have been especially concerned with the problem of conformity in political opinions. We are concerned on the one hand with the propensity of many citizens simply to follow along with the status quo, conforming passively to the given order of things as expressed in their neighborhoods and

[4]*Ibid.*, p. 41.

clubs and schools. On the other hand, there is the fear that too many citizens are so concerned with being up to date with the latest going thing in their social environments that they are easily led to follow along like sheep in mass movements led by dramatic heroes.

We have already seen some of the conservative aspects of social adjustment in our discussion of group identifications.[5] People think of themselves as Democrats or Republicans and shape their political opinions accordingly. Religious, class, and ethnic identifications serve some of the same functions. They confirm the citizen's own identity as a member of the group and help to reinforce opinions consistent with identifications.

Classic experiments in social psychology show how far conformity can go. An example is the "autokinetic" experiments. Subjects are brought together into a room that is completely dark except for one dot of light. Actually the light is stationary, but it appears to the eye as if it were moving. The subjects are asked to estimate how far the light "moves." At first the subjects vary considerably in their estimates, but with repeated trials the estimates come closer together. In other words, the individuals develop, and conform to, a group norm.[6] It is not clear how such experiments relate to political conformity in real life. But many political phenomena are something like a ray of light in a dark room—uncertain, ambiguous, indefinite—and therefore not subject to confident personal judgment.

These quotes from interviews with citizens show how this kind of conformity can work in politics:

> Just before the election it looked like Roosevelt would win so I went with the crowd. It didn't make any difference to me who won but *I wanted to vote for the winner.*

> I have always been a Democrat, but lately I've heard of so many Democrats who are going to vote Republican that *I might do the same.* Four out of five Democrats that I know are doing that.[7]

[5] See chapter iii.

[6] A. Paul Hare, *Handbook of Small Group Research* (New York: Free Press, Macmillan, 1962), p. 26.

[7] Paul F. Lazarsfeld, Bernard L. Berelson, and Hazel Gaudet, *The People's Choice* (New York: Columbia University Press, 1948), p. 108.

And we can see a special sensitivity to others in these comments by a young ex-GI who was asked whether he thought the United States had given in or had its own way too much in the United Nations.

> This will sound funny, but I think we are getting our own way too much. (Why do you say that? he was questioned.) Because we don't want the other nations to feel that we are trying to take over their countries. They know that Russia wants that and I think that's why there is so much argument. But if they feel we are trying to grab, they won't trust us either and then we won't be able to steer this whole program which is what I think we should do. So when we don't get what we want and the headlines say we have been beaten on something, I think that's really good because it makes the other countries feel that we are just like them and that we are having troubles too. That would make them more sympathetic to us and more friendly.[8]

Contrast these opinions about Russia and the world with those of John Chatwell, quoted earlier. The emphasis here is much more on the reactions of *others* to various initiatives.

Perhaps the epitome of this kind of conformity is expressed in an interview with a twelve-year-old girl, who said:

> A. I like Superman better than the others because they can't do everything Superman can do. Batman can't fly and that is very important.
> Q. Would you like to be able to fly?
> A. I would like to be able to fly if everybody else did, but otherwise it would be kind of conspicuous.[9]

getting rid of inner tensions

This is what Smith, Bruner, and White mean by "externalization":

> Externalization occurs when an individual, often responding unconsciously, senses an analogy between a perceived

[8] David Riesman *et al., The Lonely Crowd* (New Haven, Conn.: Yale University Press, 1950), p. 217.
[9] Katherine M. Wolfe and Marjorie Tiske, "The Children Talk about Comics," in Paul Lazarsfeld and Frank Stanton (eds.), *Communications Research, 1948–1949* (New York: Harper, 1949), pp. 26–27, as quoted in Riesman *et al., op. cit.,* p. 105.

environmental event and some unresolved inner problem. He adopts an attitude toward the event in question which is a transformed version of his way of dealing with his inner difficulty. By doing so, he may succeed in reducing some of the anxiety which his own difficulty has been producing.[10]

Externalization means putting uncomfortable feelings outside one's self, and it appears there is a good deal of this in political opinions. For example, many facets of race prejudice have been traced to inner psychological tensions.[11]

Such interpretations have to be made with great care. For instance, a citizen who agrees with a statement like "Almost all the public officials in this town are crooked" may be unloading some of his inner tensions on the political scene. But he may be simply giving an accurate report of reality. We might think a citizen who keeps emphasizing the conflict in his environment ("The world is a jungle") is expressing certain deep personal problems. But if we know that he lives in a metropolitan ghetto, our interpretation may take a different tack. As always, both personal and environmental factors enter into the situation, usually in ways that complement and reinforce one another.

We can see a possible example of externalization in comments by another of Smith, Bruner, and White's subjects, Hilary Sullivan. Sullivan's detailed case history shows that he was brought up in a chaotic family, in which he came to see his mother as the chief villain. His early conflicts gave rise to many themes in his personality. For instance, he came out of childhood with a strong need for security. He said he would have liked to have "a home where [there was] the semblance of security . . . a mother who gave me some affection . . . and where there was some serenity, which there wasn't."[12] Sometimes he seemed to reject the whole idea of seeking security: "I never had security, so why should I miss something I never had? I have no sense of insecurity; I never had it."[13] But this security theme seems to show up strongly in

[10] Smith, Bruner, and White, *op. cit.*, p. 43.

[11] These transformations take a variety of forms, which are best illustrated in extensive case studies. See, for example, Robert Coles, "Public Evil and Private Problems: Segregation and Psychiatry," *Yale Review*, Vol. 54 (Summer, 1965), 513–31.

[12] Smith, Bruner, and White, *op. cit.*, p. 178.

[13] *Ibid.*, p. 179.

some of Sullivan's opinions. He was asked to respond to the statement "Russians have been arrested from time to time without knowing what their crime was." Sullivan says in part:

> It probably does exist because when you have a revolution and defend it against a counterrevolution . . . then you have to resort to a police state for a while until you make things secure, then the . . . there is a relaxation of the police methods and civil liberties as we know them are restored.[14]

The link here between inner needs and political opinion seems entirely plausible. A strong personal need for security leads him to be especially sensitive to conflict and control in the external environment. His political opinions reflect inner tensions. We would want to know a good deal more about this case and others like it before making the leap from personal insecurity to political opinion. But in a good many cases, that link is fairly clear. There are personal roots to public opinion which, in conjunction with an understanding of the environment, can help us explain special public opinion themes.

One warning note: there is always a temptation to attribute opinions we don't like to personal neuroses. A moment's thought helps to correct that tendency. Many important themes of loyalty to the system, acceptance of differences, motives for action and participation and so forth are important for the maintenance of democracy. These "healthy" feelings also have their personal roots. As we shall see shortly, attitudes of allegiance to political leaders can tap strong personal needs. The question, then, is not one of finding out how troubled people develop strange attitudes, but rather one of seeing how all of us, from time to time, use political opinions to help us manage personal tensions.

Nearly every opinion serves all three functions to some degree. Opinions are part of our effort to order the messages our senses send us in some comprehensible way, so that we are not continually confused. Opinions are social phenomena; they help a person manage his relations with others. Opinions are expressive of the tensions all of us experience. We use political feelings to turn our inner fights into outer fights.

The more personalized these opinions are, the more likely

---

[14] *Ibid.,* p. 185.

they are to connect with a person's special psychological needs. This makes particularly significant for politics the uses citizens make of their opinions about leaders.

leader love

Few subsequent leaders have enjoyed George Washington's popularity. In fact, there is a peculiar strain of ambivalence in Americans' feelings about their leaders. Most citizens have a high regard for the ideals of leadership, for public service as an honorable calling, much as most have pride in the Constitution. But past these generalities, Americans express a good deal of skepticism—that they are being told the truth, that their leaders have high motives, or that political compromise is legitimate.[15]

It is easy to see some of the ways this ambivalence can help Americans manage a variety of feelings about politics. On the one hand, the positive feelings—loyalty, respect, affection for leaders—can provide a strong sense of security. Perceiving leaders as motivated by the common welfare, as warm human beings who share the citizens' sentiments, lends a feeling of comfort and confidence. Similarly a belief that leaders are strong, capable people, who can see to it that the government will act to implement these good feelings, makes us happy. These comforting, quieting, security-inducing feelings are analogous to religious faith or the confidence a family feels in the leadership of the ideal father.

The darker side of politics, the skepticism people feel, also has functions for the personality. Government is a ready target for blame. Accurate or not, perceptions that politicians are selfish or incapable help people "explain" what is not going well in their lives. Particularly "that man in the White House" can be seen as responsible for a host of troubles: when prices go up at the supermarket, when jobs are cut back at the factory, when sons and brothers are drafted, when tax time comes round, political anxieties rise and seek expression in ways that will remove the respon-

---

[15] Herbert H. Hyman and Paul B. Sheatsley, "The Current Status of American Public Opinion," in John C. Payne (ed.), *The Teaching of Contemporary Affairs* (Washington: National Council for the Social Studies, National Education Association, 1951), pp. 20–23; quoted in Wendell Bell, Richard J. Hill, and Charles Wright, *Public Leadership* (San Francisco: Chandler, 1961), pp. 134–35.

sibility from the individual to highly visible others. The citizen keeps in reserve, so to speak, a suspicion that those who govern him are not all they're cracked up to be. He listens to their words; part of him believes, part of him doubts.

Robert E. Lane gives an illustration of the ways some of these attitudes toward leaders may work:

> The President gives another kind of security; at least he does in normal times. He is a strong arm against the outside world; he is a national protector, and has the stature to be one. He does not have this soft side, this slightly lovable venality—hence he reinforces the voice of the superego; he calls for a higher morality; he is a protector against our weaker natures—the side of ourselves that might cut taxes when we should keep them high to pay for defense. He cares deeply about what happens to the nation and the people and the values for which this country stands. Part of what makes Congressmen so appealing is that they are not so seriously committed in this way; they are more human. But what makes the President appealing is that he is not "all too human" like the rest of us; while not quite a hero, he is supportive of whatever small heroic qualities we have in us, at the very least of our moral selves. Perhaps it will be misunderstood, but in a figurative sense, Congress is the group adjustment leader; the President is the task leader; Congress is the mother, the President the father.[16]

Perhaps such family analogies will be misunderstood, but there is reason to believe that underlying the superficial opinions citizens have about their political leaders, there is a strong and deep undercurrent of emotion of just this type. Such feelings may underlie certain familiar features of public attitudes toward leaders. We know that there is a tendency to give strong support to a new President as he begins his struggle with the political system and that that support tends to fall off in subsequent months and years of his term. We know that the citizenry rallies around a President in trouble: his popularity jumps upward in time of crisis, whether or not he is successful. We know that Presidents gain in respect after they leave office, particularly years later, when they have become "elder statesmen." But perhaps the most revealing evidence on the deeper themes of emotion surrounding

[16] Robert E. Lane, *Political Ideology* (New York: Free Press, Macmillan, 1962), p. 152.

the President is the reaction felt when he is suddenly and un-
expectedly removed from us.

When Lincoln was shot to death, a wave of anxiety and
suspicion swept the nation with a force far beyond normal political feelings. A similar wave of strong and deep emotion has swept
the country every time a President has died in office. This has
been true not only for the great national heroes like Lincoln and
Franklin D. Roosevelt, but also for the Hardings and Garfields. In
other words, the strength of the emotional response is not due
only to the personal popularity of the President. It focuses on the
office, on whatever man is occupying that position. The citizen, it
appears, takes his government for granted most of the time, giving it little thought or careful attention. But beneath that casual-
ness are some intense emotional linkages between the citizen and
his leaders. When these linkages are broken, particularly through
the murder of a President, that hidden emotion rises to the surface and finds expression.

what the Kennedy assassination revealed

Within five hours of the assassination of President John F.
Kennedy on November 22, 1963, virtually the entire population of
the United States (99.8 percent) had heard of the tragedy. In the
following four days, the typical American watched television or
listened to the radio at least eight hours each day.[17] Probably no
event in the history of the world was known to so many people so
fast. The emotional response was profound and immediate. Researchers conclude that "the President's assassination seems
clearly to have engaged the gut feelings" of virtually every American.[18] Many people felt nervous and tense, had difficulty getting to
sleep at night, had headaches and other physical troubles. A
majority reported crying.[19] Others said such things as "I felt like

---

[17] David O. Sears, "Political Behavior," in G. Lindzey and E. Aaronson (eds.),
Handbook of Social Psychology, rev. ed. (Reading, Mass.: Addison-Wesley, 1968).

[18] Paul B. Sheatsley and Jacob J. Feldman, "A National Survey of Public Re-
actions and Behavior," in B. S. Greenberg and E. V. Parker (eds.), *The Kennedy
Assassination and the American Public* (Stanford, Calif.: Stanford University
Press, 1965), pp. 149–77.

[19] Sears, *op. cit.,* p. 92.

I'd been struck by a thunderbolt" and "I felt sick at my stomach." This reaction recalls the impact sharply:

> Well, when I first heard, my husband ran back in and he said, "You know, Mary?"—he was on his way to work—he says, "You know, the President has been shot." I said, "Oh, turn the television on, quick, quick." We turned the television on and . . . I felt terrible, just awful, so I said to myself, "Well, he'll be all right, he'll be all right. I know he'll be all right." And then a few minutes later here it came, he's dead. Well, then I just went all to pieces and said, "Well, he will not die in vain," and I cried. That's how I felt.[20]

Among those who had opposed the President, and to a lesser extent among Republicans in general, these feelings were slightly less intense, but the broad picture is one of common national feeling throughout nearly all the groups and categories of Americans.

The intensity of the response was common. And it was nearly universally positive. But there were significant variations among groups in the special kinds of deep links to the President they revealed. In research conducted just after President Kennedy's funeral, several of these themes emerged. For example, a Protestant woman said:

> At first, people were against President Kennedy because he were a Catholic. But he was so good and so everyone has shown a feeling and expressed their feeling toward [him]. Everyone, mostly, I've talked with about how they feel about Kennedy, you don't hear them say, "Well, he was a Catholic and I don't like him because he was a Catholic." They are very upset just about the shock of his death, that he was such a wonderful man. But his religion, regardless, if he is a good man, what type of religion that he like . . . it's just only one God.[21]

A group of Negro workers agreed on these themes:

> R1: I think President Kennedy was more for the colored people than any other president.
> R2: Yeah, yeah, that's right. Because he wanted the two of them to be alike—am I right or wrong?
> R1: He wanted us to have equal rights.
> R3: That's right, he did.

[20] James D. Barber, "Peer Group Discussion and Recovery from the Kennedy Assassination," in Greenberg and Parker (eds.), *op. cit.*, p. 112.
[21] *Ibid.*, p. 116.

R1: He tried to have them integrated.
R3: Together, to get along.[22]

These quotes show how individuals selected from among all the possible ways they could have thought about the President those ways that were specially meaningful to them as individuals. They had built up in their own minds certain images closely linked with their personal lives. Probably few of these citizens had expressed these sentiments before, but they were there. And they were functional in that they linked people to their government, providing a sense of security and identification and hope. Probably these feelings are functional for the political system as a kind of bedrock emotional foundation over which the arguments of the day wash like a gentle rain or, to change the image, much as our physical health is usually taken for granted and yet forms the basis for all our activity. In politics this basic commitment to the President and the system gets little attention in normal times, but in fact forms the basis for free political debate. In a sense, such feelings are all the more important for being unexpressed. They are as much a part of our culture as the belief in reincarnation is a part of Hindu culture.[23]

These examples should be enough to convey the idea that political feelings are basic to an understanding of citizen politics, and to show some of the main functions they perform, for the system and for the person. Not nearly enough is known, as yet, about the deeper springs of political sentiments. In the aftermath of the murders of Martin Luther King, Jr., and Senator Robert F. Kennedy, the question "What kind of nation are we?" came up once more. Americans wondered whether there is some deep flaw in our national character, some emotional propensity to violence. Perhaps so. Yet the campaign and election of 1968 went on, the system continued to be accepted and legitimate, and a new President was elected. He began with a high degree of popular support. . . .

[22] *Ibid.*, p. 117.

[23] Research by David O. Sears and others shows that such supportive feelings are found even among elements of the population one might expect to be profoundly disaffected. In surveys after the Watts riots in Los Angeles in 1965, Negro respondents rated almost all thirteen elected officials, from the President to a local school-board member, in positive terms. Even 124 Negro respondents who had been arrested during the rioting, and who expressed considerable hostility, generally gave positive ratings to leading white Democrats and local Negro elected officials (Sears, *op. cit.*).

chapter vii

Political Persuasion

The firm of Whitaker and Baxter has been managing California political campaigns for decades. They are the prototype of modern political salesmanship —professional public relations experts in the business of marketing candidates. As Clem Whitaker put it:

> We do our utmost, in every campaign, to get a dollar's worth for every dollar spent, just as we would if we were merchandising *commodities* instead of selling *men* and *measures*.
> We use campaign funds, not to dispense favors, but to MOLD PUBLIC SENTIMENT, to present our candidate, or our issue, in the most favorable light possible.[1]

[1] Clem Whitaker, in an address before the Los Angeles Area Chapter of the Public Relations Society of America, July 13, 1948, as quoted in Stanley Kelley, Jr., *Professional Public Relations and Political Power* (Baltimore: Johns Hopkins Press, 1966), p. 39.

Whitaker makes no secret of his techniques. Out to win elections (not to reform the citizen), he works from a few simple assumptions:

> There are thousands of experts bidding for every man's attention—and every man has a limited amount of leisure. Then we must recognize, too, that in almost every human being there is a great craving just to be lazy, at least part of the time, and a wall goes up when you try to make Mr. and Mrs. Average Citizen work or *think* when all they want to do is relax. . . .
>
> The average American, when you catch him after hours, as we must, doesn't want to be educated; he doesn't want to improve his mind; he doesn't even want to work, consciously, at being a good citizen.
>
> But there are two ways you can interest him in a campaign, and only two that we have ever found successful.
>
> Most every American loves a *contest*. He likes a good hot battle, with no punches pulled. He likes the clash of arms! *So you can interest him if you put on a fight!*
>
> No matter what you fight for, *fight for something*, in our business, and very soon the voters will be turning out to hear you, providing you make the fight interesting.
>
> Then, too, most every American likes to be entertained. He likes the movies; he likes mysteries; he likes fireworks and parades. He likes Jack Benny and Bob Hope and Joe E. Brown!
>
> So if you can't fight, PUT ON A SHOW! And if you put on a good show, Mr. and Mrs. America will turn out to see it.[2]

The public relations man works with words and pictures to shape your thinking, to touch your feelings, and to make you take the action he wants. He is "the hidden persuader" out to make "true believers" of a "nation of sheep." He can sell you a Coke or a candidate, Ronzoni or Rockefeller, the new Nixon or the old Johnson. He can make you think Republican or feel Democratic. He knows how to make a silk purse out of a sow's ear. He even knows where to find the right quote from Abraham Lincoln:

> Public sentiment is everything. With public sentiment nothing can fail; without it nothing can succeed. He who molds public sentiment goes deeper than he who enacts

[2] *Ibid.*, p. 50.

statutes or announces public decisions. He makes statutes or decisions possible or impossible to execute.[3]

Between 1964 and 1968, the total cost of air time (mainly television) bought by Presidential, Gubernatorial, and Senatorial candidates shot up 70 percent, to nearly sixty million dollars. Candidates in 1970 outdid themselves to produce pictures that could be televised. A Senate aspirant in New York not only took a swim in the polluted Hudson River but also toured the area in a balloon filled with hot air. High-priced experts could glorify a candidate, as one did Spiro Agnew: "He was a beautiful, beautiful body, and we were selling sex. . . . We introduced him as 'my kind of man,' which really could be anything you wanted." Another in Indiana hired eight hippies at seventy-five dollars apiece to act obnoxious for a commercial (one leaked the story and the spot was never shown). There were few signs of change in imaginative bull-throwing as 1972 approached.[4] The audience was waiting: "more than 95 percent of American homes had TV sets—more than had bathtubs or telephones."[5]

pr and tv

Modern public relations men in politics agree with those critics who are appalled at what they do on at least one point: that these molders of public sentiment have immense influence over the national political community. They point with pride or horror at a radical new development in opinion-making: the rise of television as a truly *mass* medium of persuasion. Here the facts are on their side:

- Today most people say they get most of their news from television.
- When there are conflicting reports about the same news story, nearly twice as many people say they would believe

[3] Clem Whitaker, "The Public Relations of Election Campaigns," *Public Relations Journal*, Vol. 2, No. 7, p. 7, as quoted in Kelley, *op. cit.*, p. 45.
[4] "The Selling of the Candidates 1970," *Newsweek*, October 19, 1970.
[5] Milton C. Cummings, Jr. and David Wise, *Democracy Under Pressure* (New York: Harcourt Brace Jovanovich, 1971), p. 294.

the television account as say they would believe their newspaper.

- When asked, "suppose you could continue to have only one of the following — radio, television, newspapers, or magazines — which of the four would you *most* want to *keep*?" nearly twice as many citizens say they would want to keep television as say they would want to keep newspapers.
- These trends are especially strong among young voters, those between twenty-one and twenty-five who represent the emerging future.
- In judging candidates for local and state offices, newspapers and television are seen as significant sources for many voters, but when it comes to national elections it is television by a landslide. Roughly two out of three citizens see television as the source by which they get best acquainted with candidates for the Presidency, the Senate, and the House of Representatives.
- Nearly half the people feel that their local newspapers are politically biased — that they "tend to favor one political party or another." But less than one out of five thinks that local or network television programs are politically slanted in this way.[6]

The rise of the professional public relations expert, the immense sums of money spent on political television broadcasts, the public's shift toward television as the most trusted source of information, the particular strength of that shift among the young people who will make up the future electorate — all these factors point to a view of the future in which television messages dominate citizen opinion. Some see virtue in that. Frank Stanton, President of the Columbia Broadcasting System, sees these trends as drawing together a national community:

> Television, with its penetration, its wide geographic distribution and impact, provides a new, direct and sensitive link between Washington and the people. The people have once more become the nation, as they have not been since the days when we were small enough each to know his elected

[6]Elmo Roper and Associates, "The Public's View of Television and Other Media: 1959–64," in Edward C. Dreyer and Walter A. Rosenbaum (eds.), *Political Opinion and Electoral Behavior* (Belmont, Calif.: Wadsworth, 1966), pp. 309–17.

representative. As we grew, we lost this feeling of direct contact — television has now restored it.[7]

Others see great danger in a citizenry dominated by the tube, a kind of *1984* society in which "the word" is sent out in an instant from a few sources to a passive people. They envisage a new politics, not of public debate and deliberation, but of TV salesmanship. Our political decisions and actions would reflect the all-pervasive influence radiating from a few offices on Madison Avenue.

These images raise two important factual questions that are related to each other. First, to what degree and in what ways do the mass media influence a national political community? Second, at a higher level of abstraction, what practical definitions of "influence" are most useful in understanding relationships among citizens and between citizens and their leaders?

what the hidden persuaders are up against

The first and in some ways most difficult problem the PR man faces is simply *getting his message into your sense organs.* The immense cost of television time is only part of this problem. In terms of the content of television programming, politics takes up only a small proportion of the total flow of media messages. In the newspapers, sports beats politics in the competition for space. On television, messages with political content are confined largely to news programs; only rarely, mainly during national campaigns, is the citizen exposed to much *persuasive* communication from television, programs designed to make him prefer one political position over another. So even if the TV set is turned on for five or six hours every evening, only a few persuasive political programs glimmer forth.

And that which is given may not be received. At least three selective processes intervene between media content and citizen perception.

1. People select *which medium* to expose themselves to.

[7]Dr. Frank Stanton, president of Columbia Broadcasting System, quoted by Angus Campbell, "Has Television Reshaped Politics?", in Dreyer and Rosenbaum (eds.), *op. cit.*, p. 318. Cf. William A. Glaser, "Television and Voting Turnout," *Public Opinion Quarterly*, Vol. 29, No. 1 (Spring, 1965), 69–86.

Actually this is probably the least important screen, but it does operate to some degree. By and large, those who use one medium, such as newspapers, are also likely to use other media, such as radio, television, and magazines. But there are still many people in this country who are selective in choosing media: the intellectual who will not allow television in the house, the businessman who never reads a book, the unskilled laborer who can't afford magazine subscriptions, the migrant farm worker who may miss all the mass media. The higher a person's education, the more he relies on printed sources such as books, magazines, and newspapers; the *less* education he has, the more the citizen tends to rely on pictures and sounds. (What does that imply, in an age of galloping increases in educational levels, for the future power of television in political persuasion?)

2. People select the *kinds* of messages they want to attend to. One can be a TV addict without ever watching a political program. One can "read" the newspaper without ever getting beyond the headlines on the front page. People who are better educated have a preference for "serious" books and articles and programs. Every evening millions of Americans reach for the knob on their TV sets and choose whether to watch fiction or nonfiction. Many a political propagandist gets tuned out in this selective process.

3. People select from the total content of the media message certain parts to attend to, and ignore other parts. For example, much "television watching" is extremely casual. The set is turned on but the watcher is only occasionally tuned in. People are especially prone to pay attention to messages they agree with and to screen out of their perceptions messages inconsistent with their ideas or threatening to their beliefs. Republicans tend to listen much more carefully to what Republican candidates say than to the views of the Democratic opposition. Campaigns to stimulate support for the United Nations reach mainly those already in favor of the UN.[8] People inclined to buy government bonds are more likely than others to pay attention to bond-drive propaganda.[9]

[8] Bernard Berelson and Gary A. Steiner, *Human Behavior: An Inventory of Scientific Findings* (New York: Harcourt, Brace & World, 1964), p. 530.

[9] Dorwin Cartwright, "Some Principles of Mass Persuasion: Selected Findings of Research on the Sale of U.S. War Bonds," in Daniel Katz *et al.* (eds.), *Public Opinion and Propaganda* (New York: Holt, 1954), pp. 382–93. See also V. O. Key, Jr., *Public Opinion and American Democracy* (New York: Knopf, 1961), Chapter 14.

Especially just after a person has come to a decision—say, to vote for a certain candidate—he will tend to seek out and pay attention to communications that support that decision. A man trying to decide whether to buy a Ford, a Chevrolet, or a Volkswagen checks the ads for all three cars; if he buys the Ford, he is most likely to concentrate on Ford ads in the next few weeks. Similarly in a political campaign, a citizen trying to make up his mind among candidates tends to watch several, then decide on one, and then devote his attention to the one he has chosen.

So even in getting his message across to the citizen's senses, the political public relations man has problems. It is no wonder that Clem Whitaker feels it necessary to make a big noise—a fight, a drama, a circus—simply to gain the attention of an audience.

being believed

But that is just the beginning of his troubles. His objective is not just to educate the public; he wants to get people to do something, such as vote for or against a particular candidate. Here he faces additional barriers. Basically, he has to get you to believe that the action will help you. Either he must persuade you that the action will meet needs and goals that you already have, or he must change your needs and goals to ones best met by taking the action he suggests. Let us see what that implies.

1. A person is not a computer: he *interprets* what he sees and hears. Many political messages leave room for interpretation—and for misinterpretation. For example, voters who prefer a certain candidate are prone to read into that candidate's messages their own policy preferences. Prejudiced people are far more likely to "misunderstand" a cartoon series ridiculing anti-Semitism.[10] As Lane and Sears emphasize this point:

> We should counsel our mayors and newspapers and leaders: People who differ from you will tend to distort your views. When you differ slightly from your friends, they will think you agree with them. Your enemies will think you disagree with them more than you actually do. Both tendencies will

[10] Berelson and Steiner, *op. cit.,* p. 537.

weaken your capacity to influence them in the way you wish to.[11]

2. People's basic *needs, goals, and values are not easily changed.* There are certain central life concerns that grip the citizen. Propaganda that conflicts with what he sees as the fundamental welfare of his family is likely to be rejected, and he is unlikely to give up or sharply modify that central value. So most of what a persuader has to do is show people how goals they already have can best be met by a suggested course of action.

3. People have *many goals;* a message may be consistent with some and inconsistent with others. The parents of a draft-age son may be pushed toward supporting larger call-ups by appeals to patriotism. But they may be pulled more strongly by affection for the boy. So the persuader who relies on a single appeal, linking one goal with one action, may succeed in that but fail to get what he wants, because he has not dealt with a wide collection of competing goals. Persuasion takes place in a context of many mutually reinforcing and competing needs, goals, and values.

4. The *link between action and goal* must be established. The citizen has to see how to get from here to there. For instance, the World War II bond drives tried to persuade people to buy bonds in order to prevent inflation. But more than half the population did not see the link, the sequence that led from buying a bond to keeping prices steady. Similarly, some people simply did not believe that the government would pay back the money after the war, so the argument that bonds were a good investment for the future left them cold.[12]

So once the persuader has got his message into the eyes and ears of the people, he still has problems. He has to connect his message with popular goals. The message must be perceived — and received and believed.

from belief to action

There is still more. "Good intentions" are not enough. The persuader wants action. If he is wise, he knows that a citizen may get the message but skip the action. A person may believe the

---

[11] Robert E. Lane and David O. Sears, *Public Opinion* (Englewood Cliffs, N.J.: Prentice-Hall, 1964), p. 51.

[12] Cartwright, in Katz *et al.* (eds.), *op. cit.*, p. 389.

right things but do little or nothing about them. So the third set of barriers to persuasion has to do with moving people beyond thought and feeling to behavior.

The art of political timing is important here. It does not do much good to persuade a voter in January that he should be sure to get to the polls next November. Similarly, coming around to the right thoughts and feelings a week *after* the election, or getting your letter to the Congressman after his committee has reported out the bill, is not much help. To link thoughts and feelings to action, the persuader has to get to the citizen at the right time. What "the right time" is in any given case is very hard to say, even though it is clear that there are campaigns that "peak" too early or fail to get off the ground early enough. But while thought and feeling are more or less continuous, action takes place at a specific time. The persuader who misses the moment usually loses the action.

To move a person to action you usually have to tell him *specifically* what you want done. Notice that political election campaigns get very specific: "Go to the Center School between noon and eight P.M. on April 9, and pull down the lever in the row marked 1B for the Wynne slate." This focuses attention on something definite to be done, a way of translating thought and feeling into a particular step to be taken.

Many aspects of the political campaign have to be stated in broad, general terms because they cover so many different actions and circumstances. But the persuader who never gets beyond high generalities has lost his fight. It does not take much to persuade people that peace is good, racism is bad, prosperity is good, poverty is bad. But the individual citizen will remain unmoved by these general sentiments unless someone shows him just what steps he should take to fight bad and boost good.

Suppose, then, that the persuader succeeds in defining for the citizen the particular path of action he should take. There is still the problem of getting him to decide to take it. Many of us are adept at dodging decisions. Especially when an action costs us something—time, money, energy—we have a way of putting off till tomorrow a definite commitment to do the right thing. The experienced party worker knows how to set up a situation in which there is pressure for a definite decision. For example, it has been shown repeatedly that canvassing works: people who are approached by a party worker and asked to express a definite candidate choice and a definite intention to vote are more likely than others to carry through on these intentions.[13] The conversation with the party worker presses the citizen to make up his mind. Similar things happen at meetings ranging from small coffee groups to mass rallies. First come the arguments about the "situation we face." Then come the appeals about "what this means to us." And then the clincher: "What are we going to do about it?" It is at this last point that the whole process comes to fruition—or falls flat. Many a persuader has been extremely effective in carrying the process through right up to this last point and then has failed, because he cannot define clearly, and get a positive commitment to, a definite course of action.

Indeed, one of the key tasks of the political order is the translation to action, the channeling of amorphous thoughts and feelings into concrete proposals and decisions.

small and big effects

What then of the "power" of the "hidden persuaders?" What does their problem show us about the influence of propaganda, or about political influence more broadly conceived? In terms of *one-shot persuasion attempts,* the PR man in politics has a hard time of it. His message, in competition with all the other messages the citizen receives, is likely to get lost. Thus if we look only at one persuader purveying one message at a time, calling for one action, we are likely to conclude his influence is not much. In terms of the *total impact over time of all political persuasion attempts,* the picture may be much different. This is a matter much more difficult to capture in research because it involves the long-term, large-scale effects of millions of messages upon millions of citizens. So we are left with speculation, and certain gross negative findings.

By several crude indicators, the rise of the mass media has failed to revolutionize American politics. Neither radio, which exploded onto the national scene in the twenties, nor television,

---

[13] Samuel J. Eldersveld, *Political Parties: A Behavioral Analysis* (Chicago: Rand McNally, 1964), Chapter 17.

beginning in the forties, has brought quantum leaps in political participation (in both cases the charts show moderate and fairly steady rises in participation rates accompanying far more radical upswings in media use rates).[14] The basic structure of voter party loyalties does not seem to have been much affected. Nor have our political institutions — the parties, the primaries, the conventions, the whole range of representative structures — been fundamentally altered. (But what is happening to the national political conventions, as national polling makes their outcomes more predictable and national media open their deliberations to an immense audience?) So the general shape of politics remains about what it was thirty or forty years ago.

Common sense and social science come together in findings that show it is hard to change people's minds. The simplest reflection reminds us that a person is not an amoeba, reacting anew to each little message or stimulus he receives. He bears with him the lessons of a long past — not only what he has read in the history books, but what he has experienced in his own life. That includes all the lessons of his childhood, all the flag-saluting, all the dinner-table conversation, all the celebration of Columbus and Washington and Lincoln and Roosevelt, all the adolescent chatter about what's "in" and what's "out," and all the personal struggle to establish oneself in his occupation, his family, his neighborhood. And the sources of stability are not only in the past. The person has expectations and hopes for the future. Even if few citizens take a very long view of politics, very many are thinking about next month, next year, and, if only vaguely, those coming events that will be landmarks when they arrive: the time when the children will go to school or leave for college, when a new house will be needed, when retirement comes. The persuader is dealing with men and women who have to feel some strong reason for changing their minds.

Some of the difficulties the persuader is up against are evident in research on the effects of political campaigns. Of course campaigns have some effect, and of course small margins of change can make large differences sometimes, as in the 1960 and 1968 Presidential elections. But such changes rarely involve a shift from one well-defined political position to its opposite. For ex-

[14] Campbell, in Dreyer and Rosenbaum (eds.), *op. cit.*, pp. 318ff.

ample, in a careful study of one campaign, the researchers analyzed the results as follows:

- For most voters, the campaign reinforced the position the voter had already taken (53%).
- Other voters had been undecided before the campaign and it helped them make up their minds to vote as one would have predicted they would vote, given their group affiliations (20%).
- For a substantial number of voters, the campaign had no effect (16%).
- Small numbers of voters were confused by the campaign; they moved from one position to an undecided feeling (6%).
- Only a tiny minority of voters was converted by the campaign from a definite position to its opposite (2%).[15]

power effort ≠ power effect

These findings cast doubt on the view that we are prisoners of the mass mediators. More generally, they warn us against equating the *attempt* to exercise influence with *success* in exercising influence. A great deal of activity does not necessarily produce a great deal of result. Time and again observers of political persuasion attempts forget that. They see tremendous expenditures, great concentrations of talent and energy, subtle calculations, and intense desires all pouring into some attempt to influence others. The easy thing to assume is that all that exertion must have a whale of a wallop.

Maybe yes, maybe no. The answer depends on the evidence. So far the exaggerated claims and fears regarding the impact of the mass media on political opinions are not strongly supported by the facts.

brainwashing

What *does* it take to make fundamental changes in people's political thinking? A different slant on the persuader's problem is given by studies of brainwashing. One form of brainwashing in

[15] Paul F. Lazarsfeld, Bernard L. Berelson, and Hazel Gaudet, *The People's Choice* (New York: Columbia University Press, 1948), p. 102.

China shows how a program worked to train active Communist party workers.[16] Often this involved taking people who had done relatively little thinking about political action and who had grown up in a traditional environment and turning them into convinced Communist advocates. Suppose we look at some of the elements in that system and contrast them with the situation in which the citizen of a democracy finds himself.

These were the main factors in the Chinese Communist brainwashing operation:

1. *Isolation.* The trainees were taken to a special camp away from their families; no visiting was allowed. A small group of ten or twelve was kept together throughout the program. This broke the ties with their ordinary environments. Obviously most free citizens have a variety of social networks—the family, the work group, the set of casual friends—with whom they can check their opinions from time to time and who lend a kind of anchorage to the views that the person develops. For instance, a citizen may hear his neighbors expressing one view about housing integration, perhaps a fear that if Negroes move in, property values will decline. But at church he hears another view, a different set of values being invoked. And if he is a careful reader of the newspapers (or even a social science book), he may learn that the evidence is against the views of his neighbors. So the persuader seldom has an isolated audience. Even in college, in the army, and in prison, there are other folk to check with when those in charge put forth a propaganda line.

2. *Fatigue.* The Chinese brainwashees were subjected to very intense physical labor at first, about two months of demeaning physical tasks to the point of utter exhaustion, day in and day out. Later the emphasis was shifted to an endless round of meetings. So a man's time was completely taken up. He had no chance to control his own life schedule. But obviously the citizen in a democracy does have some time of his own at the end of an eight-hour day, at the end of a forty-hour week. A few minutes with the newspaper or a few hours with television must be viewed in the context of a person's full-time schedule.

3. *Tension.* The subjects of brainwashing were kept in a constant state of anxiety. Again and again they were forced to

16 William Sargant, *Battle for the Mind* (Garden City, N.Y.: Doubleday, 1957).

criticize themselves to the others in their group. As one trainee said:

> A straight narration of your past life is not enough. For every action you describe, you had to give its motives in detail. Your awakened criticism had to be apparent in every sentence. You had to say why you smoked, why you drank, why you had social connections with certain people – why? why? why?

This constant pressure got the men down. About a fifth of them cracked under the strain, developing severe symptoms of hysteria. Obviously few persuaders in a democratic context can create that kind of tension. Their audiences are not very excited about politics in the first place, and they have plenty of opportunity for relaxation and calm reflection about such tensions as they do feel. As we have seen, one of the persuader's toughest jobs is simply to arouse some interest in what he is saying.

4. *Uncertainty.* The brainwashing trainees never knew what was going to happen next. Each group had an informer in it, but the members of the group didn't know who he was. Occasionally a trainee would disappear overnight and there were many rumors about what had happened to him. There are uncertainties in the life of the democratic citizen, but seldom anything like that. Regarding politics, he knows when the elections are going to be held (at least roughly) and who the main candidates are (at least some of them). Generally speaking, he knows the range of penalties – usually quite mild ones – that might befall him for holding the "wrong" opinions. It is rarely true that the citizen is so in the dark that he will grasp at almost any solution that promises to make him feel more secure.

5. *Vicious Language.* At the camps for training Communist party workers, the Chinese brainwashing subjects encountered a whole new way of talking. The group's very language represented a sharp break with tradition. The members were encouraged to think and talk very aggressively, especially about their parents and the friends they had left behind. They were introduced to the Marxist jargon, which came to pervade all conversation. Obviously the persuader who can push his subjects into an entirely new way of thinking about reality and an entirely new way of expressing emotion has already attained a high degree of control.

The ordinary persuasion situation in a democracy is, of course, far different. Democratic discourse seldom descends to continual vituperation.

6. *Seriousness.* There was nothing funny about being brainwashed. The whole affair was infused with a puritanical seriousness, a sense that every opinion—even every thought—was a matter of life or death. But in the "carnival of bunkum" that is democratic politics, there is plenty of leeway for laughter. The persuader whose arguments cannot stand up to being ridiculed has already lost his case in our jolly politics.

The power implications of these contrasts is simple yet often neglected. The persuader very seldom has control over more than a very small part of the citizen's life. In fact, it is rare to find any political situation in which one person has control over many factors in another person's life. In democratic politics, power moves take place in complex situations, in sticky conglomerations, not in bang-zing flashes. The ability to change one facet of another citizen's politics is apt to involve the ability to affect several other facets connected with the one you want to change.

These contrasts bring sharply to mind the ways *social contexts* affect political communication. We need to move beyond a simple model that shows the persuader at one end of a wire leading into the brain of the persuadee. That single brain is wired to a whole network of social circuits and is full of switches and transformers and condensers built up over a lifetime. In what we have seen of political thinking and feeling, we have explored some of this. What are these social connections? How is communication affected by community, by the *place* of different citizens in different social contexts?

the two-step flow of communication

In 1968 there were 83 million television sets in the United States. As early as 1963 television had gained the lead over newspapers as the "primary news source" of the public.[17] This means that a very great number of Americans have *available* to them a direct line from the national network headquarters in New York.

[17] Bernard Rubin, *Political Television* (Belmont, Calif.: Wadsworth, 1967), p. 3.

In a national emergency such as the Kennedy assassination, or when the President addresses the nation, virtually the whole public is tuned in to the same source of political news. But there are few such emergencies. Most of the time only a small number of those 83 million television sets are being watched by people attending closely to matters political. In terms of attention to politics and the media, the citizenry is not uniform. It is stratified, much in the way we saw that it was stratified in regard to political participation. The better educated people, those most interested in public affairs, are more likely to pay attention to what the media have to say about politics.

But there is an additional key point. Those most interested and attentive to the media are also those most likely to try to convince their friends and neighbors. One study showed that people who had been exposed to as many as four different media were five times as likely to try to convince others as were persons who had been exposed to no media.[18] Conversely, citizens not so tuned in to the mass media depend more on conversations with other people and are most likely to seek the political advice of persons who are tuned in.

This is the two-step flow of communication mentioned briefly in a previous chapter. (There may be more than two steps, perhaps many, but there appear to be at least two.) We need to picture the television public as divided, crudely speaking, into those who keep up with public affairs and give out advice, and those who ignore public affairs and take advice. As V. O. Key summarizes it:

> The theory of the multistep flow of communications compels a modification of the conception of the world of mass communication as one in which the communications barons place their imprint directly on helpless mass man. This hypothesis brings the recognition that the flow of mass communications to people is to some degree not direct but occurs in part through the network of personal relationships within society. It might be called a "trickle down" theory of communications flow. From studies of communications generally it is known, as might be suspected, that the network of personal communications does not act as a neutral transmitter but that people "color, amplify, distort, limit or otherwise change the information as it is passed along." Instead of a pure system of influence by media, this system includes a

[18] Key, *op. cit.*, p. 361.

large element of personal influence. Between the media and at least part of their audiences is a human screen that filters and modifies the messages of the media as they are passed along.[19]

the attentive advisers

This picture again modifies our view of the political influence of the mass media. As Key says, the talkers, convincers, and advisers are not neutral channels of communication. They have their own predispositions. Like everyone else, they are especially sensitive to some messages and cold to others. They pick and choose, consciously or unconsciously, those parts of the media messages to be passed along to others. They are like editors who receive a rough manuscript and transform it into a finished argument. So here once again influence is indirect, filtered, dependent upon a chain of small influential acts. The glow of the television screen is refracted through millions of little social prisms – the attentive advisers.

Who are these advisers? In gross terms they are the higher status, better educated people, but that is too crude a view. We can see this by a look at a classic study of advice networks on different *kinds* of topics. In *Personal Influence,* Eilhu Katz and Paul Lazarsfeld[20] explore such networks of advice regarding conversations among women about marketing, about fashion and movies, and about public affairs.

Where do women turn for advice about marketing? The researchers found that there were "marketing leaders" in almost equal numbers at each of three different status levels. Social status was not very important in discriminating between advisers and advisees. But there was a strong tendency for marketing leaders to be wives in large families. These were experienced women who had to do a lot of marketing and thus became experts

[19]*Ibid.*, pp. 362–63. Copyright © 1961 by V. O. Key, Jr. Reprinted by permission of Alfred A. Knopf, Inc. The two-step flow theory may be more applicable to beliefs and behavior than to information. See Verling C. Troldahl, "A Field Test of a Modified 'Two-Step Flow of Communication' Model," *Public Opinion Quarterly,* Vol. 30, No. 3 (Fall, 1966), 609–23.

[20]Elihu Katz and Paul Lazarsfeld, *Personal Influence* (New York: Free Press, Macmillan, 1960).

in that field. The young wives and those with small children would turn to the large-family wives for counsel on what to buy. If these wives in large families were also gregarious – talkative and with many friends – their influence was even greater when it came to marketing decisions.

In regard to fashions and movies, status and gregariousness were not very clear discriminators. But when the women were classified into four categories – the girls, small-family wives, large-family wives, and matrons – a strong pattern emerged. Clearly the girls led the way when it came to fashions and movies. The influence of large-family wives was quite low.

On public affairs, still another pattern emerged. There was no regular tendency for women to turn to those older or younger, married or single, in small families or large families. But social status was a strong discriminator. On political matters, the educated, wealthier woman was the one her friends turned to for advice.

For marketing advice, the large-family wife; for advice about fashions and movies, the girls; on matters of public affairs, the educated, higher status woman: in each subject-matter area, a different set of prime advisers. What are the implications of this for the persuader? If he wants to sell the latest fashions – say the accoutrements of Ricci, Gernreich, or John Myers – he should make his pitch to the girls, not to the harassed housewife with ten children. And there are similar specialties for his marketing messages and his messages on public affairs. The picture grows complicated; the two-step flow moves down *different ladders* according to the subject matter of the communication.

Social status made a difference in patterns of advice among women regarding public affairs, and that ties in with the general picture showing the better off as more likely to be political advisers. But a moment's thought and some additional data show how social status can be misleading as a guide to the pattern of political advice. Put simply, the hodcarrier does not go to the president of the bank for political advice. He goes to someone *near his own status level, but of somewhat higher status.* He goes to his foreman or his union steward or some other member of the work crew with more education than he has. As one semi-skilled California worker put it:

> They (politics) do get complicated, but I try to understand
> and ask someone if necessary. It's no good trying to read the
> papers, they use such big words a person can't understand.
> You have to ask somebody who knows stuff.[21]

The "somebody" is likely to be someone who finds newpaper reading easier. Nearly half of the college educated who are exposed
to several media try to persuade others how to vote. But so do
nearly a third of the *grade school educated* who are exposed to
several media. So there is not a tight little hierarchy of influence,
with those at the top having immense power and those at the bottom none. (If that were so, wouldn't the Republicans win all the
elections?) A more accurate picture comes to light when we step
back, figuratively speaking, and look at all the millions of advisory
conversations in progress during a political campaign. Some are
taking place on the upper stories of Rockefeller Plaza and the Ford
Foundation, or the Top of the Mark in San Francisco. But there are
thousands more going on in shops, in locker rooms, and at ladies'
teas, in ghetto store-front churches, in groups of ranch hands and
Rotarians. In all these settings, some citizens are a little more
attentive, a little better informed than their fellows, and it is to
them that the others turn for political advice. The influence from
Madison Avenue on the man in a mine in West Virginia not only
passes through many filterings, but is changed a little at each
passage.

communities and communities

If we were able to listen in on all these conversations at once, we
would notice that they were quite different in different groups.
    Studies of mass society show how significant a rich and varied
group life is to the maintenance of freedom. We take the groupi-
ness of American life for granted as something natural and obvious in our society. When an American is faced with a problem,
one of his first impulses is to form a group, to get together and do
something about it. For every problem, we seem to say, there is
some organizational solution. We send Peace Corpsmen around

[21] Key, *op. cit.*, p. 363n.

the world to help hungry villagers get themselves organized. The very naturalness and obviousness of group life in our political culture is apt to make it hard for us to see how much our politics and the patterns of influence underlying politics are shaped by group life.

William Kornhauser has done some thinking about what the breakdown of group life can mean:

> *Mass society* requires both accessible elites and available non-elites if it is to exhibit a high rate of mass behavior. Elites are accessible and non-elites are available in that there is a paucity of independent groups between the state and the family to protect either the elites or non-elites from manipulation and mobilization by the other. In the absence of social autonomy at all levels of society, large numbers of people are pushed and pulled toward activist modes of intervention in vital centers of society; and mass-oriented leaders have the opportunity to mobilize this activism for the capture of power. As a result, freedom is precarious in mass society.[22]

In other words, groups act as a kind of insulation between leaders and followers. Citizen demands are not expressed directly to the government, but are filtered through a complicated process of groups in interaction. When groups break down, leaders in power are vulnerable to direct action—strikes, boycotts, sit-ins, disruptions of the process of governing—by intense minorities temporarily mobilized to get their way. On the other hand, groups insulate individuals and families from the direct power of government. What Kornhauser means by "available non-elites" is an unorganized mass of people without strong group connections, who are readily mobilizable by demagogues bent on capturing power. The isolated citizen feels he has no place to turn except to the leader who promises to bring utopia in exchange for absolute allegiance.

Here we are talking about real groups, about groups in which people interact with one another and have common purposes that they try to implement through group activity. Real groups are to be distinguished from groupings, from categories we set up for analytic purposes. The population between the ages of eighteen and twenty-one is an important political category, but it is not a

---

[22]William Kornhauser, *The Politics of Mass Society* (New York: Free Press, Macmillan, 1959), p. 41.

group. A group is a fraternity, a classroom of students, a football team, a student union, a caucus of the SDS. We are talking about groups as they actually enter into the life of individual citizens.

The first group is the family. The next is the peer group at school. The next is a group of fellow workers on the job. And the next is the family again – a new family to begin the cycle over. As we have seen, political viewpoints tend strongly to perpetuate themselves in this sequence. In most families, mother and father agree about politics. The closer the family ties, the more that agreement will tend to be confirmed in the future political outlook of the child. The family has a particular style of life shaped by its place in a range of occupations, incomes, educational background, and religion. It tends to send its children to a school, and thus to a new group of friends, consistent with that life style, thus reinforcing the lessons of the family dinner table. When it comes to a job, the son is likely to find a place in the occupational world not very far from that of his father, and so again there is reinforcement. And he marries a girl, chances are, who shares the life style he inherited. All of these effects tend to reinforce continuity, to strengthen over time the strain of inherited political predispositions.[23]

The significance of these long-term influences toward continuity can hardly be exaggerated. Any persuader has to cope with the fact that the group gathered around the television set is the family, a real group with its own history and future, whose members check and reinforce one another.

What does the family show us about the characteristics of politically influential groups in general? Research backs up common sense here in many respects. Groups are influential over individuals when the relationships within the group are intense –

---

[23] Herbert McClosky and Harold E. Dahlgren, "Primary Group Influence on Party Loyalty," *American Political Science Review,* Vol. 53 (September, 1959), 757–76. This is the common pattern, but there may be many important exceptions. For instance, there are families that raise their children with a sense that they should be independent, thus paving the way for later revolts from the *substance* of the going family viewpoint. Similarly, some families inculcate a predilection for political change, for adapting political techniques to current conditions, a lesson that also facilitates later deviations from the family ideology. And the lessons of the family include moral imperatives at a higher level of abstraction than the political; children may grow up taking the ethics more seriously than the politics they have learned in the family and come to use the former as a justification for altering the latter.

when the group is small, gathers together frequently, persists beyond a few meetings, and involves each member in the work of the group. Obviously groups dealing with issues important for the members are most influential. Groups composed of people with similar backgrounds, opinions, views of the future, and so on exert the most influence on the members.[24]

The broad implication is clear: real groups affect politics at every stage of the game. From the perspective of the individual, most of his real groups reinforce one another. The fact that the society as a whole is composed of a great many different groups with conflicting purposes does not necessarily imply that any given *individual* experiences, in his everyday life, group interaction involving conflicting political viewpoints. There are not any members of garbagemen's unions in Rotary Clubs, not many AT&T stockholders in the Black Panther party. So there are limits on the degree to which the persuader can manipulate the group loyalties of citizens. He cannot play on them as on an organ, shifting from one theme to another. He has to deal with a relatively stable set of fairly consistent interpersonal networks.

In understanding the influence of such groups, we need to keep in mind the distinction between labels and life, symbols and reality. Myths, images, pictures in the heads of individuals—we have seen how all that affects political thinking and feeling and how the persuader tries to use such symbols to move citizens. But the myths and symbols are not floating free in a cloud above the political landscape. They are anchored in individual needs and experiences. They are also anchored in the realities of social life, in the ways people relate to their real groups. You can get yourself labeled as a "member" of the Democratic party easily enough, and that may be very important for certain analytical purposes. But the nameless group of friends you go bowling with may turn out to have much more to do with your political opinions.

The elements of politics come together in space, in places, in communities. All the forces we have been talking about—the pull and thrust of class and ethnic loyalties, the family feelings, the economic and occupational dimensions of politics—come to bear in certain *locations*. Each has its own bundle of factors put together in its own way. Each is a little political culture within the big national one, and each has its own pattern of power which gets

[24] Lane and Sears, *op. cit.,* pp. 35–36.

its fundamental shape from the special way things are in that place. We saw how cultural differences shape political attitudes across national boundaries. But also within the nation there is not one standard structure of power, but a whole series of different ones spread out across the national landscape. In many important ways, northern California is different from southern California, as northern Italy is different from southern Italy.

We are a nation with a geography. *The whole political system is structured around geography.* The election districts, right down to the ward and precinct level, the judicial circuits, the administrative regions, even the Presidential electoral college, all are geographical units. They are the framework in space within which all the social forces we have been talking about play themselves out.

Where things happen has always been important in America. From the first settlements, the nature of the land affected the power of the ruling orders.

changing places, changing politics

Think of the Puritans. They spent over a decade in Holland after leaving England to found a community where they could build a new life infused with the tenets of their religion. But it didn't work out. They were in the wrong place. As William Bradford put it:

> That which was more lamentable, and of all sorrowes most heavie to be borne, was that many of their children, by these occasions, and the great licentiousness of youth in that countrie, and the manifold temptations of the place, were drawne away by evill examples into extravagante and dangerous courses, getting the raines off their neks, and departing from their parents. Some became souldiers, others tooke upon them farr viages by sea, and other some worse courses, tending to dissolutnes and danger of their soules, to the great greefe of their parents and dishonor of God. So that they saw the posteritie would be in danger to degenerate and be corrupted.[25]

[25]William Bradford, *History of Plymouth Plantation* (New York, 1908), p. 46, as quoted in Daniel J. Boorstin, *The Genius of American Politics* (Chicago: University of Chicago Press, 1953), p. 41.

In other words, in Holland things were getting out of hand. The children and more venturesome adults could not be well controlled and the community had begun to break down. So they went to New England and found there an environment much more consonant with their theology—and, incidentally, much more supportive of the power of the leading Puritans. The very hardship of their voyage and their struggle to wrest a living from the wilderness drew them together. As one said:

> That the spirits and hearts of men are kept in better temper by spreading wide, and by pouring as it were, from vessell to vessell . . . will [be] euident to any man, that shall consider, that the husbanding of unmanured grounds, and shifting into empty Lands, inforceth men to frugalitie, and quickneth invention: and the setling of new States requireth justice and affection to the common good: and the taking in of large Countreys presents a naturell remedy against couetousnesse, fraud, and violence; when euery man may enjoy enough without wrong or injury to his neighbour.[26]

In the New World there were Indians to be converted, there was struggle, as between God and the devil, there were hundreds of strange natural phenomena that confirmed the judgment and providence of God:

> Such Divine judgments, tempests, floods, earthquakes, thunders as are unusual, strange apparitions, or whatever else shall happen that is prodigious, witchcrafts, diabolical possessions, remarkable judgments upon noted sinners, eminent deliverances, and answers of prayer, are to be reckoned among illustrious providences.[27]

All of this fitted well with the Puritan purpose: to establish a new Zion, pure and righteous, undefiled by the corruptions of the world in a struggle with the forces of nature.

The struggle drew them together. But as the struggle was won, they began to fall apart. The community became more secure. The Indians were defeated or mollified. Colonists spread out

[26]John White, "Planter's Plea," in Peter Force, *Tracts* (New York, 1947), Vol. II, p. 3, as quoted in Boorstin, *op. cit.*, p. 43.

[27]Declaration of Ministers in General Meeting, May 12, 1681, in Preface to I. Mather's *Remarkable Providences* (London, 1856), as quoted in Boorstin, *op. cit.*, p. 47.

over the New England countryside and found good land, and, eventually, prosperity. Thanksgiving became a regular holiday on the calendar, no longer an occasion proclaimed by the magistrates to celebrate some special event of good fortune. There was a new sense of mastery, a sense that man could control his own life. Control by the church declined. As Daniel Boorstin put it, "For the circumstances which have nourished man's sense of mastery over his *natural* environment have on this continent somehow led him away from dogmatism, from the attempt to plan and control the *social* environment."[28]

Thus the place where the Puritans were living at any given time profoundly affected the character of their social community and of relationships of control in that community. Placed in Holland, they found their community falling apart. In the New World, battling to establish themselves in a harsh environment, they were welded together again. But as they spread out and found success, the bonds among them slackened. Their leaders were no longer in command of a besieged army, but of a dispersed and increasingly comfortable population of farmers and businessmen.

Those who have studied their American social history know how often such patterns have been repeated in our national experience. Again and again, our geography has channeled our politics. The sheer physical facts—the string of colonies along the eastern seaboard, the frontier, the North and the South, the cities where the rivers meet, the immense wall of the Rockies, and the golden land beyond—each in its turn acquired immense significance for our development and brought to the fore new forces, new leaders, new patterns of power. Each wave of change left behind a residue from the past, a political tradition, so that the politics of Texas today retains in the midst of an advanced and affluent economy much of the flavor of the frontier.

It is easy to get romantic about this vast land, but in fact its configurations point us to some hard political realities about the ways citizens develop their community power relationships. We see voting patterns, for example, in a new and different light when we look at them in their community settings. In 1960, voting patterns in the nation as a whole showed a *tendency* for Protestant citizens to vote against Kennedy. But there are Protes-

[28] Boorstin, *op. cit.*, p. 65.

tants and Protestants: one careful study showed that fundamentalists in Tennessee were profoundly affected by the "religious issue," while Lutherans in Minnesota were virtually unmoved by it. Perhaps there is something one could call an "Italian vote." In Providence in 1960, citizens of Italian ancestry showed a considerably stronger tendency to vote for candidates of Italian ancestry than did their neighbors a few miles up the interstate highway in Boston. In 1960, Negro voters, viewed nationwide, showed a strong tendency to prefer Kennedy, but this was not true for Negroes in Boston or in rural Tennessee.[29] From town to town, from county to county, underlying the great national trends there are many important variations.

Some cases show how they affect the flow of power.

[29] Lucy S. Dawidowicz and Leon J. Goldstein, *Politics in a Pluralist Democracy: Studies of Voting in the 1960 Election* (New York: Institute of Human Relations Press, 1963), pp. 95–96.

chapter viii

Citizen Power and Community Culture

One of the wisest interpreters of American politics wrote:

> If one views power as relational, he must hasten to reject some of the popular connotations of the term "power." The word carries by implication its own adjectives and may suggest unlimited authority. In fact, the power relationship may vary from brute force to the most gentle persuasion. Nor should the term "power" be allowed to conjure up solely visions of commands coming from "above." The power relationship is reciprocal and the subject may affect the ruler more profoundly than the ruler affects the subject. As Lasswell

161

puts it, "Power is an interpersonal situation; those who hold power are empowered. They depend upon and continue only so long as there is a continuing stream of empowering responses. . . ." Though political power in the relational sense ultimately distills down to the relations between individuals A and B, the isolated political act takes on a fuller meaning when regarded in the framework of the totality of political relations within the society. A working political system consists of a multiplicity of these individual relationships which, collectively, tend to be organized or shaped into characteristic forms.[1]

Power in politics is not just an isolated factor to be analyzed apart from the web of culture. It is a set of culture-bound relationships. The powerful in a democracy are, as Key puts it, empowered, dependent upon "a continuing stream of empowering responses" from the citizenry. An *analysis* of citizen power breaks down power relations into elements. A *synthesis* of citizen power shows how these elements combine to produce particular power contexts or situations, particular bunches of elements. This happens in all communities, from the nation to the village.

In previous chapters we have looked one at a time at many elements of the empowering process: the location, concentration, and mobility of populations; traditional activity levels and partisan loyalties; class and ethnic tensions; the expectations and hopes citizens have for the political system. Chapter vii put such factors in a context of persuasion, with the aim of conveying a sense of how situations affect persuasion attempts. Here we want to see, through some special cases, how political cultures, in a synthetic sense, bring together elements of power to make systems of power.

the "solid south"?

To the visiting European, "American culture" is an obvious reality. He sees the stark contrasts with his own way of life – and he sees them much more clearly than he sees the similarities. Furthermore, it is hard for a stranger to perceive the contrasts within "American culture." The language, the mass media, and

[1] V. O. Key, Jr., *Politics, Parties, and Pressure Groups* (New York: Crowell, 1958), pp. 3–4.

the symbols of nationhood give an impression of unity, of universally shared values and practices.

Similarly, most Yankees tend to think of the South as a region with a special, shared culture different from northern ways. To a degree, the European and the Yankee are both right. There is an American political culture and there is a southern political culture. But neither is "solid" in the sense of either uniformity or permanence. To get our bearings for the cases in the following pages, we must grasp the significance of variations in time and space — how power elements are synthesized differently in different cultural settings and how these combinations develop their own versions of growth.

Every culture is a collection of memories — often very tenacious memories. In the South, for example, the "memory" of the Civil War lingers a century after its ending. The veterans are all dead. What is remembered, then, is not personal experience, but culturally inherited experience — what fathers have told their sons. These memories are recalled selectively over the years. Some are muted and almost disappear while others are exaggerated. Some southerners do not remember, in the cultural sense, how much racial integration there was in the South — in public facilities, for instance — in the late nineteenth century.[2] Some Yankees would just as soon forget what the Union Army did to Atlanta. Cultural memories always are a mixture of myth and reality.

The past is constantly being reinterpreted to fit the needs of the present as well as the needs of the future. Political culture is a moving consensus; its second main theme is anticipation — what people expect to happen and how they come to accept or resist that. We can see the impact of anticipations in the recent history of southern racial attitudes. In the 1950's and 1960's, a great many white Southerners who did not want integration came to expect it in the future.[3] By 1968, large majorities of white southerners had come to accept civil rights laws promoting integration in voting, employment, education, and public accommodations.[4]

[2] C. Vann Woodward, *The Strange Career of Jim Crow* (New York: Oxford University Press, 1957).

[3] William Brink and Louis Harris, *The Negro Revolution in America* (New York: Simon & Schuster, 1964).

[4] Samuel Lubell, *The Hidden Crises in American Politics* (New York: Norton, 1971), pp. 174–75.

From expectation to acceptance – that seems to be the path followed by a good deal of cultural change, in the South and elsewhere. Few people have a clear-cut image of the future. But once they become convinced that certain new things are bound to happen, they eventually accept them.

The shape and movement of political cultures depend heavily on leadership. Most citizens are political consumers. They receive and digest the interpretations handed them by leaders – who, in turn, try to shape their messages to fit the public mood. In the South, whites who are active in politics (voting, interacting with community leaders, and holding office) are more likely to favor Negro voting than are inactive whites.[5]

There have been some remarkable changes: in 1965, Herman Talmadge, scion of the race-baiting Georgia Talmadges, told a Negro organization in Atlanta that race was no longer a factor in Georgia politics and that qualified Negroes should be appointed without delay to responsible government posts. In Alabama, a white candidate for sheriff courted the votes of thousands of newly registered Negroes.[6] Charles Evers, the black civil rights leader, became mayor of a Mississippi town. And by 1970, in southern states with relatively small Negro minorities, "A truly tough segregationist stands little chance of being elected to state-wide office."[7] In each such case, we want to watch for that subtle interplay between citizens and the leaders they empower and follow.

Back in the 1940's, V.O. Key found remarkable variety within southern political culture, ranging from quiet aristocracy in Virginia to tumult in Alabama. The South was changing then and it is changing now.[8] Urbanization and suburbanization, the northward migration of Negroes, changes in agriculture, air conditioning, education, integration, industrialization, health and housing and hubris have made for different forms of Dixieism, have shifted power, in many states, away from the cotton fields and canebrakes to the big cities and their suburban warrens. But the

---

[5] Charles F. Cnudde, *Democracy in the American South* (Chicago: Markham, 1971), p. 58.

[6] Donald R. Matthews and James W. Prothro, *Negroes and the New Southern Politics* (New York: Harcourt, Brace & World, 1966), p. 469.

[7] Donald S. Strong, "Further Reflections on Southern Politics," Presidential Address to the Southern Political Science Association, 1970, p. 12.

[8] V. O. Key, Jr., *Southern Politics* (New York: Random House, 1949).

links between culture and control, though changing, are always there, favoring one strategy here and dooming it to failure in a different place.[9]

When we move below regions and states to towns and cities, cultural variations and their impacts on politics are even more striking. If state patterns show how the relative placing of things and people affect political power, local patterns show how different bundles of factors come together in one place to shape the human relationships we call political power. The local community is like a little laboratory—sometimes a very big laboratory—in which the whole chemistry of politics is poured into the same beaker or, if you like, in which all the wires and circuits of the political network are tangled into a great knot. In the community, we are not dealing with single events, isolated individuals, or single variables like class or ethnicity or age, but with families and neighborhoods in which these things are woven together to make a culture. We move beyond analysis of the power implications of factors taken one at a time to the ways in which these mixes are put together. A brief look at a few of these clusters brings out the ways such factors intertwine. In each case, we shall see a somewhat different aspect of democratic political legitimacy. In other words, in each case the very way of life the citizens pursue implies a certain view of authority, a set of criteria by which some leaders, but not others, are empowered by the citizenry.

In short, why do you and I do what some politicians want us to do?

the CDC in LA

Take Los Angeles, in particular the members of the California Democratic Clubs there.[10] In that sprawling, variegated jetropolis these citizens of the sixties came together out of a common concern with issues. They were Democrats, interested in the party and its future and its organization, but even more interested in finding answers to big questions. Should there be universal dis-

[9] *Ibid.*, p. 87.
[10] As described by James Q. Wilson, *The Amateur Democrat: Club Politics in Three Cities* (Chicago: University of Chicago Press, 1962).

armament? What should be done about recognizing Communist China, abolishing capital punishment and loyalty oaths and the House Un-American Activities Committee, about discrimination and medical care for the aged, about consumer cooperatives and the oil depletion allowance? Primarily voters who had been attracted to the candidacy of Adlai Stevenson, the club members needed bigger reasons to participate than simply winning elections:

> We're volunteers. We have to have the feeling we are working for a cause in which we believe in order to work at all. . . . If we didn't have this cause to believe in . . . we wouldn't work at all.[11]

What public officials achieved—not how they got and held office—was their focus of attention.

The clubs were small groups of like-minded individuals, mostly middle class and well educated, loosely organized statewide. The clubs in Los Angeles were important to the members in part because they offered social benefits; in the Beverly Hills club, for example, the average member was a young and single female. The combination of companionship and concern for issues cemented the groups together and affected their organization. As one Los Angeles County committeeman explained:

> A lot of Easterners come out here and tell us we've got the system all wrong. What we ought to do is appoint a precinct captain in each precinct and give him the responsibility for getting out the vote, and organize the county in that way. But we've tried it. We're not closed to such ideas. We're interested in all alternatives to what we're doing now. But . . . they don't work. You can't get people to take responsibility for a precinct and . . . work in it.
>
> The basic organization of the County Committee depends on the club movement. . . . We have to have group support or consensus [for the members]. . . . You've got to realize, it's not just ideals that get people into politics. If it were only ideals, then the precinct system would work. If it were ideals simply, then you could persuade people to work alone in their precinct . . . in order to realize their ideals. But you can't persuade them to do this. You can only

[11] *Ibid.*, p. 151. This quotation and the following quotations from Wilson, *The Amateur Democrat* are reprinted by permission of the University of Chicago Press. Copyright © 1962 by the University of Chicago Press. ·

persuade them to work through a club. The club atmosphere, the "groupness," is vitally important.[12]

The general cleanliness of California politics did not provide much target for reformism in the clubs. Nor did they take much interest in *local* conditions; Watts was separated physically and even farther away psychically from these white, middle-class folk. In a fragmented system without a "machine" tradition, the issue-oriented clubs were important because they attracted many Democratic activists and raised questions many of the party's candidates would not have minded ignoring. They endorsed or withheld their endorsement from candidates *before* the primary elections.

This is the point at which they ran afoul of the regular party leadership. As the leader of the Democrats in the state legislature put it,

> The group which is concerned with agitating, with being the gadfly, with being out in left field . . . should not also be the group which makes the selection of men to run with the Democratic party label. This group has no responsibility and dreads responsibility.[13]

The CDCers thought of themselves as "the conscience of the party"—and numerous incumbents felt they could do as well with their own consciences. "I can tell you this," said one party regular, "the big contributers . . . never have been as demanding of our incumbents as some of these people in the clubs and councils try to be. . . . The representative has an obligation to all the people of his district, and not just to the members of a Democratic club in the district."[14] Yet these demands continued to be made, and grew more and more militant. The members, being amateurs, uninterested in patronage or party officialdom, could not easily be mollified. Their militancy grew, in part because they found this the best way to attract new members to replace the large numbers who dropped out each political season.

At the time James Q. Wilson studied them, the California clubs had never lost a statewide nomination, and only two of those

[12] *Ibid.*, p. 169.
[13] *Ibid.*, p. 296.
[14] *Ibid.*, p. 297.

they had endorsed at the state level had been challenged in a primary.[15] They conducted voter registration drives. Whether through their influence or not, their rise coincided with a growth in the Democratic ranks. They became a force to be reckoned with. As Wilson sums it up, after reviewing some cautions about the extent of CDC power:

> Despite all these doubts and limitations, however, probably the most significant piece of evidence on the influence of the CDC is the fact that a large number of legislators and party professionals, as well as organized labor, would like to strip CDC of the right to make pre-primary endorsements. CDC's influence, although it is difficult to establish statistically, must be sufficient to concern those who are not in favor of the endorsing process. It is probably fair to say that the label provided candidates by the endorsing process is sufficiently troublesome to be concerned about if you are an incumbent.[16]

How did culture affect power in this case? The CDC's organizational unity was based mainly on *shared values* (expressed in issues) and *shared characteristics* (mainly young, well-educated, middle-class whites). The clubs' power in state politics was in part due to their members' lack of interest in the traditional rewards (patronage) the state politicians controlled; this gave them independence from the machine and legitimacy in the eyes of the voters. By concentrating their energies on specific issues and the candidates who stood for these issues, the CDC achieved more than they might have with a scatter-shot technique. For a time, at least, they exercised important influence in California politics.

tight little village

For contrast, take "Springdale," as described by Vidich and Bensman in *Small Town in Mass Society*.[17] At the time of their research, Springdale comprised about 3,000 souls in upstate New York. A few stores and a lumber business, a central school, a

[15] *Ibid.*, p. 320.
[16] *Ibid.*, pp. 329–30.
[17] Arthur J. Vidich and Joseph Bensman, *Small Town in Mass Society: Class, Power, and Religion in a Rural Community,* rev. ed. (Princeton, N.J.: Princeton University Press, 1968).

fairly sizable group of residents who commuted elsewhere to their jobs—that in a nutshell was the Springdale economy. The social system was more complicated, but not by Los Angeles standards. Springdalers thought of themselves as "just plain folks"—a phrase that distinguishes them at once from big-city people ("How can people stand to live in cities?") and emphasizes the values they prized. "Belief in the superiority of local ways," the researchers write,

> actually conditions the way of life. Springdalers *"make an effort* to be friendly" and *"go out of their way* to help new-comers." The newspaper always emphasizes the positive side of life; it never reports local arrests, shotgun weddings, mortgage foreclosures, lawsuits, bitter exchanges in public meetings, suicides or any other unpleasant happening. By this constant focus on warm and human qualities in all public situations, the public character of the community takes on those qualities, and hence it has a tone which is distinctly different from city life.[18]

Not everyone in Springdale was everyone else's friend; even 3,000 is too large a number for that. About a tenth of the people lived in shacks on the outskirts of town; regular folks called them "no-good people" who "can't be trusted." There was a good deal of gossip, much of it about politics, and not all of it kindly. But almost all of Springdale's pejorative language was reserved for troublemakers, for those who are "always raising a ruckus" or in some lesser way disturbing the community's tranquillity.

These feelings carried over into Springdale politics. Political talk was a matter of personalities, not issues. There was a great deal of such talk, but the operation of politics itself was almost ideally arranged to prevent serious controversy. The village government avoided innovation, sidestepped decision-making, and, when something simply *had* to be done, worked things out unanimously. In this Republican town the Republican committee consisted, technically, of ten elected members, but the full committee convened only once in four years and the ordinary caucuses were managed by three citizens. A quorum of the caucus—thirteen Republicans—could be gathered when necessary, usually without

---

[18] *Ibid.*, p. 32.

anyone having to "coax or walk the street in search of another villager or two to make the required quorum."[19]

Elections happened with a similar lack of fuss. As the newspaper reported on one election:

> Perhaps it's due to the fact that people are becoming public-minded, or it may be that good citizens who accept the nomination unopposed for public office are becoming suspicious of sneaky write-in methods; regardless of the reason, 34 villagers went to the polls and voted on Tuesday afternoon. This is in comparison to 13 votes last year. However, no competition or write-ins amounting to anything developed. . . .[20]

No wonder, then, that after the election, not much happened in Springdale government. The basis for some issues was there. For example, property assessments were extremely uneven. And sometimes—very rarely—a group of citizens would get aroused about some issue and demand action. But when that happened, when action absolutely could not be avoided, the old hands in the town government quickly got the reins of the movement, doing whatever was needed to satisfy the demanders without bringing them into the process of decision-making. These ripples in the status quo were soon calmed and left behind the same system of unflurried cogitation by the traditional leaders. There may be those in Los Angeles who think their system is much the same, but the differences in degree (and, as regards the California Democratic Clubs, the differences in attitudes toward issues) are striking.

the tyranny of exclusion

Take Harlem. Kenneth Clark's book *Dark Ghetto* is an in-depth study of the culture of that community of the outcast.[21] Clark lived in Harlem for more than forty years. He brought to his home-place the eyes and ears of an expert psychologist. The Harlem he

---

[19] *Ibid.,* p. 121n.
[20] *Ibid.,* p. 124.
[21] Kenneth B. Clark, *Dark Ghetto: Dilemmas of Social Power* (New York: Harper & Row, 1965).

wrote of comes alive as an incredibly complex social and psychological tangle, all the more difficult for most outsiders to understand because the understanding involves a recognition of unbelievable suffering and disturbance in the midst of an affluent society. The life theme for many who lived in Harlem was hopelessness, as in these words by a man of thirty:

> A lot of times, when I'm working, I become as despondent as hell and I feel like crying. I'm not a man, none of us are men! I don't own anything. I'm not a man enough to own a store; none of us are.[22]

In the whole catalogue of social basics, the typical Harlem citizen was deprived—in housing, employment, education, recreation, sanitation, and the entire range of government services the suburbanite takes for granted. Drugs and crime were as natural to the Harlem youngster as baseball and ice cream to the average white American teen-ager. The very fundament of society, the family, was ripped asunder. At the time Clark was writing, "Only about half of the children under eighteen in the Harlem community are living with both parents. . . ."[23] All this in an area next door to some of the highest living in the world. The Harlem child in a rat-infested, crowded bed-living-dining-cooking room sees on television—or just a few blocks away—a fairyland of elegant comfort. Faced with this grim contrast of realities, it is no wonder that for many of the young men Clark observed in Harlem

> . . . Fantasy played a major role. Many of these marginal upward-striving teen-agers allowed others to believe that they were college students. One young man told his friends that he was a major in psychology. He had enrolled in the classes of a Negro professor with whom he had identified, and he described those lectures in detail to his friends. The fact is he was a dropout from high school. Others dressed like college students and went to college campuses where they walked among the students, attempting to feel a part of a life they longed for and could not attain. Some carried attaché cases wherever they went—often literally empty. One carried ordinary books camouflaged by college book covers and pretended to "study" in the presence of friends. Most of these young men were academically at the fifth- or sixth-grade

[22] *Ibid.*, p. 1.
[23] *Ibid.*, p. 47.

reading level; none was in college. . . . To some, this form of social schizophrenia might seem comic, but a more appropriate response is to tears, not laughter.[24]

Fantasy also affected Harlem politics. Ghetto political leaders, when Clark studied them, lacked experience and political sophistication; their difficulties grew out of the community's shared sense of helplessness: "It is difficult, if not impossible, to behave as one with power when all one's experiences have indicated that one has none."[25] These feelings lent an air of ambivalence to popular perceptions of Negroes who had "made it." On the one hand, the Ralph Bunches and Jackie Robinsons were seen as Negroes who had achieved high eminence worthy of respect and admiration. But the people of Harlem are not blind to the immense distance that separates them and their problems from United Nations headquarters and Yankee Stadium, and they see and feel the way in which success in the larger society often seems possible only at the price of denying their homeplace and adopting the ways of an alien world. Clark analyzed the career of J. Raymond Jones to show how this ambivalence affected the operations of an aggressive and realistic political leader who tried to work within the Democratic party. In 1964, Jones became the first Negro county leader of a major political party anywhere in the United States.[26] He reached that position despite many moves on the part of white party leaders to shunt him off to less powerful positions. Even as a county leader Jones was suspected by numerous Harlemites of accommodating too readily with the regular organization of Carmine De Sapio. Much would depend on his ability to produce results without appearing to sell out.

A more striking view of the connection between political authority and the culture of the ghetto, with special emphasis on the link between helplessness and fantasy, is seen in the case of Adam Clayton Powell. From the 1930's on into the 1950's, Powell had been a practical politician who used his personal popularity to wring results from the political system. But at the time Clark wrote, "In the genuine thrust of the civil rights movement, Powell is a has-been, still seeking to give the impression of leadership."[27]

[24] *Ibid.*, pp. 66–67.
[25] *Ibid.*, p. 156.
[26] *Ibid.*, p. 161.
[27] *Ibid.*, p. 165.

His primary importance had become symbolic; he was a living expression of the fantasy element in Harlem culture. Powell was an expert actor. He could sense the rapport between his own personal flamboyance and the hurt of ghetto life. As Clark sums it up:

> The Negro can in fantasy journey with Adam to the Riviera, enjoy a home in Puerto Rico, have beautiful girls at his beck and call, change wives "like rich white folks." Powell plays the role the Hollywood star may for whites but even more powerfully, for added to the magic and glamour of personal fame is the excitement and virtues of defiant racial protest.
>
> The Negro masses do not see Powell as amoral but as definitely honest in his protest against the myths and hypocrisies of racism. What whites regard as Powell's violation of elemental ethics, Negroes view as effective and amusing defiance. Whatever is the personal ethical moral standard of the individual Negro, it tends to be suspended in judgment of Powell. He is important precisely because he *is* a caricature, a burlesque, of the personal exploitation of power. His behavior merely focuses on the fact that certain respectable white congressmen, too, may use public funds for personal junkets or put their wives on the public payroll. The white power structure never successfully calls him to account and the Negro sees this and applauds.[28]

Indicted in the courts and castigated by his fellow Congressmen, rarely visiting his constituency from his home in the Bahamas, Powell nevertheless has been elected again and again as the representative of his district.

Clark reaches this conclusion:

> The effective use of the potential power of the Negro masses and the ability of Negro leaders to discipline and mobilize that power for constructive social change may well be determined by the ability of a critical mass of Negroes to control their ambivalence toward themselves and to develop the capacity for genuine and sustained respect for those Negroes who are worthy of confidence and respect. The present unreality and distortions of ghetto life make it difficult to differentiate between empty flamboyance and valid achievement; between hysterical, cynical, verbal manipulations and sound judgment. It is difficult for the uneducated, exploited and despised Negro to know whom he can trust and whom he

[28] *Ibid.*, p. 163.

must continue to suspect. He knows for sure only his own deep despair and resentment, and he sees that as long as the conditions which give rise to these feelings persist he will continue to be their victim. The compounded tragedy is that he will remain the chief victim also of himself. The real tragedy for the Negro is that he has not taken himself seriously because no one else has. The hope for the Negro is that now he is asserting that he really is a human being. If he succeeds in winning these rights he will respect and trust himself, but he cannot win the right to human dignity without the ability to respect and cherish his own humanity in spite of pervasive white rejection.[29]

Balanced on this knife edge is the future of politics in communities like Harlem. Obviously the power of a man like Powell depends profoundly on the cultural meanings of politics in the community, on the images and dreams and calculations people develop as they reach for a better life. A politics of fantasy, empowering symbolic leadership rather than realistic leadership, flourishes where the realities appear to offer so little.

middle-old-style politics in Boston

Take Boston, and in particular the Italian-American subcommunity in the West End. In *The Urban Villagers,* Herbert J. Gans[30] analyzes the social system of native-born Americans of Italian parentage who lived in the West End among other ethnic groups. Culture and power were interwoven in many patterns relating to an inherited Italian-American tradition. Unlike Harlem, the West End Italian community was made up of strong family units built upon the patriarchal model. In the family there was a whole series of ancient patterns of behavior that had long ago been established and passed down through the generations.

Gans described this traditional power situation:

Second-generation Italians grew up in a patriarchal authority system with a strictly enforced double standard of behavior for boys and girls. The boys were freer to indulge their gratifications than the girls. In order to be able to do what they

[29] *Ibid.,* pp. 197–98.
[30] Herbert J. Gans, *The Urban Villagers: Group and Class in the Life of Italian Americans* (New York: Free Press, Macmillan, 1962).

wanted, the girls thus had to learn early how to subvert the male authority by verbal means—"how to get around the men"—and what they did not learn elsewhere, they learned from the mother's wile in getting her way with her husband. . . . The father enforces discipline and administers punishment; he does not need to talk. The mother can influence her husband only by talking to him, reinterpreting the child's deeds so that he will not punish the child any more than she feels desirable. Talk is the woman's weapon for reducing inequities in power between male and female.[31]

There are obviously tensions in such situations, but the tensions are ameliorated by their regularity, by the mutual understanding of all the participants that this is the way things are.

Even more important than the small family or household, Gans found, was the peer group, the gathering of relatives and friends which took place "regularly in the kitchens and living rooms of innumerable West End apartments"[32] after dinner for a long conversation. In these gatherings and in the whole culture of the West End Italian-Americans the emphasis was on what Gans called a "person-orientation." These Italian-Americans tended not to strive to achieve some external goal or "object," such as higher status, a successful career, or some moral or social ideal; that is the pattern Gans calls "object orientation," more typical of the general middle-class American culture. The person-oriented West Enders stress "the desire to be a person within a group; to be liked and noticed by members of a group whom one likes and notices in turn."[33]

The group—that is, the specific group, the family and the cluster of friends and relatives making up the peer gatherings—came first. In cases of conflict between goals of an abstract or long-range sort and goals of developing warm human relationships, the West Ender would take the latter. People were expected to treat one another as whole persons, not according to some particular social role, such as "doctor" or "tailor." The tenants expected their landlords, for example, to behave as members of their peer groups—as friends first and landlords second. "One West Ender has never forgiven his landlord for announcing a rent increase in a tone of voice which suggested to him that he

[31] *Ibid.*, p. 48.
[32] *Ibid.*, p. 77.
[33] *Ibid.*, p. 90.

was being treated as a tenant rather than as a peer group member."[34] So the sense of personalism, of a direct and intense appreciation or rejection of specific others, was the trademark of this urban village.

What did this mean for political power? The West Enders had many grievances against the city government. In general their stance toward the political order in Boston was one of hostility and suspicion, a conviction that there was a deep and pervasive conspiracy afoot to make life hard for them. These feelings were in part the result of real experience; in many ways the government had made things hard for them. But they were also extensions of the person-orientation the Italian-Americans used to understand their own lives.

> . . . They conceive the governmental process to be much like personal relationships in the peer group society. Thus, government agencies are identified with the individuals who run them, and agency behavior is explained in terms of their personal motives. . . . Government agencies have no reality; the city is seen as a congeries of individuals, most of whom are corrupt. . . . The personalization of government operations stems in part from the West Enders' inability to recognize the existence of object-oriented bureaucracies. The idea that individual officials follow rules and regulations based not on personal morality but on concepts of efficiency, order, administrative hierarchy, and the like, is difficult to accept. For example, when the redevelopment agency initiated its procedures for taking title to the West End properties, and for relocating people and demolishing houses, West Enders refused to believe that these procedures were based on local and federal regulations. They saw them only as individual, and individually motivated, acts. Taking title to the land was described as a land grab to benefit the redeveloper. Relocation was explained in terms of the desire of the redeveloper and his governmental partners to push West Enders out of their homes as quickly as possible, so that the new buildings could be put up. The protests of redevelopment officials that they were only following standard operating procedures went unheeded.[35]

Given this viewpoint, West Enders acted accordingly. They tried to keep out of the way of contact with the alien world of a rationalized city administration bent on handling issues in the light of

[34] *Ibid.*, p. 93.
[35] *Ibid.*, pp. 164–65.

principles according to procedures. Their politicians acted as "ambassadors to the outside world" The key to the politician's success was his ability to work as a go-between, a broker managing relationships with officialdom. He moved back and forth between the exercise of personal influence and the exercise of political influence, constantly translating the one into the other. He would be expected to provide jobs and other favors, to take care of individual constituents by using the "rules and regulations" to best advantage. He was important as a channel for information—not only technical facts about the complexities of Boston government, but also believable explanations in personal terms of what was going on. As an ambassador he represented his people in the wider political arena. He, not his constituents, was responsible for doing whatever had to be done to manipulate the political machine.

As men in the middle, the politicians naturally felt a certain ambivalence. But by and large they shared their constituents' view of the political order as an arena of personal action and reaction. As Gans puts it,

> In short, the "pols" interpret political events with the same theory of government as their West End constituents and lack the detachment and insight that is common among the party leaders. This is probably one reason that they are local politicians.[36]

One can see in outline here some of the qualities an individual would have to have—or appear to have—in order to acquire and maintain power in the Boston West End Italian-American community. Essentially, he would have to do what all successful ambassadors do: extract from a strange environment rewards his constituents think are important, and explain that process in the language his people can understand.

community culture and citizen power

What do these examples say about citizen power in American communities? They suggest great variety. We see four quite different ways in which political leadership is affected by the special values, needs, perceptions, and resources citizens in the com-

[36] *Ibid.,* p. 180.

munity have come to emphasize. Much as in our outline of the effects of mass media, we see how citizens are far from being placid creatures manipulable by a community elite. These cases show in stark outline some of the limits of leadership.

What would it take for the leaders of the Los Angeles Democratic Clubs to operate like Adam Clayton Powell? What would it take for the Springdale leaders to develop a politics of issues on the Los Angeles model? What would it take to bring the Boston West Enders around to a "just plain folks" politics of unanimity and repression of controversy à la Springdale? Obviously there are themes that strike a responsive chord in some communities and fall flat in others. The impact of culture on power is evident. Culture shapes the agenda of politics. Culture decides who will decide what. Culture determines to a very large degree how power is organized and exercised in a community.

Of course, most people most of the time give little thought to the content of their political cultures. People are not in the habit of examining, in any conscious way, the premises of their political beliefs. Nor do many citizens make systematic mental surveys of the power structures of their communities. This has some important implications for research. To go around asking people vague, general questions about who runs their town is likely to produce vague, general answers about the more visible public personalities. Much research has been misled in this direction.[37]

On the other hand, looking only at actions—at specific community conflicts and who won and who lost—can also be misleading. For example, an analysis of specific disputes and their resolution in Springdale would miss the point that very few big issues get raised and that there is a strong cultural tradition against issue-raising. The outlines of power in communities emerge most clearly when one focuses on the connections between culture and action. One asks *how what people believe affects what they do.* One pays special attention to political moves that are linked to long-standing cultural values, and one pays special attention to those particular shared belief that channel events.

Perhaps this point is best made in a story Elting E. Morison relates:

[37] See especially the critique of many sociological power structure theories and findings in Nelson W. Polsby, *Community Power and Political Theory* (New Haven, Conn.: Yale University Press, 1963).

In the early days of the last war, when armaments of all kinds were in short supply, the British, I am told, made use of a venerable field piece that had come down to them from previous generations. The honorable past of this light artillery stretched back, in fact, to the Boer War. In the days of uncertainty after the fall of France, these guns, hitched to trucks, served as useful mobile units in coast defense. But it was felt that the rapidity of fire could be increased. A time-motion expert was, therefore, called in to suggest ways to simplify the firing procedures. He watched one of the gun crews of five men at practice in the field for some time. Puzzled by certain aspects of the procedures, he took some slow-motion pictures of the soldiers performing the loading, aiming and firing routines.

When he ran these pictures over once or twice, he noticed something that appeared odd to him. A moment before the firing, two members of the gun crew ceased all activity and came to attention for a three-second interval, extending throughout the discharge of the gun. He summoned an old colonel of artillery, showed him the pictures and pointed out the strange behavior. What, he asked the colonel, did it mean? The colonel, too, was puzzled. He asked to see the pictures again. "Ah," he said when the performance was over, "I have it. They are holding the horses."[38]

[38] Elting E. Morison, "A Case Study of Innovation," in Warren G. Bennis, Kenneth D. Benne, and Robert Chin (eds.), *The Planning of Change* (New York: Holt, Rinehart & Winston, 1961), p. 592.

chapter ix

Political Change

Given all the forces for stability, how do we get any action out of politics? What we have seen may make us overly aware of the limitations and difficulties of political change. In one sense, influence is the ability to cause change. A person is powerful when he can make things happen. Yet we have seen again and again how hard it is to change people. To oversimplify: citizen participation in politics is largely habitual. The ways people think about politics are pretty much traditional. Political feelings reflect a man's whole life experience – the personality he has been developing since childhood – and are closely tied in with his relatively stable network of human relationships. Often, when some new influence (like television) comes along, there is barely a ripple in the pattern of political behavior.

Even when the people are convinced, the government may take a long time to act. In January, 1971, the Gallup poll reported that 73 percent of the public agreed that American armed forces should be withdrawn from Indochina by December 31, 1971. The invasions (or "incursions," in Pentagonese) of Cambodia and Laos and the threat of an invasion of North Vietnam, the enormous increase in bombing, the skyrocketing costs of the war, its demoralizing effects on soldiers in the field and on hundreds of thousands of wandering Vietnamese survivors, and the social and economic chaos the war brought home to our own country had sunk into the public mind slowly but surely. But the war ground on into the Spring of 1971 with no definite end in view. The President dismissed the issue as a temporary one; he was, he said, "winding down" the war but would follow his own unannounced plan rather than the preferences of a large national majority.

Year after year the government rattles along with a load of stale policies. Ill-suited for any comprehensive review of policy results, the political order produces a patchwork of responses to new demands based on old assumptions. The priorities—as reflected in behavior, not rhetoric—are so clearly out of whack that many critics throw up their hands in despair. Whoever decided to pay farmers $4 billion a year not to grow food while twenty million Americans do not have enough to eat? Why did we decide to spend more than *ten times as much* to explore outer space as we spent on controlling air and water pollution during the 1960's? By what principle do scores of the very rich get away without paying any federal income taxes? Why such cautious calculation of expenses for anti-poverty programs while the defense establishment makes billion-dollar mistakes?[1]

The costs of gradualism, in human terms, are immense. To see them one needs to look past the statistics to the individual realities. Perhaps in its gross dimensions the war in Indochina is being steadily "wound down." But there is nothing gradual about sudden death for an American soldier or a Vietnamese peasant. The miner killed in an unsafe coal pit, the black child deprived of a decent education, and the sick migrant worker who cannot

[1]Duane Lockard, *The Perverted Priorities of American Politics* (New York: Macmillan, 1971).

pay a doctor take little comfort in the idea that in a decade or so, things might be better.

To meet the challenge of rapid social change we have a government designed for delay. It can be moved. It has been moved. What it takes to make progress happen is the mobilization of vast social energies behind a workable purpose. In other words, it takes focused power. How can that be done?

The power of political leaders depends not only on the legitimacy they acquire from their cultures, but also on timing. The political leader not only pulls society forward; he is also pushed by certain broad social forces that provide special opportunities for leadership. Across the country as conditions of life change for millions of citizens, the political order tends to respond, to grow and develop in ways to meet new challenges. A key question is whether or not the political system can respond quickly and accurately enough to maintain itself and to meet the needs of citizens in an era of escalating rates of social change and complexity.

Processes of political change are some of the hardest phenomena to capture in an analysis. That requires a close look at relationships among factors *in motion*. Here we shall look at some examples to show how, for change to succeed, the changers need to act

at the right *time,*
on the right *issue,*
with the right *leaders,*
and the right *people,*
in the right *place.*

the farmers go to town

How does social change shape political action? In agriculture, once the backbone of the American economy, we see a strange set of trends: the decline of farming accompanied by the rise of large, powerful farm organizations. By 1960 only about 9 percent of the population lived on farms, yet the three largest farm organizations, the National Grange, the American Farm Bureau Federation, and the National Farmers Union, have become powers to be reckoned with in Washington and in the state capitols.[2] This apparent correlation between declining fortunes and political organization historically does not seem accidental. As Key points out, trouble—especially sudden deprivation—can be a powerful force for bringing citizens together around their common grievances and mobilizing them for political action.

> A factor of great significance in the setting off of political movements is an abrupt change for the worse in the status of one group relative to that of other groups in society. The economics of politics is by no means solely a matter of the poor against the rich; the rich and the poor may live together peacefully for decades, each accepting its status quietly. A rapid change for the worse, however, in the relative status of any group, rich or poor, is likely to precipitate political action. Depressions have been closely associated with intensification of farmers' political activity. Agrarian agitation, at times boisterous and disturbing to the conservative elements of the society, has not occurred at a uniform pitch. It has had its dull periods and its shrill points correlated somewhat with variations in the fortunes of farmers.[3]

For a long time, farmers bore the ups and downs of the market as isolated individuals, enduring whatever fortune delivered to them. In the late nineteenth and early twentieth centuries, farmers' movements sprang up in times of depression and then withered away as times got better. "When the pain left, the farmer quit squawking and went back to the plow."[4]

But then came the massive and persistent agricultural depression of the 1920's, which merged with the total depression of the 1930's. The outlines of a national farm organization were already in existence. Small groups of farmers had organized around the Department of Agriculture's county-agent system, mainly to help with the spreading of new farming techniques. But suddenly millions of citizens living on farms were in deep trouble. Suddenly millions of farm families found their standard of living radically reduced. They turned to the government for help and they turned to their emerging organization to get that help. The American Farm Bureau Federation came forward as a broadly

[2] V. O. Key, Jr., *Politics, Parties, and Pressure Groups* (New York: Crowell, 1958), p. 21.
[3] *Ibid.*, p. 24.
[4] *Ibid.*, p. 30.

based national organization to press the farmers' cause in Washington. For years their proposals were defeated in Congress or vetoed by the President. Finally the farmers' organizations turned to politics, expressing their demands in the national party conventions and making clear which candidates they favored.

In other words, strong national organizations of rural citizens (though rarely the poorest among them) had emerged as a prime factor in American politics. "Instead of a slumbering, rustic giant roused only by depression and adversity, farm organizations, well organized and competently led, maintain an interest in public policy as keen and continuous as that of any business or labor group."[5]

This history shows that citizens in trouble—*when that trouble hits a great many of them at the same time*—are likely to seek government action through political organization. The very weakness that has put them in dire straits becomes a cause of strength, a spur to power. The conditions for such organization must be right. For example, the fact that the farmers had already in existence the framework of a national organization was an important factor in their success. As Harold D. Lasswell wrote: "Although political movements begin in unrest, all social unrest does not find expression in political movements. Under some conditions, a community which is visited by plague may pray; under other conditions, the community will demand the retirement of the health commissioner."[6]

So a change in power relationships among citizens and their leaders may arise at certain key moments, particularly when leaders help citizens become *conscious* of the fact that their trouble is widely shared, and that there is a remedy in government action.

labored progress

Once organized for one purpose, a social movement may develop other purposes, other goals, other techniques more or less suited to the needs of their constituents. Labor unions in the United States illustrate this. The main thrust of union organizations

---

[5] *Ibid.*, p. 30. Other factors, such as alliances with business groups and malapportionment of legislatures, also contributed to agricultural clout in politics.

[6] Harold D. Lasswell, "The Measurement of Public Opinion," *American Political Science Review*, Vol. 25 (1931), 311–36, quoted in Key, *op. cit.*, p. 41.

came with fundamental changes in the American economy. As farming declined, industrialization escalated; by 1870, about as many people were earning their livings in manufacturing as in agriculture. Like farming organizations, unions leaped forward in numbers and power in times of depression, culminating in the massive organizations of the 1930's, the American Federation of Labor and the Congress of Industrial Organizations, which merged to form the AFL–CIO in 1955.

The basic purpose of unions was economic rather than political. They were formed to get benefits from industry for workers, and the means for this were strong, recognized organizations with the right to bargain collectively with employers. But almost inevitably national workers' organizations have become involved in politics. In Washington, the AFL-CIO is a major lobby analogous to national farm organizations.

But labor's fortunes in party politics — in mobilizing members for campaigns and elections — have been mixed. Early in the game, a separate national political party for labor was rejected and labor adopted a nonpartisan doctrine of rewarding its friends and punishing its enemies in whatever party they might appear. Eventually the major national unions developed political arms to mobilize workers in elections. There is evidence that union members are more likely to vote Democratic than people who do not belong to unions, but the influence of specific union drives on this picture is not clear.[7]

If union leaders had tight control over their millions of members, they would be able to shift their votes from candidates of one party to candidates of the other party freely, as the goals of labor demanded. But in fact that is very hard to do. As national organizations, the major unions are confederations — loose congeries of local workers' organizations. Workers are split up into thousands of craft and industrial categories; there is not in this country a strong class consciousness among workers. One study showed that more than a fourth of the skilled manual workers in the country consider themselves middle class, while more than a third of white-collar workers consider themselves working class.[8]

[7] Key, *op. cit.*, p. 67. For a perceptive analysis of this, see Grant McConnell, *Private Power and American Democracy* (Mew York: Knopf, 1966), Chapter 9.

[8] Richard Centers, *The Psychology of Social Class* (Princeton, N.J.: Princeton University Press, 1949), p. 86.

There are places, such as New York, Michigan, and Minnesota, in which labor unions are powerful forces in the actions of political parties. And some unions, like the United Auto Workers, are much stronger than others in the political realm. But it is generally true that union members, as such, are mobilizable mainly when there is some relatively clear labor issue involved in an election.[9]

Thus, labor's *political* activities—a line of attack tangential to its economic purposes—come to the fore when politics is perceived as an important mechanism for getting what the members want. This happens primarily when there are political issues affecting the *economic* status of labor. At other times, other loyalties move the members.

issues and organization power

The implication is that citizen organizations are not infinitely plastic. They can be bent but not molded into any shape the leaders desire. An organization is in part a prisoner of its history, particularly of the conditions under which it was originally put together. Members are attracted to organizations for certain special purposes to meet certain special needs. One has only to imagine the shifts that would be necessary to make of the AMA an organization to elect Democratic candidates, the Ku Klux Klan a champion of racial integration, the League of Women Voters a competitor for patronage. The shift, one supposes, would be too much to bear. The organization would rapidly lose members, dues would fall off, and the leaders who advocated such moves would be deposed. Particularly when we are talking about voluntary organizations of citizens we are talking about a fairly fragile set of structures not easily altered in their fundamental frameworks and directions.

Other new groups have gained power when the time was ripe, when some critical set of events brought forward a new basis for connecting the needs of many citizens. The large-scale veterans' groups are an example, as are the many rising organizations concerned with the Negro in America. And many other groups formed

[9] *Ibid.*, p. 67.

originally on other bases have turned toward politics with more or less success. One thinks of the way business organizations have taken on public relations and lobbying in Washington as major enterprises. Or the way the National Council of Churches has spoken out on various public issues. Both themes—successful timing and successful politicalization—point to power as a *historical* phenomenon, one in which much depends on the development of general changes in the society and the relationship of those changes to the history of a particular organization.

who governs when?

Much as the culture of a group affects the kinds of leaders it empowers, so historical change is reflected in leadership echelons. A set of leaders may enjoy almost automatic legitimacy at one historical stage and then may be almost completely excluded at another, owing to changes in the composition and functions of the group. In *Who Governs?*, a study of power in New Haven, Connecticut, Robert A. Dahl shows how historical changes have altered the power accorded various categories of leaders.[10] New Haven was incorporated in 1784; up to about 1842, the patricians, a small collection of aristocratic families, had a monopoly of public offices. These were the wealthy, highly educated folk, those who could trace their ancestry back to the English aristocracy or squirearchy. They stood at the top of a social structure embracing nearly all important aspects of life. In the beginning they had everything—except numbers. And in the early years numbers were not very important. Voting rights were restricted and turnout was sporadic. There were 225 voters in 1813; only 648 New Haveners voted in the 1818 referendum on the state constitution.[11]

But the 1834 elections were a watershed: two nationwide political parties had been developed, the Democrats and the Whigs, and each had organized voters down to the town and ward level. Candidates began to compete for votes from a growing electorate. *Numbers* became an important political resource, and the patricians lacked numbers.

The new democracy replaced the patricians with the entrepre-

---

[10] Robert A. Dahl, *Who Governs? Democracy and Power in an American City* (New Haven, Conn.: Yale University Press, 1961), Chapters 1–7.

[11] *Ibid.*, p. 23.

neurs. From about 1842 to the turn of the century, "Mayor after mayor was a successful manufacturer, and businessmen virtually crowded all other occupations from the Board of Aldermen and the newly established Board of Finance."[12] With industrialization, businessmen got money. These were the self-made men who grasped a new technology and new forms of industrial organization and exploited them for all they were worth. Eli Whitney marked the transition. His father, the story goes, mortgaged his farm to send his son to Yale. Whitney went to Georgia, where he invented the cotton gin, only to lose out on the profits of that innovation, but he came back to New Haven to develop techniques of producing firearms with standardized, interchangeable parts. This paved the way for mass production, and the methods were imitated in enterprises for making light carriages, clocks, and ships. A whole new segment of rich men was added to the patrician aristocrats. One's pedigree was no longer a good measure of the size of one's pocketbook. The urban workers, now able to vote but lacking their own leaders, gave support to the entrepreneurs. From 1856 to 1899, twenty-two of the thirty-two candidates for mayor in New Haven were businessmen.[13] Dahl explains:

> The patricians had been almost totally displaced from the center of public attention; in fact, most of the voters probably could not even distinguish between the patricians and the new rich. Moreover, the whole emergent style of life in politics and business was against them. In the course of the century, politics had taken on some of the flavor of the lower middle classes, with their enthusiasms, emotionalism, and evangelistic religions; frequently the decorum of the preceding period now gave way to buffoonery, dignity was undone by the horse laugh, and the deadly seriousness of the Puritan was replaced by ballyhoo. . . . The monopoly that leading entrepreneurs enjoyed over the chief elective offices of New Haven depended to a considerable extent on a third resource that need not always go with wealth or social standing, namely, popularity. The popularity of the businessman as an elected official in turn required a wide belief on the part of the rank-and-file voter in the peculiar virtues and meritorious attainments of the businessman, a certain measure of respect, and perhaps even some sympathetic identification.[14]

[12] *Ibid.*, p. 25.
[13] *Ibid.*, p. 28.
[14] *Ibid.*, pp. 29–31.

The first Irishman was elected to the Board of Aldermen in 1857. By 1910, one out of every three New Haveners was foreign-born and another one of the three had at least one immigrant parent. The population makeup of the city had been transformed; eventually these new voices would be heard in politics. At first too poor and confused to develop effective organization, the immigrants slowly began to produce their own leaders. The Irish, first on the scene in large numbers, elected their first mayor in 1899; since then every Democratic mayor has been an Irish Catholic. The election of 1917 was a contest between one David Fitzgerald, and Irish Catholic, and Samuel Campner, a Russian Jew. "From that time on, both parties usually nominated candidates who did not suffer from the handicap of being Yankee."[15] By 1933 the Irish had almost half the jobs in city government. The Italians, who had come later, competed intensively through the Republican party, and in 1945 the first Italian mayor was elected.

Not many of the ethnic candidates were top businessmen; the shift in population was reflected in a shift away from business dominance. As Dahl explains:

> What the immigrants and the ex-plebs had accomplished . . . was a further split in political resources. Popularity had been split off from both wealth and social standing. Popularity meant votes; votes meant office; office meant influence. Thus the ex-plebs completed the transition from the old pattern of oligarchy based upon cumulative inequalities to new patterns of leadership based upon dispersed inequalities.[16]

Beginning in the 1950's, Dahl saw still another pattern of power emerging. The outlines of this pattern were not entirely clear as yet. But the emphasis had shifted, particularly with the election of Mayor Richard C. Lee, from "divisible" political benefits—things like jobs, contracts, and welfare payments, which could be split up among competing individuals—to "indivisible" political goods—such things as parks, playgrounds, and schools, which affect large neighborhoods or the city as a whole. Still another set of leaders, under Lee's direction, emerged: the bureaucrats and experts who know how to acquire and manage these new political benefits.[17]

[15] *Ibid.,* p. 40.
[16] *Ibid.,* p. 51.
[17] *Ibid.,* Chapter 5.

changing power resources

Even this sketchy account of leadership changes in New Haven shows clearly how mistaken we would be to identify a pattern of community power in one slice of time and infer its permanence. The recruitment and selection of leaders is a developing process, a shifting system that reflects, to a large degree, the fundamental changes going on in a community or a nation. Power is transformed with changing conditions. New names appear on the voting machines, but perhaps even more important, new combinations of political *resources* become relevant. As the history of New Haven shows, there was a trend away from the concentration of resources in the hands of the patricians who controlled wealth and status, and could largely ignore their lack of popular support, to a more dispersed pattern of resources, where numbers – votes – became essential. Political power is not some set substance you can put in a bucket, but an animal that may turn against you if you don't treat him right.

changed minds or changed places?

We saw how much leadership shifts in New Haven reflected population shifts. An analyst who simply compared Democratic and Republican percentages of the New Haven vote over all these years might well be misled: he might think of New Haven as having changed "its" mind. Similarly in other settings aggregate voting statistics – vote totals for different groups or areas – may obscure the difference between the same people changing their minds and a change in the composition of the population itself.

For example, in the Eisenhower landslides of 1952 and 1956 the Republican Presidential candidate piled up large votes in the suburbs. The suburbs had been growing fast in population while the cities – particularly the twelve biggest ones (except Los Angeles) – were losing population. One interpretation, plausible on the surface, would be that Democratic voters moved out of the cities to the suburbs and switched to the Republican party. This is the idea that "the working man moves to the suburbs as a Democrat, but there associates with Republicans and with greater or lesser speed he takes on Republican characteristics."[18]

[18] Angus Campbell *et al., The American Voter* (New York: Wiley, 1960), p. 443.

Already from what we have learned of the persistence of basic political loyalties, we should be suspicious of that theory. Close analysis of data on *individual* voters shows that the apparent change in attitudes, when viewed in the aggregate, was far more extensively a change in population distributions. That is, the suburbs, which were growing three times as fast as the nation as a whole, were being populated by many new *Republican* migrants. Roughly speaking, these voting patterns were not due to people moving out to the suburbs and changing their political predispositions, but were due to the *kinds* of people who moved to the suburbs—in this case, Republicans.[19]

Similarly, looking only at aggregate patterns can give a false impression of stability. For example, the Survey Research Center of the University of Michigan was able to show that massive population changes were going on beneath the apparently stable balance between Republicans and Democrats in the cities. The overall party balance was not changing much, but there was a rapid flow of Republicans out of the cities (primarily better-off people moving to the suburbs) at the same time that roughly the same number of rural Republicans (most of them not so well off) were moving into the cities.[20] The "net result of the two streams of movement, in and out of the major metropolitan centers, apparently has been to leave the partisan balance within the metropolitan center almost unchanged."[21] These complementary flows of people may be having profound effects on the nature of urban Republicanism, changes that are very difficult to see when one views only the aggregate picture.

These basic changes are less likely to result from sudden conversions than from changes in the mix of community population. The interplay and mutual adjustment of new people and old communities takes time. The new people carry along their experiences, their identifications and loyalties from the past. They learn their way into a new culture over a period of years; few are suddenly transformed by a new environment. But the fact that California has been doubling its population every twenty years, at

---

[19] For an analysis of these arguments, see David Wallace, "Suburbia—Predestined Republicanism," in Edward C. Dreyer and Walter A. Rosenbaum (eds.), *Political Opinion and Electoral Behavior* (Belmont, Calif.: Wadsworth, 1966), pp. 102–11.

[20] Campbell *et al., op. cit.,* p. 465.

[21] *Ibid.*

the rate of about half a million people a year in the last decade, and that more than four-fifths of the increase has been taking place in California's nine metropolitan areas, is obviously extremely important for the state's politics.[22] *Individuals* may be changing slowly, but *communities* are changing much more rapidly.

Very many Americans are on the move. From March, 1965, to March, 1966, 36,703,000 Americans moved from one house to another. Of these, 12,538,000 moved to a different county.[23] Between 1960 and 1965, New York state gained 410,000 more people than it lost. Florida had a surplus by migration of 518,000, California a surplus of 1,447,000. Meanwhile, Mississippi, Massachusetts, and many of the midwestern states, among others, lost population in net terms.[24] About half the southern Negro college students surveyed for one study expected to live outside the South; of those who expected to move out of the South, 41 percent thought they would live on the Pacific coast.[25]

The many implications of these massive shifts cannot be surveyed here. But they bring to mind with special force some power implications of a highly mobile citizenry. For one thing, the character of a community's leadership depends on its supply of available leaders. In many communities throughout the country—and the world—there is a constant drain on this supply as the better educated parts of the population move away. Someone must govern, and that someone will be found among those who stay behind. So in many places the hometown boy, the one who has come home again from college or has acquired his schooling in the local community, stands a good chance of gaining political influence. No matter how much a community would like to have itself governed by modern-day George Washingtons or Thomas Jeffersons, it must make do with the material at hand. Thus in every leadership recruitment system there is always a compromise between the ideal and the available. This becomes a special kind of national political problem when some areas of the country attract a great many of the politically talented (and thus

[22] Joseph P. Harris, *California Politics*, 3rd ed. (Stanford, Calif.: Stanford University Press, 1961), p. 9.

[23] *Statistical Abstract of the United States: 1967* (United States Bureau of the Census), p. 34.

[24] *Ibid.*, p. 6.

[25] Donald R. Matthews and James W. Prothro, *Negroes and the New Southern Politics* (New York: Harcourt, Brace & World, 1966), pp. 447–48.

experience a scramble for power) while other areas of the country are constantly losing the politically talented (and thus experience a continual search for the minimally acceptable).[26]

Not only the talented move around. In recent years the migration of the poor and uneducated to urban centers has escalated rapidly. These are people, by and large, who are most in need of help from the political order, and least able to organize effectively for political action. Several factors combine to make it difficult for transients in politics to adapt rapidly to the urban environment and to wring from the system what they need.

They have come from a very different physical environment, one in which there was lots of space in which to move around. In the city there is an intense spatial compression of life, a jamming together of people accustomed to distances. The migrant from the farm leaves behind a life style attuned to the pace of the seasons and takes up the pace of the clock, the tight schedule of rapid urban movement. Many of these migrants lack strongly developed abilities to learn quickly; from a life dominated by tangible things, they move into a life of words and numbers and abstractions. They get lost; they cannot understand the newspapers. Thrown together with millions of other strangers, they are also brought into close juxtaposition with the affluent society. The impersonality and "fast living" of the city contrasts with the "just plain folks" attitude of the small town or farm community.

Millions of these new core city residents are Negroes; they must bear all the burdens of discrimination on top of the other disabilities. A survey by *Fortune* as early as 1962 showed that Negroes in cities with populations of over 50,000 were increasing five times as fast as whites. Harlem had become the largest Negro community in the world. In 1910, 80 percent of the Negroes lived in the South; by 1960 only 52 percent of Negroes were southern. And within the South, many Negroes had moved to the cities. In 1910, 90 percent of southern Negroes were rural residents; by 1960, that had declined to 69 percent. Eight major American cities were more than 30 percent black in 1969.

Even if the Negro newcomers were free to organize for political action, their disabilities would make that difficult. But they also have to contend with established power holders who resist

---

[26] See James David Barber, *The Lawmakers: Recruitment and Adaptation to Legislative Life* (New Haven, Conn.: Yale University Press, 1965), pp. 233ff.

their demands and often subvert their attempts at organization. Clearly one of the critical questions for the future of the city is whether or not the masses of citizens concentrated in dilapidated ghettos will succeed, through organization, in establishing a base of political power capable of meeting their demands for a chance at progress within the framework of the political system. If that does not happen, the outlook for peace and a decent standard of living in the cities is dim.

Whatever the profound and disquieting practical implications are, these patterns of movement illustrate one of the main dynamics of power in American communities. This is the interplay between *a system constructed around geography* and a *population moving about in great numbers*. Throughout the world, it is the groups of country people coming to the city, of students temporarily residing in colleges and universities, of racial and ethnic minorities in new places, who are frustrated—by their own inabilities to organize effectively for political action and by the failure of established institutions in the community to respond to their needs. The temptation to bypass the established political order is strong. The temptation to violence is ever present. Even in the oldest of democracies—in England and the United States and France, systems that have managed to cope with many severe challenges in the past—it is not yet clear whether the machinery of government is flexible and efficient enough to meet these challenges.

votes for youth

These factors show up clearly in a political change that is happening now. In 1972, people between the ages of eighteen and twenty-one would be eligible to vote in federal elections. How did this happen? What are its implications?

Over the centuries the electorate was gradually expanded to include religious dissenters, the propertyless, Negroes, and women, but one barrier held firm: age twenty-one. In the nineteenth century millions of American teenagers—proportionally many more than today—held full-time jobs and fought in the wars. Yet until recently, there was relatively little agitation for lowering the voting age. When it came to voting and other legal rights and obligations, the child became a man on his twenty-first birthday.[27]

But in the 1960's, several forces combined to spur this issue toward the front of the pack. First, there were suddenly a great many more voteless young adults. When the G.I.s came home from World War II they promptly married and their wives promptly produced babies. By the sixties, this postwar fecundity sent the youth population curves bounding upward. In 1964 there were 1,401,000 eighteen-year-old males. Just one year later there were 1,897,000 – a leap of 35 percent. By 1972 there would be more than two million.[28] So the first requirement for political change – large numbers – was massively and suddenly present.

By a quirk of history, this youth population explosion coincided with Lyndon Johnson's escalation of the war in Vietnam. Young people were dismayed. They were concerned not only about the morality of the war, but with a specific deprivation: the draft. Bad enough that tens of thousands would die and hundreds of thousands be hurt in this dismal venture. The political effect of the draft law in effect at that time was probably even greater. Every youth subject to the draft – millions more than would ever be called up – was living in seven years' suspense: would he be drafted, and if so – when? Thus personal frustration added to moral outrage, producing a motivational basis for mobilization. And the source of the problem was clearly the government. Protest turned naturally toward the political order.

There were many issues; votes for youth was one of them. The major resources for this move probably rested in three widespread American values: support for the American soldier, respect for education, and the perennial American excitement with youth. The argument "old enough to fight, old enough to vote" gained significance as the troop commitment in Vietnam escalated. Many citizens contrasted their own easy life with the lot of the draftee in the jungle, so consciences were stirred. Then the issue tapped into the American love affair with education. Youth today are certainly more educated than the youth of yesterday, and most people are ready to think that education – plus television – makes young people smarter than their parents and grandparents. Surely,

---

[27] Twenty-one was the medieval age of eligibility for knighthood: three (for the Trinity) times the lucky number seven.

[28] Samuel Lubell, *The Hidden Crisis in American Politics* (New York: Norton, 1971), pp. 182–83.

the argument went, these well-trained intelligences could make a contribution in voting. Finally, there is a vaguer value: the American fascination with youth—the sense that it is better to be young, vital, alive, the association of youth with joy and with the future. Older people often try to look and feel young. In the midst of the ambivalence aroused by hippies, drug freaks, protesters, and commune-dwellers, the basic American liking for youth probably supports the movement to let young people vote.[29]

The organizational opportunity that completed the requisites for the eighteen-year-old vote movement was primarily the concentration of new masses of students in institutions of higher learning. Most young people are not students; they are workers. But students are, comparatively speaking, much more organizable. They live in close community in their colleges. Communication is easy, schedules are flexible enough for extracurricular politics, and leadership is available. Furthermore, politicians and activists in labor and other organized interests saw the potential force of this new voter category and calculated its impact on their fortunes. So the organizability of students met the opportunities of politics.

The *national* enfranchisement of youth was a new factor in politics. In the four states allowing eighteen to twenty-one year olds to vote in 1968, only 44.2 percent of them registered. But those isolated examples gave little clue to 1972; the scope of the situation was radically expanded. Young people eighteen to twenty-one tend to identify with their peers (57 percent) somewhat more than with their families (43 percent) and are generally more liberal and more strongly opposed to the war. But how these perceptions and opinions would be translated into votes remained to be seen.[30]

There are still many uncertainties about the youth vote. Will it turn out to be a conservative influence, with young people following their parents as they generally have done in the past? Will it lapse into a cycle of apathy and activism, accelerating the swings of temper in American politics? Will the "youth vote"

[29] For extended argument on these points see William G. Carleton, "Votes for Teen-Agers," *Yale Review*, Vol. 58, No. 1 (Autumn, 1968), reprinted in William R. Nelson (ed.), *American Government and Political Change* (New York: Oxford University Press, 1970).

[30] Richard Reeves, "Any Number Can Play 'Scenario,'" *New York Times Magazine*, April 11, 1971, p. 52.

concept only momentarily obscure the great variety among youth in values, memories, and career plans? Or, as many advocates of the change have hoped, will we see here a new progressive force, a force not just for change, but for a better brand of politics?

Some change is likely. Which way it goes is a matter of political choice.

how change happens

Political change never just happens. People make it happen, purposefully or inadvertently. Organized action to bring about change, like individual political action, is a product of motives, resources, and opportunities on the part of citizens and of their leaders.

The motivational thrust for large-scale, organized political action has usually come from an *awareness* on the part of *significant numbers* of citizens that they are being subjected, *relatively suddenly,* to *important deprivation,* and that the *political* system can alleviate their distress. The history of agricultural and labor organizations illustrates these combined factors.

Resources for organized political action, especially the resources leaders can call upon, depend primarily on *what the society values.* The changing patterns of leadership in New Haven reflected changes in the availability of valued political goods — status, wealth, popularity, skill. The potential leader who can perceive in a fluid situation which resources are available but underutilized has grasped lesson number one.

Organizational opportunities are always related to and largely defined by the political motives and resources at hand. Perhaps the hardest problems — and the most challenging opportunities — for organized political change arise from *massive changes in the distribution of people in the social structure.* Geographical and occupational redistributions — changes in such fundamentals as where citizens live and how they work — are galloping forward in the United States. So is the proportion of youth in institutions of higher education, and the proportion of women in the labor market.

The question is whether the political system can respond to, or even anticipate, the meanings of these changes before they overwhelm us.

chapter x

The Darker Side of Change

Political power takes many forms. The significance —the political *meaning*—of power varies with the situation. The power to resist change can be just as important in some circumstances as the power to make things happen. To understand organized resistance as a form of citizen power we need to grasp how certain social structures with certain shared purposes are more or less vulnerable to change. As some cases make clear, not all change is for the best and not all resistance to change is heroic. In the midst of a fast-moving society, the political system balances power. The way that balance is achieved or upset in the short run may shape the long-run fate of citizens by the millions.

The political order of things we take as natural

has often come close to disintegration. Power does not disappear in a society; when the democratic machinery stops working, people find other ways, other kinds of power, to get what they want. The history of modern totalitarianism is the most striking example in our era of the breakdown of democratic power procedures.

Both of the major totalitarian movements of our age—Nazism and communism—have had to come to terms with the power of groups in the political order. The success these movements had in establishing totalitarian regimes was not simply a matter of their strategies in regard to groups. They came to power after mass social crises, economic breakdowns, in times of great confusion and instability. It was more than a matter of persuasion. The whole society was in an uproar, and thus all institutions were called into question. The totalitarians were working in a context conducive to political change; their attacks on independent group life did not take place in isolation. But their success was in no small measure a success in subverting or rendering helpless many groups thought nearly invulnerable.

The object of the totalitarian is simple: to control every group. Groups with a certain independence, a sphere of autonomy, a degree of detachment from the political order, are anathema to the totalitarians. Those they cannot control they destroy—or at least render irrelevant by removing them from an active role in the political system. Thus the ability of groups to resist totalitarian incursions depends both on their ability to stand somewhat apart from politics *and* their ability to affect the political order through participation.

The Nazis and the Bolsheviks undertook the task of molding groups to their purposes from the first.[1]

home and hearth

They had least success with the family, although in an indirect way they managed to affect even that bastion of independence. Originally the Bolsheviks were antifamily—the family was seen

[1] The following section is based primarily on Carl J. Friedrich and Zbigniew K. Brzezinski, *Totalitarian Dictatorship and Autocracy* (Cambridge Mass.: Harvard University Press, 1956), Part IV, Chapters 22–24.

as a typically bourgeois institution linked to private property—while the Nazis glorified the family as the core of the culture. But the Soviets came around to the recognition that family life could not be destroyed, and so turned to manipulating it for the benefit of the regime. Both governments encouraged child-bearing; Hitler wrote in *Mein Kampf,* "The object of woman's education must be immovably directed to making the future mothers."[2] The Soviet government gave medals and money to large families; mothers of six or seven children got Medals of Motherhood, and those with more than seven children received Medals of Maternal Glory. But beyond this, the dictatorial regimes tried to break down the family—to turn it into a propaganda institution—by encouraging children to spy and report on their parents. This met with only limited success. Sometimes the terror reached within the family circle, but more often "the anxiety-ridden subject of a totalitarian dictatorship, in his isolation and alienation from all ordinary community living, seeks refuge in the intimate relations of family life."[3]

The family was a refuge, an island of trust in the midst of a chaotic and dangerous social environment. In many cases family ties were strengthened by the threat, but at the same time in many ways the family became an escape, a comforting retreat, *a substitute for action in the wider environment.* In this sense the failure of the totalitarians to subvert the family was only a partial failure. There were many variants, but the family as an escape probably tended to deprive politics of persons who might otherwise have acted on a broader scale to resist the totalitarian thrust.

church and school

Originally the Bolsheviks set out to destroy the churches, while the Nazis posed as defenders of the Christian religion. Lenin wrote that "religion is a kind of spiritual vodka in which the slaves of capital drown their human shapes and their claims to any decent human life."[4] In the 1920's the regime began a campaign to destroy the resistance of the Russian Orthodox church

[2] *Ibid.,* p. 241.
[3] *Ibid.,* p. 245.
[4] *Ibid.,* p. 248.

by means of violence and propaganda, and by taking advantage of the traditional submissiveness of the church to state authority, the Bolsheviks managed first to reduce religion to a kind of ritualism shut off from concern with wider issues, and then, during the Second World War, to mobilize the church as an arm of the Communist party, giving its blessing to the patriotic war. At first, "Render unto Caesar that which is Caesar's" meant "Stay out of politics"; then it came to mean "Do what Caesar says." There were those in the Russian church who resisted heroically, but the ability of the regime to prevent any independent stand on the part of the church seems to have been successful.

The Nazis took a totalitarian view of all man's soul: "Every thought and idea, every doctrine and all knowledge have to serve this purpose," Hitler said of his fight for the racial fatherland.[5] Nazism itself was to be a "political faith." It would use the church when convenient as a mechanism for propaganda. Hitler saw the advantage of traditional religion concerned only with the rituals of spirituality: "I do not permit priests to concern themselves with secular matters."[6] In other words, like the Bolsheviks at one stage, Hitler hoped to remove the influence of a group he could not completely control by depoliticizing it, rendering it irrelevant to the concerns of practical affairs. Again the choices open to the totalitarians were to dominate and control such organizations if they could, and to render them irrelevant if they could not.

For the most part, these efforts failed. The story of the resistance of churchmen, Protestant and Catholic, in Nazi Germany is one of the most striking examples in all time of the personal heroism of men and women who knew what they believed in. While "the Nazi government never quite dared to take vigorous action against the high dignitaries of the church,"[7] they were forced to rely on torture and murder to combat the persistent refusal of the clergy to give in. Thousands of teachers and priests died in concentration camps, but *public* resistance to the Nazi regime continued even in the midst of the Second World War. The clash between the totalitarian claims of Nazism and the claim of Christianity to speak to the whole man in life rather than to a religious fragment of man in church — these rival total claims

[5] *Ibid.*, p. 249.
[6] *Ibid.*, p. 250.
[7] *Ibid.*, p. 258.

could not be reconciled. Resistance did not succeed in preventing tyranny, but the resistant powers of the church were highlighted even as they failed.

The totalitarians needed the universities. Central to the success of both Nazism and Bolshevism was the exploitation of technology for military, industrial, and agricultural development. But technology depends on science, and science, in the modern state, is the province of the university. They needed the universities for indoctrination, to mobilize the new generation. Therefore both regimes undertook to control the institutions of higher learning. The policies of the Nazis and Communists in the field of higher education were remarkably alike. They consisted of the following process: The universities are deprived of their autonomy and are subjected to rigid bureaucratic controls. More particularly, the rectors (presidents) and deans are made appointees of government agencies and the teaching staff is made removable at pleasure. At the same time, programs of ideological indoctrination are instituted in which the

> "true science" of certain laws is expounded to faculty and students alike. In all institutions of higher learning, party and youth group cells are instituted . . . which control, and terrorize, not only their fellow students, but also the faculty. Ideological and party qualifications are given increasing weight in the selection of students, as well as faculty.[8]

Many of these measures worked to destroy the autonomy of universities by exploiting their inner tensions. Was the administration to be brought under the control of the government? Well, many students and professors had not had much use for the administration anyway. Was there to be a new emphasis on technology? Particularly in some universities that had been dominated by the humanities and philosophy, this was good news for the scientists, who felt that they would now come into their own. Were the students to be organized and encouraged to report on their professors and fellow students for ideological deviations? Many students felt alienated and disgruntled; this would give them a chance to have a say in their own education.

The result was mixed. The basic contradictions between the pseudoscience of the dictatorships and the free scientific inquiry

[8] *Ibid.*, p. 268.

of the universities continued. But the universities did not—as the churches did—show strong signs of resistance to the totalitarian movement. Many scholars simply retreated "into the inner sanctum of the intimate group and the esoteric communication" by which they could protect themselves and their work from political incursion.[9] The universities were not completely transformed, not easily made into arms of the movement. Built into their work was a fundamentally antitotalitarian theme:

> Science is a method of human beings who are engaged in a search for the truth, and that truth is a hard mistress who expects to be wooed in accordance with her nature. As the totalitarians marshal youth to try and conquer her, they are likely to find those youth who are capable of pursuing truth, who have the imagination and the sensitiveness and sharpness of mind to discover new truths, become new recruits for a value which transcends their totalitarian enterprise. As they enter the island where the quiet of study and inquiry reigns, they become separated from the loud battle cries of the totalitarian regime.[10]

Thus in different ways and with different degrees of success, citizens in a political holocaust retained some independence through their institutions. In the last analysis, not even these immensely powerful dictatorships could completely control group life. There was always at least some residue of independence, some islands of separateness. In a sense these island fortresses never fell. But they failed to prevent the rise of dictatorship.

one by one

It was the strength of these social island fortresses, not simply their numbers, which counted most as forces of resistance. That is, a mere multiplicity of groups in a community was not sufficient to resist the totalitarian movement. Rather, resistance depended on the degree to which such groups were important to their members; if a group held enough meaning to its members, it could draw upon much social energy to maintain independence and effectiveness. Citizens may "belong" to many groups of only

[9] *Ibid.*, p. 271.
[10] *Ibid.*, p. 273.

peripheral importance to them, groups that are easily subverted by a small, determined active minority ready to take advantage of other members' apathy.

A fascinating study by William S. Allen of one German town in the thirties shows how the Nazis used the very profusion of groups as a tool for gaining control.[11] The town had hundreds of organizations. By an "enormous social reshuffle" the Nazis eventually eliminated the independence of a tremendous range of them. Initially there were sports clubs, unions, business and professional societies, guilds, cooperatives, patriotic societies, youth clubs, singing societies, shooting societies, religious organizations, supporters of the schools, a library organization, the Social Democratic party, and a city band.[12]

To this melange of group life, the Nazis brought demands for social rationalization—what they called *Gleichschaltung* (coordination). An overabundance of groups was inefficient and confusing. Why have several sports clubs, with their "senseless competition," when a single unified club could manage sports affairs more efficiently and bring together the best athletes from each club? Why have five or six unions when one would do at least as well? In short, why not coordinate, unify, and energize the organized social forces of the whole community?

Step by step, that is what the Nazis in this community managed to do, with few exceptions. At each step, there were plausible reasons for the move. Few citizens could see clearly what was happening. Allen concludes that "the problem of Nazism was primarily a problem of perception"; there was no single moment at which it became obvious that the Nazis were taking over the entire town. Allen summarizes the results this way:

> Thus by the summer of 1933, the Nazis had either broken up, altered, fused, or brought under control most of the clubs and societies of Thalburg. The complex and diversified social organization of the town had been almost completely uprooted. In most cases the Nazis tried to fill the vacuum, but often people simply stopped coming together. Either there was no more club, or the attractiveness of the club had been

[11] William S. Allen, *The Nazi Seizure of Power: The Experience of a Single German Town 1930–1935* (Chicago: Quadrangle Books, 1965). Reprinted by permission of Quadrangle Books. Copyright © 1965 by William Sheridan Allen.
[12] *Ibid.*, Chapter 14.

destroyed by *Gleichschaltung,* or people no longer had the leisure or the desire to continue with their club. What social life there was continued in the most basic groupings: the *Stammtisch,* the beer-and-cards evenings, or small social gatherings in homes.

Even these were threatened as people began to distrust one another. What was the value of getting together with others to talk if you had to be careful about what you said? Thus to a great extent the individual was atomized. By the process of *Gleichschaltung* individuals had a choice: solitude or mass relationship via some Nazi organization. None of the Nazi measures in the first six months of the Third Reich had a greater ultimate effect than *Gleichschaltung.* By it the externals of the rigid class structure were destroyed, and Thalburgers were moulded into the kind of unorganized mass that dictators like so well.[13]

the power to resist

These observations on group life and social power may seem cold and foreign to Americans. And indeed analogies and comparisons drawn from distant cultures are risky. America is not Germany or Russia. This is not the thirties. But these examples in extreme form show how one particular kind of group power—the power to resist—operates. We usually think of political power as the ability to get something done, to cause change. This is the active, striving dimension of citizen power expressed through groups. This is the kind of thrust toward control exemplified in the emergence of new organizations with new purposes and, negatively, in the difficulties transient populations have in grasping political power. But in our society as well as in the totalitarian cases we have examined, citizens' groups exercise also the power of resistance, the ability to keep things from happening. Indeed, this kind of stopping power may be the major trend of development for politically relevant groups in the United States. As David Reisman explains:

> The shifting nature of the lobby provides us with an important clue as to the difference between the present American political scene and that of the age of McKinley. The ruling class of businessmen could relatively easily (though

13 *Ibid.,* pp. 225–26.

perhaps mistakenly) decide where their interests lay and what editors, lawyers, and legislators might be paid to advance them. The lobby ministered to the clear leadership, privilege, and imperative of the business ruling class.

Today we have substituted for that leadership a series of groups, each of which has struggled for and finally attained a power to stop things conceivably inimical to its interests and, within far narrower limits, to start things. The various business groups, large and small, the movie-censoring groups, the farm groups and the labor and professional groups, the major ethnic groups and major regional groups, have in many instances succeeded in maneuvering themselves into a position in which they are able to neutralize those who might attack them. The very increase in the number of these groups, and in the kinds of interests "practical" and "fictional" they are protecting, marks, therefore, a decisive change from the lobbies of an earlier day.[14]

In other words, intense and organized minorities throughout our system have radically increased their ability to prevent other forces, including the government, from harming them. But it is easy to see how the growth of this kind of power can work against the effectiveness of positive political power, the power to bring about social change. The citizen who aims to prevent something is strengthened, while the citizen who wants to change something is weakened. The danger in this development is evident: a political system increasingly incapable of taking progressive action. Often this danger hits hardest at those who most need progress; the disadvantaged, the excluded, the losers in the midst of an affluent society.

power and perception

Allen saw the Nazi tragedy as primarily a failure of perception, a strangely soft and indefinite thing when one thinks of the mass of material cruelties of the Hitler regime. But in our own country, we see some prime examples of how the whole power system is profoundly shaped by distortions of perception.

Perhaps it is unfortunate that the word "power" has attained

[14]David Riesman *et al.*, *The Lonely Crowd* (New Haven, Conn.: Yale University Press, 1950), pp. 246–47.

over many years the status of political science's main concept. For when we think of power, we usually think of some direct and obvious act of domination: the policeman forcibly arresting a law-breaker, a lobbyist pressuring a legislator for his vote, a politician forcing his views on a following. Then when we look around at the way real people actually relate to one another in the political system, we are puzzled to see how rarely we are able to find such "power." Our attention is diverted by an emphasis on "power" from the vast number of ordinary events that shape the course of our lives to a few sharply defined crises in which issues are starkly posed and clearly resolved. "Power" throws our attention to the news that the National Guard has been sent into a city to suppress violence and diverts our attention from the web of human conditions that brought about the crisis. We see the breakdown of community in a great university in a direct power confrontation between students and administration. But it is more difficult to perceive how that dramatic crisis represented only the surface of a longer, more basic and pervasive set of indirect and ill-perceived relationships of influence, authority, persuasion, and neglect.

institutional racism

We can see this problem—a fundamental one in the development of political science—in a last example. In 1968, the *Report of the National Advisory Commission on Civil Disorders* described part of the problem of housing discrimination in this way:

> Thousands of Negro families have attained incomes, living standards, and cultural levels matching or surpassing those of whites who have "upgraded" themselves from distinctly ethnic neighborhoods. Yet most Negro families have remained within predominantly Negro neighborhoods, primarily because they have been effectively excluded from white residential areas.
>
> Their exclusion has been accomplished through various discriminatory practices, some obvious and overt, others subtle and hidden. Deliberate efforts are sometimes made to discourage Negro families from purchasing or renting homes in all-white neighborhoods. Intimidation and threats of violence have ranged from throwing garbage on lawns and making threatening phone calls to burning crosses in yards

and even dynamiting property. More often, real estate agents simply refuse to show homes to Negro buyers.

Many middle-class Negro families, therefore, cease looking for homes beyond all-Negro areas or nearby "changing" neighborhoods. For them, trying to move into all-white neighborhoods is not worth the psychological efforts and costs required.[15]

Notice what is described here. There *are* some direct and overt acts of power such as dynamiting property. Obviously it is not the *number* of such events which is important; it takes only a very few dynamitings in a community to affect profoundly the entire picture of population movement from the ghetto to the suburbs. The significance of such acts is not to be derived from their frequency, but from the meaning attached to them by the participants in the power process. Thus it would be a gross analytic error to see the rarity of such acts as indicating a system in which "power" was rarely operative. From another perspective, a community in which the racists must resort to dynamiting is one in which their power rests on such shaky ground that they are forced to resort to violence. As Karl Deutsch has argued, the use of force in a political system, like the use of gold in an economic system, is more often a sign of failure in control than a sign of success.

But the Commission report goes on to say that an effective technique for preventing Negroes from buying suburban homes is simply the failure of real estate agents to show them to Negro buyers. In this situation, the Negro is not encountering some direct and overt act of exclusion; he is simply not made aware that certain houses are for sale. The real estate agent exerts a form of power by withholding information—by *not* doing something rather than by taking some positive action. The home owner who is putting his house on the market may find it difficult in this situation to see himself as a "white racist." He may not even know that the real estate agent pursues such a policy. He will not be put into the position of confronting a potential buyer on his doorstep and refusing to sell to him. All that is necessary on his part to maintain a power system that effectively excludes Negroes from his neighborhood is to list his property for sale by a real estate

[15]*Report of the National Advisory Commission on Civil Disorders* (New York: The New York Times Company, 1968), p. 244.

agent who practices discrimination. No drama, no crisis, no definite issue, no clear-cut act of domination is required.

Finally, notice the effect such a situation has on middle-class Negro families. Many simply stop trying. Possibly a Negro citizen could, with great persistence, beat the system. He could try to find out from other sources what housing was in fact on the market, approach sellers directly even if that meant some unpleasant situations, take the case to court, and so forth. The power system, in other words, may not have made it impossible for him to get what he wants, only extremely difficult. The cost for him is made higher—not only in money, but in time and trouble and his tolerance for experiencing rejection.

So an important way of exercising power over another person is to raise the cost he must pay to get what he wants. One may not have to lock the door; one can hide the entrance, or make the road to success so full of ruts and holes as to exclude all but the most determined and capable. The victory in gaining formal access to the vote through registration may mask a thousand little defeats in actually getting past all the barriers between a black Mississippian and the polling place. The point is that effective political power involves a great deal more than formal opportunities. One must consider the costs a citizen must pay to take real advantage of those opportunities.

We notice also how misled we would be to estimate the power situation by some sort of count of Negroes who had tried and failed to buy housing in white suburbs. It does not take many such failures to get the point across to the Negro community. If we were to insist on a view of power as determinative action on numerous issues, we would miss the dynamic of the situation. For a political power holder, the best indicator of the extent of his power may in fact be how *infrequently* he has to use it. And as indicator of the powerlessness of other citizens may be how rarely they think it worthwhile to try to overcome the power holders.

It is a mistake to read the quiet of the prison as an indication that the guards and the convicts are not in a power situation.

groups in the changing power system

Much of what we ordinarily mean by political change is change in the power position of groups. Group politics is a dynamic process, a shifting, developing set of balances and upsets among organizations. Individual citizens take part in politics through their groups. The categories citizens use to understand politics are most often group categories, referring to the person's collection of more or less meaningful memberships. The way people feel about politics both reflects and affects their group affiliations.

Within politically relevant groups there is always a structure, an ordering of activity and leadership. The central members of a group mediate between the members and the larger society, conducting relations in both directions in accordance with major cultural values.

None of this is static. We have seen some of the definable conditions under which some groups come to power while others are fading away. When effective group life dies out of democratic politics, either through the alienation of those who have given up or through the violence of those who would take over by any means, the path is paved for a rerun of the totalitarian story. In the long stretch of history, democratic group politics is young. And most democracies, unlike the United States, have been temporary.

a postscript
on the future

As a divided America limped into the 1970's, prospects for the future were probably as unclear as at any time in the nation's past. There were many reasons for despair—that ultimate political sin that drags the good into apathy and the bad into violence. For the new political generation had grown up through the murders of the Kennedys and Martin Luther King, the "credibility gap," the numbing reality of Chicago in 1968 and Kent State and Jackson State in 1970, the Calley trial in 1971, and, most depressing of all, the seemingly endless killing and maiming by and of Americans in Indochina. Little wonder, then, that the fundamentals are again in question—that Americans young and old are asking what this country is all about and what, if anything, can be done to fix it.

Three answers seem to be emerging. There are those who see American politics as the last vestige of a dying liberalism, a hopelessly tangled knot of corruption and lies, fundamentally beyond repair. For a tiny minority of angry blacks and disillusioned white children of the upper-middle-

213

class, made visible by the excited media, the answer is "revolution!" Their pathetic attempts to bring down the system with guns and bombs and screaming rhetoric only serve to alienate them further from the great American middle. But many thousands who do not buy revolution but share the disgust at government by thieves simply shrug and turn away. The feeling is most evident among the young dropouts who leave home and school and jobs —and politics—either to flock together in isolated groups or, as individuals, to demote themselves from leadership roles to house painting, cab driving, meditation, or other jobs, leaving direction of the country to the ambitious sons of straightness. The same slice of youth that supplied the verve and dedication of the Peace Corps and VISTA and the earthly work of the church only a few years ago now contains many who turn away, not to careerism as in the fifties, but to a kind of private submersion in the self. Nor is this strictly a youth phenomenon. Hidden in their work nests and retirement villages, multitudes of post-youth adults, beadless and beardless, have given up on politics to cultivate the minor pleasures of the barbecue pit.

In a crude political calculus, these open and hidden dropouts score zero for the future. In a more sophisticated analysis, they come out minus because their desertion leaves the field to the very people they disdain.

A different response to the frustration of the seventies is a cleaving to that special version of patriotism that sees control as the answer to chaos. Perceiving an America out of hand, cut apart by dissent, endangered by the spectre of crime at home and communism abroad, an active minority preaches the morality of the flag, the oath, and the law against the confusions of modern society. To many, a country in trouble needs support, not criticism. Faltering leaders should be able to count on the citizen's commitment; those who have fallen out of love with America should find another place to live.

Like the passive dropouts, patriotic controllers have a political effect. In its extreme form, their protest mocks that part of our variegated tradition that celebrates an open society. They forget that forced conformity is a sham in a democracy and that fear is a weak weapon against doubt. Political wiretaps, search without warrant, imprisonment to prevent crime, armed police to cut down mobs, threats to deport nonconforming aliens, use of the draft to punish dissenters, censorship of mail to GIs, Draconian sentences for minor offenses, and the whole apparatus for spying on peaceful political groups – all that proceeds from the assumption (proved false time and again in our history) that coercion, rather than persuasion, is the way to build loyalty. Along a different dimension, the super-patriot relies on coercion also with respect to international relations; caught in the logic of suspicion and force, he sees war as the key to peace and blindly approves any escalation thought "necessary" to cane the recalcitrant into submission.

Such mentality costs the future heavily. The greatest cost is an immense diversion of political energy and a distraction of political attention. There is only so much of each. Fundamental problems – the structuring of enduring peace, the advancement of liberty and equality in America, the development of an environment in which the pursuit of happiness is possible, and the rescue of the sick and illiterate and hungry – are obscured while the nation drifts aimlessly in a fog of recrimination above a sea of patriotic gore.

But there were signs of a third way, not so much between these extremes as moving beyond both of them. People who have neither given up nor chained themselves to some narrow ideology are at work, defining a new vision of the future and designing the new approaches that vision requires. The signs are not entirely clear in the first years of the seventies, but there were at least these glimmers:

> • In the midst of much furor about the "generation gap," certain values widespread among youth began to penetrate the general political culture. Scholars and the media began to look beyond the clothes and the hair and to see the vestiges of a new humanism, a culture in which sharing, openness, honesty and personal simplicity are valued in a way not easily dissolved by the acids of cynicism. In a giant act of political inclusion, the older generation admitted youth to the electorate.

> Few could foresee what the revolution in political opportunity would mean. But the *potential* impact of the youth vote was immense. In just four years – between 1968 and 1972 – more than 25,000,000 young citizens became eligible to vote.

In every state except one (Alabama), the number of these new voters was greater than the margin of votes by which the winning candidate carried that state in 1968. For example, Nixon carried California by 233,346 votes in 1968; between then and 1972, some 2,580,000 young Californians became eligible to vote. Nixon carried Kentucky by 64,870 in 1968; in 1972, there were 254,000 new young eligibles in Kentucky.

The biggest question remained registration: would young people find a way and a will to get their names on the voting lists? Traditionally that has been the hardest barrier to voting. Once registered, people are quite likely to vote; 89.4 percent of registered voters actually voted in 1968.

• Amidst much rubbish about the "sexual revolution," people who are also women begin to gain a new dignity and to demand, in highly practical terms, acceptance as full-fledged human beings. Far from liberated, American women broke through the web of stereotypes and lame humor to seek, half a century after their enfranchisement, the rights and responsibilities men had won at work, in school, in the home, and in the political order.

• After agonizing years of war in Indochina, the longest war in our history, the great American middle class at last declared for peace. Pushed by mounting evidence contradicting the rationale for the pursuit of "victory," the public moved —and moved their leaders—to a new assessment of the meaning of national honor.

• Black Americans, far from full citizenship in practice, began to register and vote in massive numbers, particularly in the South. Within three years after passage of the Voting Rights Act of 1965, black voter registration in the Old Confederacy had increased by 1,280,000 to 62 percent of voting-age blacks and the number of elected black officials in the South rose from 72 to 665. New southern governors, those in Georgia and South Carolina, for example, spoke of an end to the politics of race and matched their words with new appointments and policies.

• The American imagination produced new organizational forms—new ways of grasping at the machinery of government. One ascetic researcher with a penchant for hard facts and vigorous propaganda established Nader's Raiders as a force to be reckoned with; as the seventies began, this little band of competent enthusiasts had moved beyond exposing sin to solid achievement on a range of environmental and consumer issues. The public interest law firm and a host of arrangements for doing part time good were invented. Dr. John Cashin's National Democratic Party of Alabama bypassed the regular parties to win effective control of three Alabama counties. College student volunteers, organized in the Movement for a New Congress, developed new sophistication in canvassing techniques, won some elections, and set a pattern for intense spurts of action by temporary participants. An implausible "citizen's lobby," Common Cause, quickly recruited more than 100,000 members to press for governmental change, and both parties set into motion reforms to widen popular participation in Presidential nominating politics. In many respects "the system" was as rigid as ever. But in the early 1970's, the groping activist could find a varied collection of opportunities to achieve his political will.

Politics is a continual interaction between what people have and what they want. In Utopia there is a perfect match; when what the system wants diverges too far from what the public wants, there is revolution and dictatorship. The real future will be shaped not by isolated individuals crying in the wilderness, but by political organization guided, hopefully, by a vision of what we as a nation have been and might be. It is organization that begets response from the power system.

If organization is the key to citizen power, leadership is the key to organization. Organizations are always put together by someone, by individuals who acquire legitimacy and who exercise responsibility. In our communities, we do not just join spontaneously with others for political purposes. We come together when someone gets us together; we stay together while someone continues to lead us effectively. Within the boundaries of our cultural and political inheritance, organizational leadership is continually in the process of reshaping the alignments of power. So a major consideration in understanding citizen politics is who is in the game and who is out. Competing leaders are continually deciding that question for millions of citizens. The basis for organization arises from disparities between social needs and political performance. Leaders who perceive the character of that disparity, as it is emerging in a particular historical and community context, play the central role in organizational development for political action.

Among all the organizations in politics, the political parties are the most significant for democracy. There are thousands of organizations but none of them does what the parties do. Parties aggregate interests, communitywide, around the winning of elections. That is, they are the key organizations in putting together in two packages all the major organizational thrusts for change and stability. We have barely been able to touch here on the parties' role in organizing democratic politics. Suffice it to suggest that it is the Democratic and Republican parties, more than any other factors on the political scene, which account for such success as we have had and such failure as we have suffered in adapting our institutions to our common purposes. The activist, leadership echelons of the citizenry will in the main continue to find in the parties the most effective instruments for satisfying political demands.

Beyond citizen politics, then, is the politics of organization, particularly party organization. Systems in which the major social conflicts are worked out in comprehensive parties survive as democracies. Systems in which large numbers of citizens become disillusioned with party politics and withdraw into alienated apathy or seek an answer through direct, violent action or bypass the public arena by quiet stealing—such systems are in danger of their democratic lives.

In the emerging future, the purposes of American politics again come into question against a background of stubborn social facts. We will have our galloping philosophers with their heads in the stars and our grubbing bureaucrats who cannot see beyond their desks. What will the new generation do with the opportunity to create, from facts and visions, new directions for the political order? And having planned and dreamed, will we have the spunk to make it happen?

index